✓HOLD FOR NLS ⸺

PAISLEY PUBLIC LIBRARIES

..............Branch

This book is to be returned on or before
the last date above. It may be borrowed
for a further period if not in demand.

The POTTERS and POTTERIES of BENNINGTON

By JOHN SPARGO

President *of the* BENNINGTON BATTLE MONUMENT
AND HISTORICAL ASSOCIATION

DOVER PUBLICATIONS, INC.
NEW YORK

738.2

TO
MY GOOD FRIEND AND FELLOW COLLECTOR
GEORGE S. McKEARIN
THIS STUDY OF THE HOBBY IN WHICH
WE ARE MUTUALLY INTERESTED
IS DEDICATED AS A MARK OF MY FRIENDSHIP

2 079495 21

Published in Canada by General Publishing Company, Ltd., 30 Lesmill Road, Don Mills, Toronto,
Ontario.
Published in the United Kingdom by Constable
and Company, Ltd., 10 Orange Street, London WC 2.

This Dover edition, first published in 1972, is an
unabridged republication of the work originally
published in Boston, 1926, by the Houghton Mifflin
Company and Antiques Incorporated, in a limited
edition of 800 copies.

International Standard Book Number: 0-486-22876-2
Library of Congress Catalog Card Number: 72-80878

Manufactured in the United States of America
Dover Publications, Inc.
180 Varick Street
New York, N.Y. 10014

PREFACE

NO apology is offered for this book, except, of course, for its deficiencies and defects. Of these I am more acutely conscious than any of my readers is likely to be. With all its shortcomings, the book must be its own justification. It can have no other.

A word of personal explanation may not be out of place. In many books and pamphlets published during the last quarter of a century, I have dealt with great and perplexing problems, social, economic, and political. Just as many of my personal friends have been surprised to find me interested in 'old cracked tea-pots and dishes,' as one of them expressed it, so some of those who have paid me the compliment of reading what I have written upon social and economic questions may be surprised that in times like these I should be found devoting time and energy to something so remote from social and political controversy as this historical and descriptive account of an old New England industry.

It would be idle to deny the incongruence, of course. When one turns from the impassioned controversies over Bolshevism and our national policy toward the Soviet Government of Russia to a study of the simple products of a little Vermont pottery, the most sensible thing to do, so far as I can see, is to avow, and if need be to defend, a diversion which is, at least, quite harmless. Surely one may 'strive to set the crooked straight' and still be human enough to ride a hobby! I venture to believe, moreover, that a moderate devotion to some innocent hobby that requires patience, contemplation, and, above all, contact and association with other devotees of the same hobby, would, for all mankind, make for better and wiser thinking upon graver matters, and so help in the work of setting the crooked straight.

Be that as it may, I confess that, from my boyhood days, I have always been interested in old china and pottery, and even fascinated by them. A modest publicist, one of the humblest of the citizens of the great republic of letters, may confess so much without apology in view of the many illustrious names upon the roster of the same hobby. The immortal Washington was an enthusiastic and discriminating collector of china, and, when he returned to private life at Mount Vernon, his collection of Sèvres china and porcelain figures was extensive enough to require the setting apart of a small room for them. Benjamin Franklin was astonished when his wife set his breakfast of bread and milk before him in a china bowl, the first appearance of china in his household. All the world knows how fond of good china he became. Judging by the quantities of the ware which he sent to his wife from England and France, he must have devoted much time to this hobby. For his everyday use he shared Washington's preference for blue and white Canton ware. 'I fell in love with it at first sight,' he wrote to his wife of 'a large fine jug for beer to stand in the cooler.' What would he think of Mr. Volstead, I wonder?

The great Dr. Johnson was an enthusiastic devotee of this same hobby. Crown-Derby delighted his soul, though he bemoaned its costliness. He was keenly interested in the soft paste porcelain of Chelsea, and went so far as to spend considerable time at the pottery, trying his hand at mixing bodies and glazes, hoping to 'improve the manufacture of china.' Gladstone could find time in the midst of the gravest ministerial crises to revel in the beauties of old Wedgwood, which he appreciated as few have ever done, and concerning which he knew as much as any man in England. We may not take our hobby quite so seriously as did Horace Walpole, 'the best letter writer in the English language,' whose great collection at Strawberry Hill bore witness to his enthusiasm and his discrimination. It was written of him:

> China's the passion of his soul;
> A cup, a plate, a dish, a bowl,
> Can kindle wishes in his breast,
> Inflame with joy or break his rest.

But though we may not thus enslave ourselves — and, of course, Horace Walpole didn't — there is ample justification for an intelligent devotion to this gentlest of hobbies, whose devotees are such amiable folk.

When I settled in this delightful Vermont village it was inevitable that I should become interested in the quaint old pottery and porcelain that was made here in the middle of the nineteenth century, good specimens of which are more sought after by collectors than are those of any other American potteries. My principal interest, however, was in collecting facts concerning the potteries and potters rather than in collecting specimens. Bennington is one of the most historic spots in America; the romance of history is in every shadow of its hills. One who has an instinctive liking for historical study, even though he be a Vermonter only by adoption, if he has grown to love the place, finds himself drawn to a study of its inspiring past. My interest in the history of the pottery industry at Bennington, therefore, was part and parcel of my interest in the history of the foundation of the Commonwealth itself.

As will appear to the reader, this book would never have been written at all were it not for the disappointment resulting from a study of the books and articles previously published on the subject, and comparison of them with such evidence as I had accumulated in the course of my own studies. When, therefore, the state of my health made it imperative that I should cease troubling about graver and weightier problems for a time, it seemed worth while to gather together, and set down for the benefit of collectors and students of such matters, all that I had learned about the potters of old Bennington and their work.

I desire to express my thanks to many helpers for valuable assistance. To my colleague Mr. Edward L. Bates, Secretary of the Bennington Battle Monument and Historical Association, I am indebted for much valuable research, without which the book would not have been possible. To my good friend Mr. W. G. Leake, one of the old potters, I am likewise under heavy obligation. Not only has he furnished me with technical and other information not otherwise accessible, but he has been untiring in his investigation of the history of special and unusual specimens. Mrs. Edward Norton, Miss Helena Norton, and Mrs. Luman S. Norton, of Bennington, have kindly placed at my disposal valuable family papers, documents, and portraits without which it would have been impossible to trace so fully the history of the Norton potteries. My fellow collector Mr. George S. McKearin, of Hoosick Falls, New York, has not only given me the free range of his notable collection, but has aided at every step with most valuable advice and suggestions. Mr. Herbert Williams Denio, Librarian of the Vermont Historical Society, Mr. Harold G. Rugg, Librarian of Dartmouth College, and Mr. Harry J. Podmore, of Trenton, New Jersey, have been of great service in looking up old records. To Mrs. Anne R. Congdon, of Nashua, New Hampshire, Dr. and Mrs. W. B. Walker, Mrs. Charles H. Dewey, Mrs. W. J. Meagher, Mr. John Norton, Dr. S. R. Wilcox, Mr. H. D. Fillmore, Mr. John

Moore, and Mrs. Mary H. Adams — all of Bennington — I am indebted for many friendly courtesies.

Most of the illustrations in the book are from photographs of specimens in my own collection, though other collectors have kindly helped by placing individual specimens at my disposal. For such courtesies I am indebted to Mr. George S. McKearin, Mrs. Anne R. Congdon, the Reverend Joseph Lyman, of Sharon, Massachusetts, Mrs. W. J. Meagher, Mrs. Buel Sibley, Miss Helena Norton, and Mrs. Ralph H. White, of Bennington. My thanks are hereby tendered to them. My good friend Mr. W. J. Hickmott, of Hartford, Connecticut, was good enough to make the admirable photographs of the pottery marks for me, and I am also indebted to him for other helpful courtesies. Mrs. Florence Paull Berger, Curator of the Wadsworth Atheneum, Hartford, Connecticut, kindly arranged to have photographs made for me of pieces in that institution.

With few exceptions the photographs were made under my personal supervision, some by my friend, Mr. E. C. Hamilton, formerly of Bennington, but the greater part by another friend and fellow townsman, Mr. Wills T. White. I am greatly obliged to both gentlemen for their painstaking care and skill. Whatever measure of success the book attains in presenting clearly the work of the Bennington potteries is due in no small measure to their efficient coöperation. It is doubtful if any pottery made anywhere ever presented greater difficulties to the photographer than the highly glazed Rockingham and Flint Enamel Wares of Bennington, and it is equally doubtful if, on the whole, greater success has been attained.

JOHN SPARGO

NESTLEDOWN
OLD BENNINGTON, VERMONT
January, 1926

CONTENTS

PART ONE

The Norton Potteries: 1793–1894

LIST OF ILLUSTRATIONS

All the plates follow page 14, the color plates preceding the rest.

THE POTTERS AND
POTTERIES OF BENNINGTON

. .

PART ONE
THE NORTON POTTERIES
1793–1894

NOTE

THE widespread interest in Bennington pottery, the frequency with which it is mentioned in books and magazines relating to American ceramics, and the high prices paid for specimens by numerous collectors have had the natural result of arousing the interest of numerous dealers and amateur collectors. It is not surprising that any piece of pottery marked *Bennington* has seemed to many dealers and private owners to be valuable. It has not been understood that the Bennington pottery sought by most collectors is that which was made at the potteries conducted by C. W. Fenton, all of which was made within a space of less than fifteen years, and that the pottery industry was carried on in Bennington by the Norton family for a full century — the marked pieces covering ninety years.

At the same time, a smaller but not inconsiderable number of collectors to whom the foregoing distinction is clearly known, collect the coarser and less costly stoneware pottery made at Bennington by the Norton family. Sometimes they collect this ware only, and sometimes they collect it in conjunction with the finer and more expensive products of Christopher Webber Fenton and his associates.

Because this volume is intended to serve all classes of collectors, it has been my aim to keep sharp and clear the distinction between the Norton Potteries and their products, and the products of Fenton and his associates. Accordingly, the first part of the book is devoted to the Norton family's work — 1793-1894.

J. S.

PART ONE

THE NORTON POTTERIES

I

VERMONT'S FIRST POTTERY

THE first pottery in Bennington was established in 1793, two years after the admission of Vermont into the Union. That this was the first pottery to be established in Vermont seems reasonably certain. The founder and proprietor of the enterprise was a stalwart patriot who had seen much service in the Revolutionary War, Captain John Norton, a native of Goshen, Connecticut.*

In the spring of 1785 John Norton — then aged twenty-seven years — left Williamstown, Massachusetts, and came to Bennington with his wife and their firstborn, an infant three or four months old. They had lived in Williamstown only a short time. A man of modest substance, Norton now purchased a large farm, said to have been then regarded as one of the finest in the town. It lay little more than a mile south of the Meeting House, traversed by the main highway between Canada and Massachusetts Bay, on the road from Bennington to Pownal. At that time Vermont had not yet been admitted into the

* Edwin Atlee Barber says (*The Pottery and Porcelain of the United States*, p. 104) that William Norton was associated with his brother in the establishment and operation of this pottery. While William Norton settled in Bennington near his brother, he never was connected with the pottery in any way whatsoever, either as part proprietor or workman.

Union. Its claims for admission were stoutly resisted by New York and as a result it was virtually an independent republic, with its own coinage, post-offices and post-roads; its own naturalization laws and its own independent foreign relations.

John Norton had served in the Revolutionary Army from 1776 to 1781. He was a Captain in the Eighteenth Connecticut Regiment and took part in important engagements at Long Island, Haarlem Heights, and White Plains. He heard the guns roar at the siege of Fort Washington, and he was one of the guards of Major André, and present at his execution. One of his Bennington neighbors, Hiram Harwood, to whose diaries we are indebted for much of our knowledge of the pioneer potter and his work, greatly agitated by the charges made by one historian, asked Captain John Norton about that tragic event. The incident is recorded under the date, December 12, 1820:

I went to Capt. N.'s to get our fanning mill — talked with him on the execution of André to which he was an eye-witness — instead of its being an affair of revenge, as Bisset would have it, every American officer and soldier mourned and regretted it most affectionately. Any man doubting the disposition of that author toward this country will here find sufficient testimony to condemn him.

The Norton Genealogy traces the family ancestry back to one Seigneur de Norville who accompanied William the Conqueror when he landed in England, in September, 1066. In the year 1639 Thomas Norton and Grace, his wife, with their children and several neighbors, left Guildford, Surrey, England, and came to this country. They landed at Boston and settled the town of Guilford, Connecticut. Thomas Norton, who was a strict Puritan, was the first miller in the town, and the place where his mill stood — about half a mile east of the present boundaries of the town — was, until quite recently, commonly known as 'Norton's Quarters.'

David Norton, of Goshen, was a lineal descendant of the Puritan miller, and the first Vermont potter was the fourth son of David, and was born at Goshen, November 29, 1758. He married Lucretia Buel, youngest daughter of the distinguished patriot Jonathan Buel. Captain Norton was a man of considerably more than the average education.

In so far as can be learned, during the first seven years of his residence in Bennington, Captain Norton devoted himself entirely to farming. He established a distillery, but whether that was in operation before 1793 is not positively known. The date of the beginning of the pottery business is shown by family records, amply supported by contemporary evidence. The first kiln was erected in 1793. Pitkin says in his book: 'Presumably Capt. Norton was originally a maker of what are now known as red wares. Every indication tends to show, that in his first pottery, at Bennington, only salt-glazed stoneware was produced.' * This does not at all accord with the available evidence. In the first place, the confounding of 'red ware' and 'stoneware' is misleading. In the second place, the earliest well-authenticated specimens of Captain Norton's pottery are *not* salt-glazed.

What is probably the earliest, as well as the best authenticated, piece made at the original pottery is a small brown earthenware jug, made of the local clay covered with what old potters call 'Albany Slip.' It was made not later than 1798, and probably somewhat earlier. Its history is unimpeachable. Omindia Armstrong was born at Bennington in 1788. She lived there uninterruptedly until 1880, when she died at the age of ninety-two. As Omindia Gerry (Mrs. Jethro Gerry) she was one of the best known inhabitants of the town. She gave the

---

* Albert Hastings Pitkin: *Early American Folk Pottery, including the History of the Bennington Pottery*, p. 17. I have corrected the impossible punctuation of Pitkin, here and elsewhere.

first subscription — one hundred dollars — toward the cost of building the Bennington Battle Monument.

When she was a little girl, not quite ten years old, the jug was made for her at the original Norton pottery by Abel Wadsworth, who was a potter there. Mrs. Gerry never let the jug go out of her possession until she was in her ninetieth year. On March 22, 1878, she presented the piece to Mr. George Wadsworth Robinson, one of Bennington's most respected citizens. Mr. Robinson at once wrote out an account of the jug and its history and placed the document in the jug, where it was always kept until, with great difficulty, I removed it, in the early part of 1922, for the purpose of mounting it for its preservation. From 1878 until their removal to my house neither jug nor paper had ever left the Robinson homestead.

The jug is an altogether charming bit of pottery. It is about six inches high. Upon each side there is a rather crude decoration in the shape of a spray of leaves rather lighter than the rest of the coat of 'slip' with which it is glazed. That it is a coating of 'slip,' and not salt glaze, is beyond dispute. It is easy to see how it was dipped. The body is like other red ware known to have been made at the Norton Pottery. It was baked exceedingly hard.

Another specimen of the ware produced at the original pottery of Captain Norton, though perhaps at a somewhat later date than the jug, is in my collection. It is just as well authenticated as 'Aunt Mindy' Gerry's little jug. It is a gracefully shaped jar or pot, about nine and one half inches high, with handles for carrying. It is of red ware, lead-glazed. This piece belonged to Sarah Ostrander, wife of Peter Ostrander. Mrs. Ostrander died in 1827, and her husband in the following year — the same year in which Captain Norton died. The jar had long belonged to Mrs. Peter Ostrander and had been treasured by members of the Ostrander family for considerably more than a century before it passed into my possession. Its original owner, Mrs. Peter Ostrander, gave it to her daughter, charging her to preserve it carefully because it was made by Captain John Norton. The Ostrander jar has long been known locally as one of the few pieces undoubtedly made at the first pottery. Its date is certainly not later than 1800.

Somewhat earlier, I am disposed to think, is an old milkpan associated with the name of Asahel Wright, one of the pioneer settlers of Hubbardton, Vermont. Wright, a native of Lenox, Massachusetts, located at Hubbardton and built a log house as early as 1774. He returned to Massachusetts when the war broke out and served six years in the Revolutionary Army. In 1787 he returned to his claim at Hubbardton. Because of the fact that he used a pair of stags in harness to draw in logs he attained considerable notoriety. To the end of his long life of ninety-seven years the sturdy old pioneer treasured a milkpan of red ware, salt-glazed, which he said he had carried, with other things, on horseback from Bennington a few years after his return to Hubbardton. The old milkpan is quite like a number of others that have been found in the locality, and there is nothing save Asahel Wright's story to identify it. Yet there appears no good reason to doubt that it is one of the few pieces which can be definitely attributed to Captain John Norton's Pottery during the first five years of its existence.

Mrs. Luman S. Norton, of Bennington, has two interesting pieces which have been treasured in the family as products of the original Norton Pottery. The cup-shaped vase [Plate II] was owned originally by Julia Knox Pratt, who was born in 1789 and died in 1873. It descended to her great-granddaughter, Elizabeth Pratt Norton. This vase is unlike any other piece of early Vermont pottery known to me. The body is rather lighter in color than is customary in ordinary brown or red ware, and it is lead-glazed.

The other piece [Plate II] was given to the late Luman Spooner Norton by Miss Julia Bingham, one of Bennington's well-known and honored residents until her death some years ago. It came to Miss Bingham from her mother, Mrs. Sophronia Dewey Bingham, who was born in 1791 and was married in 1820. This specimen is thinner than any other piece of the early brown ware that I have come across and is exceedingly light in weight. I judge that this piece and the vase as well belong to a somewhat later period than the other two, perhaps 1810–1820.

In addition to the foregoing, several examples of pottery have been either ploughed up or dug up near the site of the second works (1823–1833). It is a tolerably fair presumption that most of these were made on the premises. So far as is known at present, however, the only specimens from the original pottery concerning whose history there is indisputable evidence are those above described. Neither these nor any of the fragments that have been ploughed or dug up show any trace of a pottery mark, and we are justified in assuming that none was used during the early years. In keeping with one of the universal practices of the trade, jugs and other utensils were sometimes marked with the name or the initials of the person for whom they were made. None of the marked pieces made at the first Norton Pottery has survived, so far as is known. Possibly they all encountered the fate of Hiram Harwood's jugs as told in the following entries:

1821. *Nov.* 19. We worked half a day on the highway and were allowed for it by Capt. N. & Sons. Settled accounts with friend Luman. . . . SettleT. being ended assisted him in marking an unburnt galln. jug the initials of my name & the year being inscribed on the bott. of it.

1821. *Friday, Dec.* 14: Looked for sheep — father & I together — were at Luman's * shop awhile — Saw Capt. N., † L. & J. ‡ & old Mr. Bovee & Capt. D. N. Bratt after brandy. L. & I talked of books — marked a jug 'H. H.'

1822. *Tuesday, Jan.* 22: Didn't see Luman — visited the shop with Corey, Henry & Parsons boys — marked another gall jug because Aust. Dimm'k had broken my 3 qt. one.

1822. *Friday, June* 14: Our ladies visited Uncle Sam's — broke a galon jug marked 'H. H.' filled with molasses, which however they saved as only the nuzzle and handle were broken off — we raved awhile on the subject and let it pass for a bad bargain.

1822. *Saturday, October* 12th. . . . Capt. Norton informed me that he was a soldier on Long Island in 1776 — was in that masterly retreat from that place under Washington — more he told me but I do not recollect nor have I time to record it. Had a gallon jug at Norton's which Norman had curiously marked with the initials of my name and the word 'Rum' annexed.

A large stoneware cider jar, with two handles and a place for a spigot, is marked *I. Judd, Jr. Bennington.* [Plate III.] This piece has been attributed to the original pottery of Captain Norton, but erroneously. Isaac Judd, Jr., was born in 1811, and was, therefore, a lad of twelve when Captain Norton retired from the pottery business in 1823. It is exceedingly improbable that a six-gallon cider jug would have been made for such a lad. It is much more likely that the jar was made between 1830 and 1835 — perhaps soon after the Pottery was removed to the lower village in 1833. This jar is especially interesting from the fact that it is one of the rare examples of Bennington stoneware in which the design was incised and partly filled with cobalt before firing. The potting is admirable and the design shows greater precision than is usual in ware of this kind.

---

* Oldest son of Capt. Norton.   † *Idem.*
‡ John, second son of Capt. Norton.

Outside the meager family records and the recorded deeds that give dates of property transfers, we are indebted for most of our knowledge of Captain Norton to the remarkable diaries kept by Benjamin Harwood and his son Hiram. From these it is possible to obtain a fairly complete picture of the man himself, his family life and his enterprise. Concerning no other early American potter is our information so extensive.

Benjamin Harwood was the first child born in the town of Bennington, the date of his birth being January 12, 1762.* He was past twenty-three years of age, therefore, when Captain Norton came to occupy the neighboring farm, and thirty-one when the latter started his pottery. The elder Harwood began his diary in 1805 and continued it for about four years † when the task was turned over to his son Hiram, who continued it to 1837. Hiram was a much more copious diarist than his father, a man of more diversified interests. It would appear that nothing of importance ever escaped the younger man's attention. Benjamin was content to record the incidents connected with the life of his farm and his family. It is not surprising, therefore, that he does not even mention the pottery of his neighbor and friend. His references to Captain Norton have to do only with farming and trading:

This day Capt. Norton inoculated several trees in my young orchard. — *August* 30, 1806.

I dont think there are many orchards of the same bigness with so much bad tasted fruit in them, but I have promised myself that, if I live till next spring, and have the care of this orchard, that it shall be ingrafted with better fruit. There are a number of grafts or scions, in many of the trees, but they are not old enough yet to produce any fruit. Capt. Norton put them in about two years ago, he has this year inoculated many of the trees. (See 30th of Augu^t, page 39.) — *September* 20, 1806.

* Isaac Jennings: *Memorials of a Century*, p. 22.
† In his own handwriting little more than a year — the son then acting as scribe.

Made a rough cast on the sum received of Capt. Norton for a mare I sold him in June last, which amounts to thirty-six dollars and sixty-nine cents — 15 Ds in cash and the other in merchandise. — *August* 10, 1810.

What appears to be the first entry concerning the pottery was made by Hiram later in the same year — October 23, 1810:

This morning father sent off 44 bushels of wheat to Troy by three waggons — two of which belong to Capt. Norton. — They carry wheat for father and he brings back a load of clay for them — or at least causes it to be bro't by Ira who went with his team.

With the cart and oxen I carried Capt. Norton's fanning mill home — I should rather say to Mr. Mellen's barn.

This entry is interesting in that it bears upon the subject of the kind of ware that was made by Captain Norton. For ordinary red ware — or brown ware, as it was more often called — it would have been foolish to draw clay from Troy. For such ware there was an abundance of clay close to the pottery on Captain Norton's own land. Clay was dug there for many years. It is evident that the Troy clay was wanted either for 'slip-covering' or for stoneware bodies. Until well past the middle of the nineteenth century it continued to be the practice for drivers of teams sent to Troy or Albany with ware to stop wherever they saw a cellar being dug, and, if they found clay, to offer to load up with it. Thus the builder was saved the expense of hauling and clay for 'slip' or for stoneware body was obtained without cost to the pottery.

There is a tradition that, during the first seven years, red earthenware only was made by Captain Norton, and that, in 1800, the first stoneware was manufactured, an additional kiln being erected for that purpose. This tradition is wholly unsupported by documentary evidence of any kind. There is not a scrap of such evidence in any of the papers possessed by the Norton family, nor has the most diligent search of contemporary newspapers revealed anything of the sort. Nevertheless, the tradition may be accepted as substantially correct. The authenticated specimens of pottery that have survived are of red earthenware. Furthermore, red earthenware was much easier to make than stoneware. It was simpler to burn, and the kiln for its firing was cheaper and easier to build. Virtually all of the early potteries began with the red or brown earthenware; and it is reasonable to believe that Captain Norton confined himself to that ware at first, adding a stoneware kiln somewhat later.

That there were two kilns is quite evident from some of the entries made by Hiram Harwood in his diaries, for he is careful to particularize as to when he found the Nortons working upon earthenware and when upon stoneware. Here is a typical entry, dated Friday, August 23, 1811.

I enjoyed my friend James' company, and with him went to Capt. Norton's shop that he might see them turning ware, of that however he was disappointed, Mr. Luman, who generally worked at that business, being absent. Capt. Norton was there burning a kiln of brown ware and entered into conversation with us which happened to turn on the weather in the Summer as well as in the Winter; It was remarked that the sun seemed to have very little influence at that season of the year . . . Capt. N. said it did not give out much more heat than a yellow dog hung up in its stead.

If the characteristics of the diarist are taken into account, the fact that he specifically mentions that it was 'a kiln of brown ware' which the good Captain was burning would justify the conclusion that there were at least two kilns at that time. We are not dependent upon such inferences, however. Many other entries scattered through the closely written pages of the diary abundantly prove that there were two kilns, one for each kind of ware. Of course, this accords with the general practice of the industry.

In the diary for 1815 there is an entry, dated January 6th, showing that on that day Hiram Harwood wrote to N. Judd, a potter, residing at Rome, New York, concerning their mutual friends Captain and Luman Norton, that 'they were making ware, of both kinds, stone and clay, very fast.' Then, under date of April 10, 1816, he notes that they were 'burning brown ware kiln.' On November 22, 1820, he records that he 'Paid a friendly visit to fr'd L. Norton — play'd the flute — bo't stone pot for 4/o.' Another entry, dated July 18, 1821, refers again to brown ware: 'On our return called a mom't at Capt. N's — found him heating a kiln of brown ware — some lively things were said & we departed.' On Monday, December 31, 1821, the record reads, 'Made it our chief business to collect strays from our flock — 3 from Capt. N's (where they were setting the stone kiln — rec'd a ld of corn from Col. Brownell who came out with it himself).'

It is believed that Captain Norton and his sons made brick and burned lime. Evidences of brick-making have been found upon the original Captain Norton farm, lately known as the Tudor farm. Under date of December 14, 1832, Hiram Harwood notes that 'trees were felled on the hill W. of the limekiln of 1794–5.' There are a number of references to the purchase of bricks at Captain Norton's. For example, in 1818 we read:

Saturday, December 12: . . . Bo't at capt. Norton's 130 bricks at $1.00 pr hun'd & 1 bush! lime at the limekiln for setting up the stove.

The younger Isaac Jennings quotes from the same diarist the following note, dated December 26, 1818:

This day drew from Capt. Norton's one hundred and fifty bricks and one and a half bushels lime to the meeting-house where E. Montague built a short chimney. The stove was set up on a high box level with the top railing of the pews, the pipe standing perpendicular. After its completion fire was kindled in the stove and operated well.*

* Isaac Jennings: *The Old Meeting House*, p. 44.

Reference has already been made to the fact that the red ware was sometimes lead-glazed. The Ostrander jar already described * is, undoubtedly lead-glazed. It is probable that by far the larger part of the output of such domestic utensils as milkpans and platters were so finished. Although Pitkin notes † the fact that several pieces of ware made at the original pottery were known to exist, he could not have examined them, otherwise he could not have written that 'only salt-glazed ware was produced' at the first pottery. The surviving specimens speak for themselves; but, to place the matter beyond dispute, here is a note from the Harwood diary for Wednesday, April 25, 1827:

Visited the shop of L. Norton — in the road talked a good deal with the Capt., who could not see through the mysterious changes in doctrines now preached up — talked awhile with our old friend L. who was washing milk pans with red lead. Visited the house & got papers — went to the corn house where they were thrashing Ind. corn in a kind of box with a bottom calculated for letting through the corn & retaining the cobs.

That they also made salt-glazed ware is equally certain. The red — or brown — ware was lead-glazed as a rule, though 'slip' was sometimes used. Under date of March 20, 1826, the same patient chronicler tells us that he 'March'd to the shop of L. & J. Norton. Saw friend John throwing salt into the hot kiln. Esqr. Bates appeared to be tending the fire.'

We can hardly know too much concerning our early industries and the manner of their development, and we may well be grateful for the industry and persistence with which our diarist wrote of men and events as he saw them. He heard and saw everything, and forgot nothing. The thousands of pages that he wrote, many of them now so faded as to be almost illegible, give us such a picture of life in early Vermont as can be found nowhere else. It is to be hoped that they will

* See p. 6.   † Pitkin, *op. cit.*, p. 17.

PLATES

Plates I, VIII, XII, XV, XXV, XXXIII, XXXVII and XL, which are in color, precede the remainder of the plates.

Except as otherwise noted in the captions, the examples illustrated are from the author's collection.

PLATE I. Lion on Base with *Cold-Slaw* Mane—Flint Enamel Ware
Illustration from specimen *owned by Gilbert Balkam.*

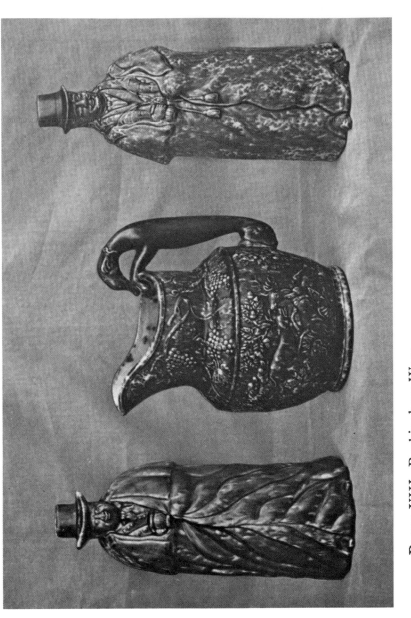

PLATE VIII. Rockingham Ware

The plate illustrates the *Monk* and *Coachman* bottles and the famous hound-handled pitcher modelled by Greatbach. For identifying the latter close attention should be given to three points, viz., (*a*) the neck of the dog is arched well above the forepaws; (*b*) the collar of the dog is a chain with clearly defined links, not a flat band; (*c*) the belly of the dog is a rather sharp ridge, not flattened or rounded as in many other models. Each of these points is to be found in various other hound pitchers, *but in no other case are the*

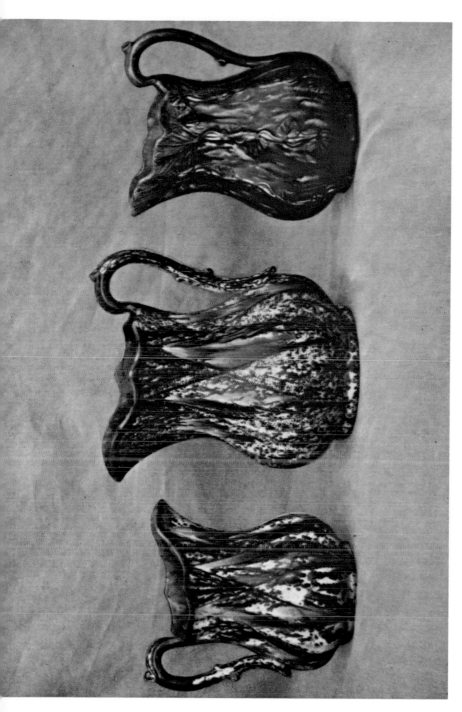

PLATE XII. Flint Enamel Ware Pitchers

The one in the center was formerly owned by Decius W. Clark, and is believed to have been his handiwork.

PLATE XV. Dog Carrying Basket of Fruit — Flint Enamel Ware
Made at the United States Pottery. Never marked.

PLATE XXV. Flint Enamel Ware
Made at the United States Pottery.

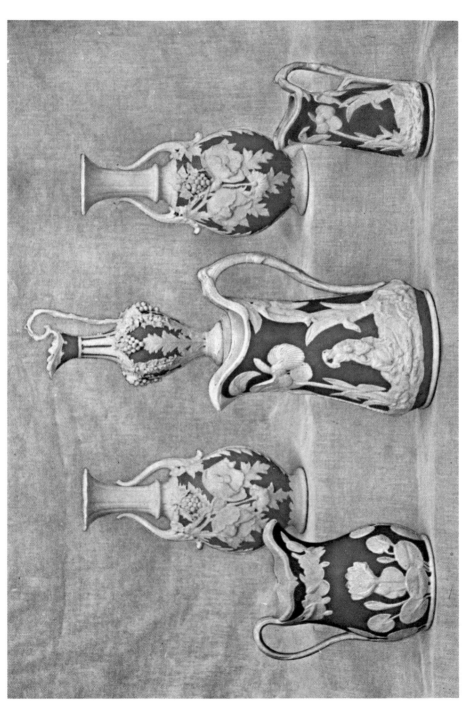

PLATE XXXIII. Colored Porcelain Vases and Pitchers Made at the United States Pottery.

PLATE XXXVII. Presentation Pitcher

Made for Samuel H. Johnson, 76 Pearl Street, New York City, Vice-President of the United States Pottery Company.

PLATE XL. Granite Ware Slop Jar
Made at the United States Pottery for C. W. Fenton and inscribed with his name.
Now owned by his son-in-law, H. D. Fillmore.

PLATE II. Examples from the First Norton Pottery
1. The Omindia Gerry jug. (See p. 6.) 2. The Ostrander jar. (See p. 6.) 3. The Julia Knox Pratt vase. (See p. 7.) 4. The Sophronia Dewey Bingham jar. (See p. 8.)

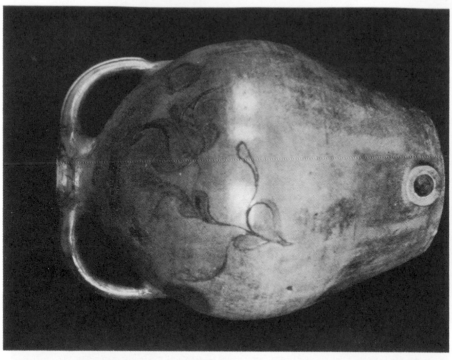

PLATE III. Early Norton Stoneware

1. (*left*). Stoneware jar with umber decoration, bearing the earliest Norton mark. 2.
The Isaac Judd jar. (See p. 9.)

PLATE IV. Stoneware Jars with Cobalt Decorations
Made at the Norton Potteries.

PLATE V. Pitchers

Made by Norton and Fenton. Rockingham Ware or "**Dark Lustre**," as the manufacturers called it. (See p. 87.)

PLATE VI.
Julius Norton (*top*); Christopher Webber Fenton (*lower left*); Decius W. Clark (*lower right*).

PLATE VII.

1. (*above*). Stoneware inkstand with cobalt decorations, made by Julius Norton. (See p. 76). 2. Slip-covered red earthenware pitchers, made at the United States Pottery. *Owned by G. S. McKearin.* (See p. 165.)

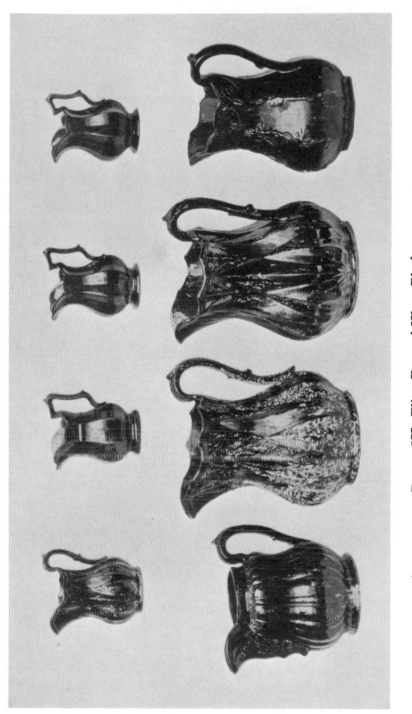

PLATE IX. Flint Enamel Ware Pitchers
Made at the United States Pottery.

PLATE X. Flint Enamel Ware
Made at the United States Pottery.

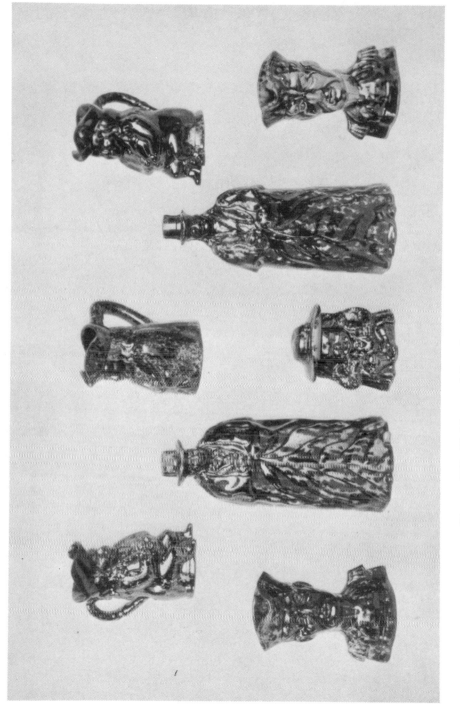

PLATE XI. Tobies and Bottles in Rockingham Ware
Made at the United States Pottery.

PLATE XIII. Porcelain Pitchers

Made at the United States Pottery. All marked. *Upper row*, white; various glazes. *Bottom row*, first on left tan and white, the others blue and white. The one third from the left, with oak-leaf design, is *owned by Mrs. W. Meagher, of Bennington.*

PLATE XIV. Recurbent Cow in Flint Enamel Ware

The tips of the horns have been broken off. United States Pottery Co. mark. *From a specimen owned by Mrs. Joseph Lyman.*

PLATE XVI. White Earthenware Ornaments — Granite Ware

The Swan has a blue line around the cushion base. The Cow-Creamer is decorated in gold. *Former owned by Mrs. Harriet L. M. Sibley; the latter by G. S. McKearin.*

PLATE XVII. Presentation Piece by John Harrison
The first porcelain successfully made at Bennington. (See p. 79.)

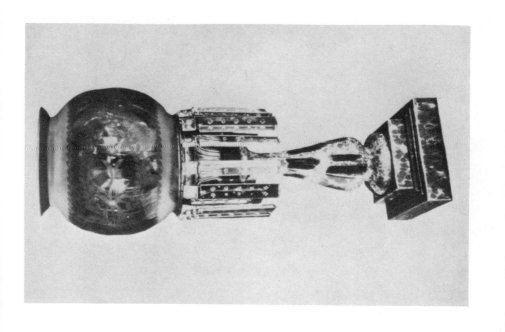

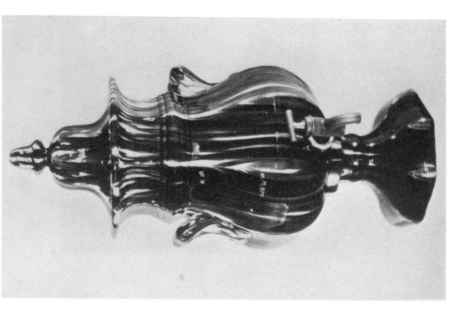

PLATE XVIII. Flint Enamel Ware

1. Brilliantly colored hot water urn. 2. Table lamp with base and standard. Both made at the United States Pottery. *Lamp owned by G. S. McKearin.*

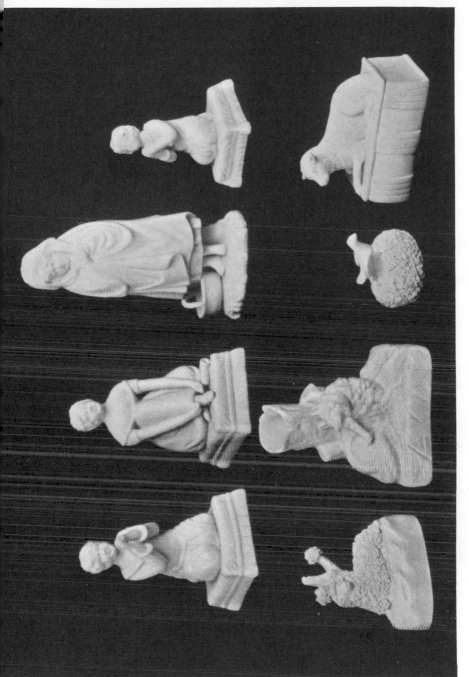

PLATE XIX. Porcelain Figurines
Made at the United States Pottery.

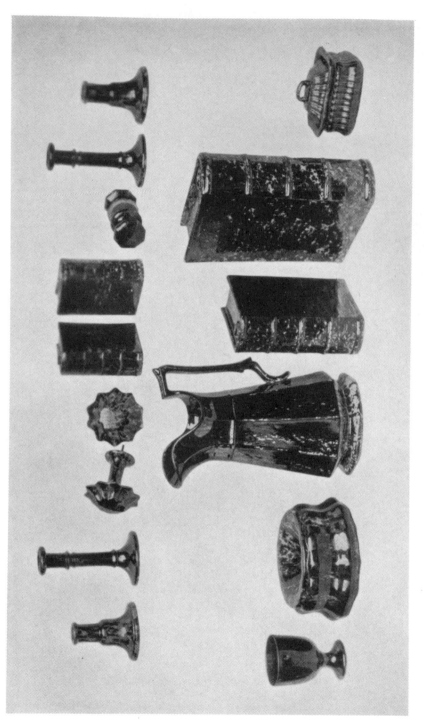

PLATE XX. Articles in Flint Enamel and Rockingham Wares

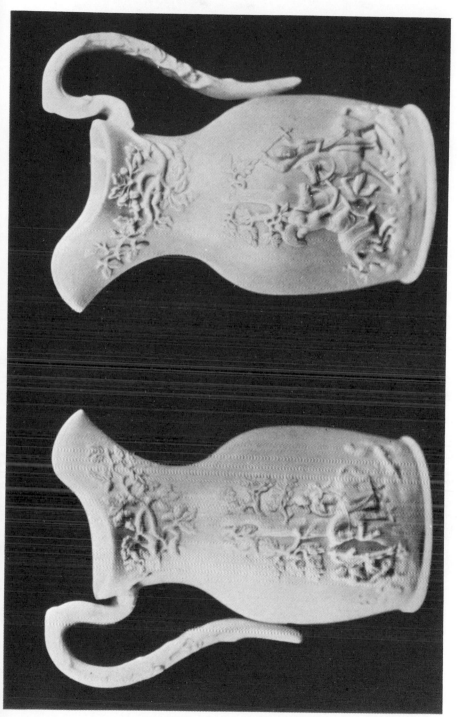

PLATE XXI. White Porcelain Pitcher, *Love and War*
Made a: Fenton's Works. An early piece. (See p. 116.)

PLATE XXII. Blue and White Porcelain Vases
Made at the United States Pottery. Never marked.

PLATE XXIII. Flint Enamel Ware
Made at the United States Pottery.

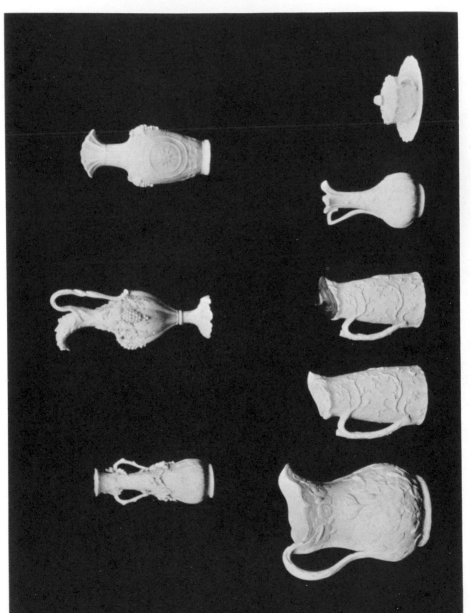

PLATE XXIV. White Porcelain
Made at the United States Pottery.

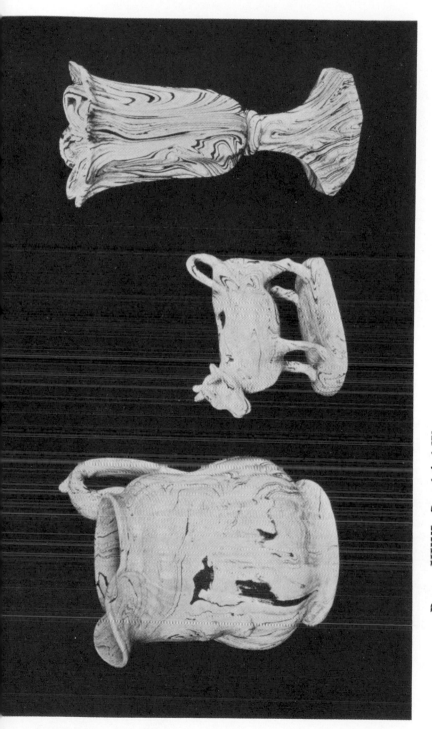

PLATE XXVI. Scrodcled Ware

Made at the United States Pottery. (See p. 185.) *Illustration from specimens in the Wadsworth Atheneum, Morgan Memorial Museum, Hartford, Connecticut.*

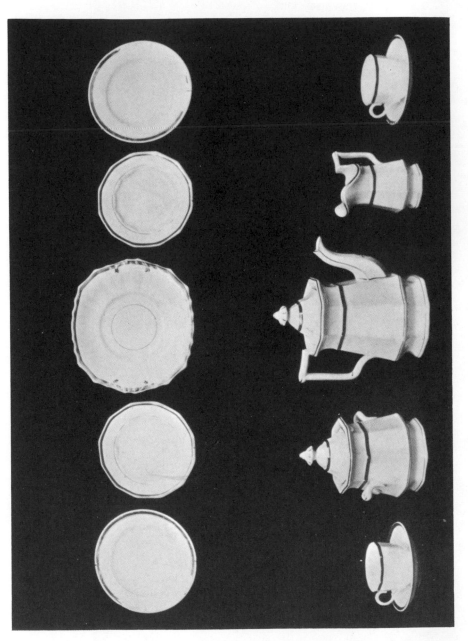

PLATE XXVII. Gold-Banded White Porcelain Table Ware
Made at the United States Pottery. *Illustration from service owned by Mrs. Charles H.*

PLATE XXVIII. Porcelain Jewelry

These brooches and pendants were not manufactured commercially, but were made by individual workmen for relatives and friends as personal favors. They are practically identical with others made at numerous other potteries, both American and European. Those illustrated have been carefully traced to the United States Pottery.

PLATE XXIX. Jewel Casket in Gold-Decorated White Granite Ware
(See p. 164.)

PLATE XXX. Pair of Deer in Flint Enamel Ware
Marked. *The Doe* (below) *is owned by W. J. Hickmott.*

PLATE XXXI. Parian Dogs
   The one above has had mustachios added by a whimsical potter. *It is owned by W. J. Hickmott.*

PLATE XXXII. Pair of White Pottery Dogs — Heavily Enamelled
Formerly owned by Decius W. Clark. (See p. 137.) *Owned by George S. McKearin.*

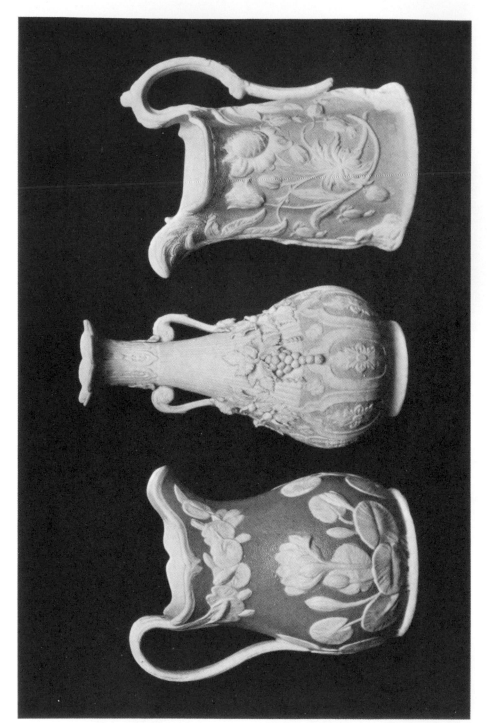

PLATE XXXIV. Blue and White Porcelain
Made at the United States Pottery

PLATE XXXV. Animals in Light Rockingham Ware
1. Dog Carrying Basket of Fruit. 2. Cow-Creamer.

PLATE XXXVI. Earthenware Presentation Pitchers — Granite Ware

The one at the extreme left is owned by Fenton's granddaughter, Mrs. Ralph H. White, of North Bennington.

PLATE XXXVIII. Lions without Base

1 (*above*). The *cold-slaw* or *rough-cast* mane type. 2. (*below*). The smooth curly mane type. *The latter is owned by G. S. McKearin.*

PLATE XXXIX. Rockingham Ware

All of the articles here represented are true Rockingham, and not Flint Enamel Ware, though some are so marked and practically all are commonly so classified. (See p. 174.)

PLATE XLI. Flint Enamel Ware Pitcher
Made at the United States Pottery. Illustrated in color in Plate XII.

PLATE XLII. Granite Ware Presentation Pitcher
Obverse and reverse of the example shown in colors in Plate XXXVII.

PLATE XLIII. Tulip Vases
Flint Enamel Ware made at the United States Pottery.

PLATE XLIV. Hound-Handled Pitcher

Rockingham Ware. Modelled by Greatbach. For points of identification compare note on Plate VIII.

be published and so rescued from obliteration. Even such items as the following note from the diary for 1816 are of value to the student:

Monday, March 18th: ... Carried to L. Norton's, this morning, Sophia W's foot wheel — Sarah sent her a thousand million thanks for the use of it. Visited the ship — Friend L. and his father were taking down some frozen green ware, spoiled by the frost — The boys had been in the shop Sabbath-day and left the door unlatched. Nothing of the kind had occurred since the completion of the cell, 4 Winters past.

There are no records extant which enable us to determine with accuracy at what date Captain Norton took his two sons into partnership with him. We shall not be far wrong, however, if we say that it was probably in 1811 or 1812. This conjecture is based principally upon the fact that, up to 1812, Hiram Harwood always refers to the pottery as 'Capt. Norton's.' From 1812 to 1823 he refers to it variously as 'Capt. Norton and Sons,' 'J. & L. Norton's,' and 'The Nortons.' This statement is subject to some qualification, however. For instance, there is an entry, dated June 24, 1815, in which 'Captain Norton's Pottery' is referred to:

Between 4 & 5 P. M. entered Capt. Norton's Pottery — Staid half an hour and saw nobody — Wrote a few words expressive of my astonishment at not seeing friend Luman laboring at his wheel, so *rare* was the instance. What surprised me *more* was, to find an open bowl standing on his mould bench, with paper money in it.

Now, at this time Captain Norton and his two sons were in partnership, the firm's name being John Norton & Sons. It may well be that the oldest son, Luman, was first taken into partnership with his father and the firm name of J. & L. Norton adopted. John's, the second son's, admission to partnership later on probably necessitated the change of the firm name to John Norton & Sons. This, however, is merely conjecture. Removals and disastrous fires destroyed the early business records of the Nortons and there exist no known records of any kind which would enable us to determine the matter with finality. Perhaps it is immaterial.

It is known that in 1815 Captain Norton and his two sons, Luman and John, were acting in partnership, the firm name being John Norton & Sons. No piece of pottery bears the mark of this firm, but there exists an old receipted bill, dated July 21, 1815, which shows that William Henry, Esqr., bought wares from the firm of John Norton & Sons to the value of $20.51. The bill is interesting and valuable for the information it affords concerning the types of ware made and the prices charged for them. Mr. Henry purchased the following items:

12 Doz.	Milk Pans		@ 9/	$18.00
1 "	Large Platters		" 6/	1.0
1 "	2nd. Size	"	" 5/	0.84
1 "	3rd.	" "	" 4/	0.67
				$20.51

The partnership of Captain Norton and his two older sons embraced more than the pottery business. It covered the farming and the distillery business as well. Captain Norton, besides assisting at the pottery, was principally responsible for the management of the distillery. When his youngest child, Norman J. Norton, who was born in 1806, grew old enough, he assisted his father in this work. From about 1812 Luman was primarily concerned with managing the pottery, while John, who was two years his junior, managed the farm. There was a good deal of overlapping, but in general the labors were divided as stated. In 1823 the copartnership of father and sons was dissolved by mutual consent, and a division of the firm's properties was amicably arranged. The Harwood diary for 1823, contains this record — dated April 11th:

Capt. Norton & his Sons lately dissolved partnership — Capt. N. takes his old farm and the Still — Luman takes the pottery with the S. third of the Atwood farm — John takes the other two-thirds & continues in the pottery with his brother — farther I am not able to state.

Actually Luman received a three-fourths interest in the pottery, John receiving the other fourth and remaining in the business for some time as partner. Soon afterward the pottery was moved to a new site. The old pottery had stood a little to the north of Captain Norton's house, on the site of what was later known as the 'Davenport house,' and still more recently, as the 'Tudor house.' Luman moved the establishment farther south, to his own property. This second site was opposite the house, which he had erected for himself in 1817, known to old residents of Bennington as the 'Rockwood farmhouse.' Two entries from the Harwood diaries bear upon this phase of our history:

All hands went to L. Norton's raising. Through misunderstanding between Oliver Abel & L. Taft, his head carpenter at this building, the front part (42 × 26) only was raised — Being in height two stories — The kitchen and woodhouse were raised next day. Ephraim Smith Esqr. who attended among others and appeared in a very unusual strain of playful gaiety and good humor died very suddenly about 8 in the evening, in an apoplectic fit — Sixty years of age in April last.' * — *May 9,* 1817.

Accompanied Montague to Major L. Norton's — 'They were sometime in trying to make a bargain about laying the walls of the great old shop which L. intended in May or June to remove on to his part of the Atwood farm just above Machey's. They could not agree whether it should be by the job or by the day — $20 parted them — L. offered him $50 — Montague asked $70 — The only thing they finally established was that M. should have the job at all events. At the time Mrs. N. had her dinner ready M. L. Selden came to get bricks for the furnace which they had lately blown out, to fix the hearth — Our friend went to wait on him — M. & I sat down to dinner —

---

* This Ephraim Smith was the father of the wife of John Norton, Jr. He and his father, John Smith, were both in the Battle of Bennington.

Luman returned with an Englishman who transacted business for Hunt — who had just rec'd bricks to the am't, I think, of $13 — 87½ at 0/9 a piece. I got a two gall. jug which was included in our settl'mt (p. 318) — had put in it 2 galls high wines — equal to 2½ reduced. — *March* 12, 1823.

. . . Carried List for 1823 to L. Norton one of the Listers. . . . Visited capt. N. & Z. Pierce. Luman was by his wheel in his new situation N. of Mackey's. The whole establishment was now removed & removing to sd spot. — *Wednesday, July* 9, 1823.

These entries are significant in that they enable us to determine a matter long in dispute locally. One tradition has named the Tudor farm as the site of the original pottery, while another has named the Rockwood farm. What appear to be remains of kilns have been found in both places, and as a result there has been no little uncertainty with regard to the matter. Thanks to the good Hiram Harwood, we can regard the question as definitely settled.

After the removal of the pottery building to its new site, Captain Norton is rarely mentioned in connection with it. There is one entry in the diary for 1825, however, which would seem to indicate that, notwithstanding the dissolution of the partnership, the Captain and his two sons, on occasion, still acted jointly, under the old firm name, as though there had been no dissolution:

Tuesday, Nov. 22: In the eveg I settled accounts in full with Majr. L. Norton. We rec'd credit for cider 1890 gallons — 2 less than my minutes shewed — that is 59 bbls 2 Gs. His book acct against us from Nov. 11, 1823 to this date arose to $7.10 — my charge was only a flat file — .50, which reduced his demand to $6.60, which I balanced with cider at 87½ per bbl — say 7½ bbls. The price I did not much like — but could do no better — & there was rec'd in Nov. & Dec. 1823 IG 3 qts.1pt. more brandy than our due, which being subtracted from what was now coming — there remained due 88 galls. & 1 pt., for which rec'd due-bill signed J. Norton & Sons. The remainder of the eveg taken up with conversing about the N. River — the situation of N. Y. City, Staten Island, the Theatres in N. Y. &c &c.

Other entries show that, notwithstanding the division made in 1823, the several Norton enterprises, and the Norton interests in general, remained interlocked almost, if not quite, as closely as before. Customers who owed for wares supplied by the pottery firm delivered cider to Captain Norton at his distillery in payment, and debts to Captain Norton the distiller were paid by supplying goods or giving service to the pottery firm which was known both as L. & J. Norton and as L. Norton & Co. The Norton family interests and enterprises at this time were extensive and varied. In combinations of members and under trade-names as varied, they embraced farming, distilling, blacksmithing, storekeeping, and pottery manufacture, as well as other business activities.

From 1823 to the end of 1827 the pottery was owned and operated by the two sons, Luman and John. I believe the earliest mark used is that of *L. Norton & Co.* Pieces so marked are occasionally found. They belong to the period 1823–1827. Thereafter, throughout the whole history of the pottery industry in Bennington — so far as the Norton Potteries were concerned, at any rate — this practice of marking the wares was maintained. Consequently, from this point onward, we can ascribe approximate dates to most of the wares produced.

Hiram Harwood, despite his habitual precision in such matters of detail, refers to the pottery during this period in such a variety of ways as to suggest that he was not always sure how things stood or how the firm should be designated. Under date of August 25, 1825, he writes: 'Father rode to L. Nort's in the big wagg. accompᵈ by litt. Hopkins & bro't home a crate of ware made by L. N. & Co. for S. Waters now Mrs. Ashley.' On March 20, 1826, he refers to the pottery as 'Maj. L. N's'; on May 8, 1826, he refers to it as 'L. & J. Norton's pottery'; on November 10, 1826, he speaks of the 'shop of L. & J.

Norton' and describes the operations going on there. On March 8, 1827, he describes a meeting with Esquire Bates who 'said he had watched last night with L. & J. Norton's kiln.' But, on April 25th of the same year, he writes that he 'visited the shop of L. Norton,' and then, on June 18, 1827, he records that 'Damia & mother went abroad together they bro't from L. Norton & Co's a stone churn & other articles.' Finally, we have this record made on July 16, 1827: 'My little boy visited by my request Maj. L. Norton's & returned with 3 N. Y. pap's. he particularly described in what manner he saw them making pans at the Maj's shop.'

The co-partnership between Luman and John Norton was terminated at or near the end of 1827, and Luman became sole proprietor. What arrangement was made between them we do not know. That it was amicable and mutually satisfactory is evident from the subsequent history of the two. We may conjecture, upon the basis of facts known to us, that John did not care for the business in which his older brother found such keen delight. Be that as it may, our concern is with the fact that, when the year 1828 opened, Luman Norton was sole proprietor of the pottery. He pursued the practice of stamping his wares with his name. All pieces bearing the name *L. Norton* were made in the period 1828–1833, for, in the latter year, Luman Norton took his son Julius into partnership, as we shall see later on, and the firm name became L. Norton & Son.

Soon after John's withdrawal from the partnership, Luman began to improve and to extend the business, thus inaugurating a policy of progressive improvement which lasted over many years. Julius, Luman's only son, was at this time — 1828 — in his nineteenth year. He had shown himself to be possessed of both a liking for the potter's trade and an aptitude for business. Intensely proud of his son, Luman

Norton was, we may surmise, to no small degree influenced by the consciousness that the young man was rapidly reaching an age at which he might be expected to assume a large part of the burden and responsibility of a growing business. An entry made by Hiram Harwood in his diary for June 27, 1829, tells us that he 'rode with Sylvanus to major L. Norton's where the maj. with Montague & journeyman was employed in building a brown-ware kiln.' This was probably an additional kiln, for at this time we note an increase in the number of men employed.

Judged by the standards of later days, the pottery industry in Bennington prior to 1830 was so small in its scope as to be almost insignificant. During its first thirty years — from 1793 to 1823 — there is little likelihood that, at any one time, more than six hands had been employed, including Captain Norton himself and his two older sons. As already noted, in 1828 the business passed into the hands of Luman Norton. In the *Vermont Gazette*, January 11, 1831, was published a 'Bennington Business Directory for 1831.' Its description of the pottery reads as follows: 'One Stone Ware Manufactory. — L. Norton. Employs 12 hands.'

Small and unimportant as this seems to us nowadays, we must remember what was the condition of Vermont nearly a century ago. A pottery employing half a dozen men would measure well above the average of the potteries that were scattered throughout New York and New England. Furthermore, it would be capable of turning out a volume of wares such as would seem almost incredible to the uninitiated. Various records in the diaries of Hiram Harwood demonstrate this. I cite a few examples:

Staid after dinner, sometime in the shop. A Mr. Stone from Arlington took off a load of ware — Saw several orders from merchants in different towns for ware, yet to be answered. — *June* 13, 1815.

1819. *Saturday, December* 18: Settled accounts with capt. Norton. . . . Mr. Godfrey came there to get a load of ware to carry to Lenox Furnace to exchange for stoves &c.

. . . Visited friend Luman N. — Montague and John Jr. were present. We talked of History, the Iliad, Gods and Godesses &c in fact we could hardly break off for other concerns — I left them loading ware & came home. — *Sunday, May* 28, 1820.

Spent the eveg at Capt. Norton's very agreeably — played the flute — an amusement not often taken up these days — Luman & John packed a ld of ware bound to Berlin, N. Y. — Searls & Deacon E. Fay were present at the shop. — *Monday, Nov.* 17, 1823.

. . . L. & J. Nort. Jr. were preparing a load of ware for W. Creek. — *Thursday, Apr.* 29, 1824.

. . . C. Brown arrived from Berlin much agitated about paying for his horse and wagg. — considered himself ill used — p^d $1.75 for 21 miles — the terms were 8¢ pr mile — he bro't news of my friend Luman Norton, who was on his way to N. York, falling from his wagg. & breaking his left arm — on the road to Troy. . . . . was seated on the top of a load of ware — the wheels suddenly falling into a deep rut occasioned the catastrophe. — *Wednesday, May* 19, 1824.

Walked to Capt. Norton's — visited L. N. — found him engaged with the 2d. Vol. of State Papers, U. S. — my visit was rather spoiled by their (L. & J.) * being obliged to continue about carrying off ware. — *Sunday, July* 11, 1824.

Returning from Troy on Wed'y the 6th near the summit of the hill just mentioned met my fr'd Judd, had not time to speak with him J. Nort. & Hummiston were in rear with loads of stone ware. — *Saturday, October* 9, 1824.

. . . met J. Norton Jr. & B. Loomis with their (team) returning from carrying off ware to Woodstock, Vt. — *February* 10, 1827.

Evening with Geo & Hopkins visited maj. L. Norton & people — Julius,

* Luman and John.

Bates, &c. were making fine music. (Jas. P. Godfrey having returned from trip of carrying off ware made settle^t with maj. L.) that business being ended drew up and made settl^t in full with him for ware had since he was last paid in Jan. of the present year — amt'g to $6.33. — *Saturday, Dec. 24,* 1830.

After starting home was overtaken and conveyed by our neighbor J. Pitts Godfrey, who was on his return from carrying a load of ware to Chesterfield N. H. in wagg. to Mr. Fay's where I called and paid Mrs. Lydia Fay $4., Bennington money towards weaving. — *January 6,* 1831.

In addition to sending loads of wares to neighboring towns, the establishment catered to the community, supplying most, if not all, of the local demand for such domestic utensils as were made there. People went to the pottery to buy what they needed, and, judging by the purchases made for the Harwood household, the total volume of this trade must have been considerable. Turning over the pages of the old diaries from which I have quoted so much, without making any effort to tabulate all the purchases of earthenware and stoneware utensils therein recorded, I note the purchase of quart and two-quart jugs (1815), milkpans and slop-bowls (1818), butter pots and preserve pots (1821), wash-bowl (1822), Dutch pan (1825), stone churn (1827), large milkpans in half-dozen and one and two dozen lots (1817, '18, '22, '25, '26, '27, '28, '29), six-gallon pot (1829), two-gallon pot (1830), crock and four-gallon pot (1831). Add to these the large jugs elsewhere mentioned by the same writer, the platters of different sizes enumerated in the Henry bill, the other items of a similar character to which reference has been made, and the casual mention of milk pails being turned — the result is an illuminating list, which shows how important the industry must have been to the community.

The items mentioned are typical, and they prove that the products of the pottery were important from a purely utilitarian point of view.

Pewter was both too expensive and too heavy for many purposes, besides being unsuited to not a few of the uses to which earthenware or stoneware was adapted. Tinware was not cheap and abundant as it was destined later to be.

Of course, we labor under the disadvantage of having only the account of a single family's purchases. Were it possible to obtain a score of diaries like Hiram Harwood's, we should find, doubtless, that practically every family represented in them made similarly liberal purchases at the pottery. Here is an entry from the Harwood diary for the year 1822, which gives a glimpse of the retail trading at the pottery itself:

July 25: Visited L. Nort. with whom as usual talked of books &c. Reynolds Carpenter called — L. enquired earnestly as to the success of the subscription for the new publication — did not distinctly hear the reply. Old Mr. Martindale came to buy ware — Brown, Temple of W[oo]df[or]d & H. Potter were there. A negro man sold a few whortle-berries — took his pay in ware.

According to present standards, there is something ludicrous in the spectacle of the negro peddler trading whortle-berries for crockery. We must bear in mind, however, that money was scarce in those days and that a considerable part of the trade of the people took the form of simple barter. It was common for customers to pay for their pots and pans with cider, beef, wood, apples, cheese, and so on. Sometimes they paid with labor. A typical transaction is recorded by Hiram Harwood in the following entry, dated October 20, 1829:

Agreed to furnish major L. Norton with 12 bbls cider at 4/0 per bbl in payment of a ware debt and for what I might call for over and above that. Should not have contracted so low if I had not supposed the article to be unusually plenty — for he told me he could buy as much as he pleased at 3/0, payable in ware.

It is worth while noting the prices that were charged for the various wares. In the Henry bill, milkpans are charged at $1.50 per dozen, 'large platters' at $1.00 per dozen, medium-sized at 84 cents, and small ones at 67 cents per dozen. That was in 1815. In the Harwood diary for 1818 we note, under date of September 30th, this entry:

This morning went to capt. Norton's — received ½ doz. milk pans & 2 slop bowls on friend Champney's acct. — amounting to $1.25. They were burning the stone ware kiln.

In 1821 butter pots and preserve pots were charged at nine pence each, for on November 21st of that year Hiram Harwood made this record:

I visited Luman twice — got two butter pots of one of which made a crock — and two small preserve pots at 0/9; the whole amtd to 3/6.* Mentioned to him that I was reading Prince Eugene.

In 1822 the price of a wash-bowl was one shilling, according to this entry for November 11th:

In the eveg settled accts at L. Norton's — found due for 1821, 62 glls. 3 qrts brandy — and for 1822 after deducting 9 gs. 1qt. & pt. for ware ($4.93) 46. .1. .00 — Talked over many old things, bo't a wash-bowl at 1/0 & came home

Prices did not change much during the first forty years, judging by such records as we have.

So far as is now known, no ornamental wares of any kind were produced at the first pottery. The age was one of utility pure and simple, with little time for ornament or thought concerning it. The practice of decorating stoneware jugs, pots, crocks, churns, and other articles with designs representing birds, animals, fruits, and flowers, done in cobalt or raw umber, was adopted later. Pieces marked *L. Norton & Co.*, made from 1823 to 1828, are frequently so decorated.

* The figures in the diary appear to be 8/6. Probably what looks like an '8' was intended to be a '3.'

The only evidence of such ornamentation in the wares produced during the first thirty years is the crude but pleasing bit of decoration upon the little jug that Abel Wadsworth made for his ten-year-old friend, Omindia Armstrong, in 1798 or thereabouts. Art has been defined as 'the little extra flourish which a man adds to his work.' Judged by that definition, the little friendship token made by Abel Wadsworth is the one example of that early craftsmanship touched with conscious art. Let it be added, however, that the other early pieces are characterized by a grace of line which makes them things of simple beauty.

It would appear from the scanty records which we now possess that, from 1828 to the end of 1832, the manufacture of stoneware increased at the Norton Pottery and that of red earthenware declined in relative importance. To improve the quality of his product the enterprising potter went farther afield for his clay. Although the statement has often been made that, as early as 1800–1802, clay from Long Island and New Jersey was used, there is no evidence of it, and we may dismiss the statement as a mere conjecture. Neither in the Harwood diaries nor in any other contemporary records is there any mention of the transportation of clay from such a distance.* Not until toward the end of 1833 is there any positive evidence of the use of New Jersey clay. November 17, 1833, Hiram Harwood recorded that he was 'very badly jolted coming from Troy with Mr. Scrivener — teamster of Stephen Dewey, 3 horses — wagg. loaded with about 16 hund. Amboy Clay for maj. L. Norton.' It may well be that there were earlier importations of this clay, but it is unlikely that the material had been largely used much before that time.

* Aldrich's *History of Bennington County* says (p. 333), 'Up to about 1825 native clay only was used in the manufacture of earthenware, but at that time the proprietors commenced using clays from South Amboy and Long Island, continuing, however, the partial use of the native material for some time.'

II

THE EARLY POTTERS

WE can hardly help being as much interested in the early potters of Bennington themselves, as in such examples of their work as have come down to us, or in the accounts of the industry penned by our indefatigable diarist. Who these men were, how they worked and lived, and in what manner they influenced the development of the industry in Vermont, cannot fail to interest us, if we are at all interested in this history. At all events, this book is concerned with the potters of Bennington as well as with their pottery.

CAPTAIN JOHN NORTON

The first person to claim our attention, naturally, is the good Captain Norton himself. We have already learned enough of his ancestry to be prepared to find him 'a man of parts,' as the old saying has it. Of his youth we know very little. That he was a man of intelligence and ability, unusually well educated for his day, we are sure; but we do not know how or when or where he learned the potter's trade. We may surmise, as Pitkin does, that he learned it at Lichfield, Connecticut, as an apprentice to some of the Lichfield potters.*

A pottery had been established at Lichfield, an adjoining town to Goshen, five years before the birth of John Norton — in 1753. Its founder was John Pierce, and among those who worked at the Lichfield Pottery were Jesse Wadhams and Hervey Brooks. If we bear in mind that Captain Jonathan Buel — whose daughter Lucretia the young Captain John Norton married in 1782 — lived at Lichfield, we

* Pitkin, *op. cit.*, p. 16.

shall not find it difficult to assume that the groom served his apprenticeship to some of the Lichfield potters.

Nine children were born to John and Lucretia Norton — four sons and five daughters, all of whom survived their father. As Hiram Harwood, John's friend and neighbor, duly noted in his diary, 'His was the first death that occurred in his family during a course of 44 years.' Although he lived to his seventieth year, and had quite a large number of grandchildren, he was never called upon to mourn the loss of child or grandchild. Because we are — or ought to be — as much interested in the man as in his work, I shall copy from Hiram Harwood's diaries a few entries which will show something of the delightful character of his family life. There are not many equally attractive domestic accounts in early Vermont:

1810. *Wednesday, Dec. 5th:* . . . came to Capt. Norton's and went into his son's part of the house. Capt. Norton and Mr. Loomis were there. The former gentleman requested me to play on my flute. I granted it. After awhile friend John came down stairs; & in the course of the evening his three sisters took seats in the room. I kept up a pretty steady stream of music — perhaps rendered myself odious on that account, but I hope not. I had my notes with me and went over with several pieces of music with Miss Lucretia, who has a soft melodious voice. The girls scattered off — and in a little time I tucked up my spectacles and tune-book — and came whistling, musing and fluting along home.

1811. *Saturday, March* 16: I invited Mr. Locke to take a walk — 'down South' in the evening and so we did — and had music too. I fifed and he whistled. — O we marched along as happy, as happy as could be, — through the meadows and pastures. Back of Capt. Norton's orchard we met with Mr. Luther Smith, who took my flute and joined us in our march. We wheeled to the left, round the S. W. corner of Capt. Norton's barn — having previously made a halt and consulted together about going into the house, to which I was opposed. Locke said he should not have come down there, had it not been for the sake of seeing the girls — he and Smith too, urged me very earnestly to go in, but I obstinately refus'd to comply. Our march was continued down by the house into the road. Smith and Locke went into the house. Locke made a short tarry and came out and had a serious scuffle with Mr. Henry Mellen. I intended not to visit the house — sent word to Smith to borrow Mr. L. Norton's flute and come and play a march or two with me, but I couldn't start him. After amusing myself, and a few boys who came to hear me, with music, I was about to go home, but Mr. Luman, who had once before given me a call, came to the door and again invited me into his apartment. Locke, Mellen and I marched along in, and took seats. Mr. Elisha Smith, who I had not seen before in many months, was taking a game of chess with Mr. John Norton, Junr. Several tunes were blown out, some of which I did without assistance, others Mr. Luman helped me to perform. Capt. Norton called us up into his room, where I had the pleasure of seeing him encircled by his numerous and very respectable family — a sight which, in all probability cannot occur but seldom in a few short years — perhaps never again. Enjoy'd no small degree of pleasure in playing several pieces of music, in which I was joined, sometimes by Mr. Luman with his flute, and by his sister Lucretia, whose soft and melodious voice gave all the beauties and graces which belong'd to our concert. Having, as I suppos'd, worn out the patience of my hearers, I began to make preparations to depart, but Capt. Norton would not consent to have me go yet — said it was not late — and after some droll things were said — I had the question decided by hand-vote — in the negative. I gave them a few more tunes and then, in company with Mister Ault, Mr. Smith (who came with us only a little way) and Mr. Locke — came fifing and potching along the road as far as Mr. Ault's, Mr. Ault having exercised the authority of a military officer in a very lively and spirited manner in the meantime; Now earnestly beset us to go to his house and take some cider with him, which we accordingly did and tarried there, I believe, two hours, hearing him relate some funny anecdotes. Twelve o'clock when I arrived home and had retir'd to rest.

1813. *Thursday, July* 29: Performed the greatest day's work at mowing that I was ever the author of in my life. Carried violin and flute to Capt. Norton's in the eve'g on which Smith and myself played 2 or 3 hours — Smith's drollery provoked a great deal of laughter.

1816. *April* 10: Found the 2 inch auger at Capt. Norton's. Burning brown-ware kiln — Clarissa spinning — Eliza tow. Informed Capt. N. respecting Mr. West.

1816. *Saturday, October* 19: The band met at Capt. Norton's this evening — Young folks went to hear.

1817. *Thursday, July* 17, 1817: We generally attended a religious meeting at Capt. Norton's — mother took care of the children.

1821. *Sunday, October* 21: . . . heard a man halloo in the road half-way from Hunt's to the Bluehill as if in distress — on enquiry found that it was Capt. Norton with his lady going to meeting in their 1 h. waggon. Their horse took fright at the carcase of Waters' cow, became ungovernable — sheared off very abruptly — threw them from the wag. & broke out both thills, but without doing any other serious injury. Of course, the meeting-ride was at an end and they returned home.

1827. *Sunday, July* 22: Late in the day visited Capt. J. Norton — talked upon the Campaign of 1776 — he was at the battles of L. Island, Haarlem Height [*sic!*] & White Plains — recollected hearing the great guns at the seige of Ft. Washington. Saw and spoke with Mrs. C. Barney * whose health was poor — Borrowed N. Y. Spect. of July 10 & 13 & returned home after dark.

While not a 'Christian professor,' to use a phrase common in his day, Captain John Norton was a stout upholder of the Christian Church. He was, according to all accounts, above everything else a reverent man. Religious services were held frequently at his home. He was one of the original square pew proprietors in the Church of Christ in Bennington, built in 1806, and a constant attendant at its services. At the same time he seems not to have refused to do business on Sundays when opportunity offered.

He was a Freemason and a charter member of Temple Lodge, which was chartered by the Grand Lodge of Connecticut in 1793. Among the other members of this Lodge were several close friends: Anthony Haswell, Vermont's pioneer printer and publisher, founder of the *Vermont Gazette* and the *Rutland Herald;* Joseph and David Fay; Noah Smith, the first Grand Master of Vermont; General David Robinson; Isaac Tichenor, elected Governor in 1797. If we are to judge a man by his friends, surely we must accord high rank to Vermont's first potter.

* Captain Norton's daughter.

A genial man, fond of music, happiest when surrounded by his children and grandchildren; an ardent patriot, but quiet and unassuming withal; sagacious in business, persistent in industry, generous to a fault — such is the picture of the man that results from piecing together the many fragments of information that have come down to us. Unlike his two older sons, he never aspired to public office. He was a simple, upright, progressive citizen, respected and beloved by his neighbors. A man of considerable education and a lover of books — a trait which he passed on to his children — it is not surprising to find that he was one of the directors of the first public library established in Bennington, in 1796.* Whether or not that was the first public library established in Vermont I am unable to state. Captain Norton took a keen interest in the Bennington Academy, of which his second son, John Norton, Jr., was one of the directors.

Like most of the men who had participated in the great struggle for American independence, Captain Norton was an intense patriot. He attached great importance to the proper celebration of the 'Glorious Fourth,' the anniversary of Bennington Battle, and similar occasions. He gloried in marching with other veterans of the Revolutionary War to the Meeting House on the sixteenth of August, all wearing evergreen in their hats, afterward proceeding to the tavern to drink loyal and patriotic toasts. He loved to talk to younger men of the great events in which he had participated — the retreat from Long Island under General Washington, in 1776, the execution of André, and so on. We may be quite certain that he cherished for the all too brief remainder of his life the memory of his interview with Lafayette, in New York, July 4, 1825, when the famous French soldier conversed with him and his son Luman 'in the most easy and familiar style.'

* John V. D. S. and Caroline R. Merrill: *Historic Bennington*, p. 59.

Writing in his diary under date of August 17, 1828, Hiram Harwood gives an account of his own last conversation with his old friend. It is perhaps worth while to transcribe enough of the account to complete the picture of the fine old patriot and pioneer potter:

...got time to pay a short visit to our old friend and neighbor, Capt Norton — which proved to be the last. We talked of the shortness of time — of the reputation of gen. E. Allen of Green Mountain Boy memory, for courage which had been disputed, but which our friend could not give up — something was said of B[ennington] B[attle] gr[oun]d — particulars of the day were alluded to — said he had the pleasure of visiting it many years since in the company of gen. Sam. Safford, col. Joseph Safford, capt. Jacob Safford, Lieut. W. Henry and others who could very accurately describe the parts they severally acted, the situation of the enemy, etc. Capt. N. said it was really very entertaining to hear their relation of the deeds of that important day. The Capt. informed me that if he should live until the 29th of Nov. next, he should be 70 years of age — At the period of the battle he was not a resident of this town — commenced his residence here if I mistake not in the year 1784.* At Maj. L's saw S. Loomis — Mrs. N. had very sore eyes — were getting better — borrowed papers — came home reading of gen. Jackson's conduct at the Capital in March 1819 — showing the man's character in full.

Captain Norton did not survive long after the foregoing conversation. He died August 24, 1828, in his seventieth year. The *Vermont Gazette*, the local newspaper founded by his old friend Anthony Haswell, in its issue of August 26, 1828, published the following announcement of his death:

DIED

In this town on Saturday night last, very suddenly, and without any previous sickness, Captain John Norton, aged 69 years. He went to rest in usual health, and was found a corpse in the morning. He was one of the most respectable of our citizens, and has left a numerous circle of relations and friends to lament their loss. This year has been remarkable for the coming of death in an unexpected hour; as if to exemplify the admonition — 'in the midst of life we are in death.'

* An error. It was in 1785.

The faithful and methodical Hiram Harwood committed to the pages of his journal, under date of Sunday, August 24, 1828, a much fuller account of the death of his beloved and venerated friend. His description of the personal appearance of the old potter is the more interesting by reason of the fact that no portrait of him is known to exist, and this is the only description we have:

Sunday, Aug. 24. The heat increased beyond what it was on the 23d. We were very early informed this morning of the sudden departure of our excellent friend & neighbor capt. John Norton to the World of Spirits. He died, as was supposed, in a fit of apoplexy, not however without some little notice of his illness. — He was taken about an hour previous to his exit, with a violent cough — which threw him into a kind of convulsion. Dr. Swift was sent for — meantime he became more easy, but ere the doctor arrived he was no more. So instantaneous and unexpected was the event that although Maj. L. Norton his eldest son was sent for with the utmost despatch — the distance being but short, he only got there in time to witness the final extinguishment of the lamp of life.

On Saturday the deceased was observed to be unusually lively — seemed to enjoy a high flow of spirits — apparently in as good health as he had been for many months before, which made his family and friends very ill-prepared for the melancholy catastrophe. Thus has community suffered the loss of a most amiable man, beloved and respected by all who were so fortunate as to become acquainted with him. Had resided in this town a few months over 43 years. Commenced his pottery on the spot where he lived and died. Raised a family of 9 children of unblemished reputation — 4 sons and 5 daughters — all married excepting 2 & with the exception of Mrs. Hill, all inhabitants of Bennington — Mrs. Hill at no greater distance than Arlington Church. Prosperity had uniformly attended this family with but few exceptions and those only of a pecuniary kind.

Our departed friend himself never endured the frowns of fortune since coming to this town in any degree at all compared with what usually falls to the lot of many of our unhappy race. On the contrary, he seemed to pass gaily and cheerfully along the stream of life without caring to make more than a decent and respectable appearance, or feeling ambitious to acquire much wealth in order to dash out and make a grand display of the fripperies of this world. In common conversation he was a most agreeable, lively and instructive companion, always seasoning his discourse with some smart little anecdote or aptly introducing an unoffending pun or in some such way giving entertainment to persons of all descriptions & of whatever age with whom he associated. He never appeared to manifest any partialities on account of station in life; with him the poor and the rich were on even ground; merit constituted the only distinction he recognized in society. These are some of the principal traits in this good man's character.

With regard to property his circumstances were entirely unembarassed and independent. For the age of Capt. Norton turn to Aug. 17. He served a few campaigns in the Revolutionary Army, beginning with the eventful period of 1776 and ending with 1780 or '81 — was at Long Island, Haarlem Heights, Whiteplains &c; saw Andre executed in the neighborhood of W. P. The scenes of his Revolutionary exploits I never heard him mention in regular order — if I had and could recollect them well enough, it would afford me real satisfaction to record the same in this humble repository of trifles.

It is a singular fact that a man should live to the age at which Capt. N. arrived without being called, after seeing several of his children settled in life with a numerous offspring during a period of from 13 to 19 years, to mourn the loss of a single grandchild. His was the first death that occurred in his family during a course of 44 years. As to Religion it will be sufficient to say that he was not a Professor of Christianity, yet no one could find fault with his general course of life — was always of a friendly, manly, frank and noble disposition; his mind was too enlarged to permit him to stoop to the commission of an act of meanness in any circumstances whatever — fair and perfectly honorable in all his dealings amongst men. In short he was a good man in every sense of the word except that of being a 'Christian.'

I was one of those who assisted in laying out the corpse — my services however were hardly worth mentioning. Mr. E. Fay Jun. was most active; those beside him were Mr. Loomis, Senr., S. Loomis, Dr. N. Swift, Mr. Fenton * I believe and near the end of the melancholy performance Lieut. Saff[or]d & Capt. O. Abell. This day was passed afterwards in much the usual way with books & papers. In the evening offered to watch the corpse in conjunction with Mr. S. Loomis, but S. H. Brown and G. House relieved us from the task. Staid awhile conversing with neighbors Loomis and House and returned home.

Some sort of description of the person of our departed friend must close these rude remarks. He was about 5 feet 10 inches in height — every way well-proportioned — serene cheerful countenance with a full expressive eye. I might if my abilities were equal to the task draw out this article to a very

* Not Christopher W. Fenton, but his brother, Richard L. Fenton. See p. 48.

considerable length, but must content myself with the feeble attempt exhibited above. One thing however is very necessary to mention — that for a number of the last years of his life he became very corpulent — walking any considerable distance say 40 or 50 rods became extremely irksome to him — suffered much from the asthma — weighed a few days previous to his decease 256 lbs.

To the same chronicler we are indebted for an account of the old Captain's funeral. It is an account which is of interest not only as a fitting close to our sketch of the life of Vermont's first potter, but even more for the light it throws upon one phase of our religious history. The brief characterization of the sermon that was preached at the funeral reveals much of the harsh, austere, and unlovable character of the theology then prevailing. An old man lay dead and ready for burial. He had served in the Revolutionary War and had long been venerated as a patriot. He had lived in Bennington for forty-three years, and was esteemed as an upright man, a loyal citizen, and a helpful and considerate neighbor. Generous in his support of the church, in which he was a pewholder, a constant attendant at its services, he yet failed — in the stern and unbending judgment of the minister — in one important respect: he was not 'a professor.' Says our diarist:

Monday, Aug. 25: Most unusually warm — hardly ever known to be more so . . . At 12 o'clock walked with Mr. Southworth to the house of mourning where a prayer was offered up by Mr. D. A. Clark. Mr. A. Bingham was also present — likewise all the children & most if not all the grandchildren. The concourse of people attending was very great — marched in procession with my good friend H. Dimmick. The corpse was carried by hand from near Brooks to the meeting house where it was deposited as usual. A sermon was preached by D. A. Clark from Romans 13th. C., verse 12th. — The discourse was a pretty powerful one, but not calculated to suit everyone — made some rather harsh remarks on the religious principles of the deceased &c. When the exercises were closed the corpse was conveyed across the old Burying Ground to the new, lately purchased of F. Blackmer, by the Town and with all due respect laid in the first grave open there — on the left of the entrance. Visited the P. Office — saw the account of Capt. N's death which was incorrect — on my suggestion it was corrected.

Greatly to the surprise of most of his friends and neighbors, Captain Norton was quite a poor man at the time of his death. Fond of good living, boundless in hospitality, extravagant in his expenditures upon his children according to the standards of his day, he had lived beyond his means and his affairs were found to be involved. He died intestate, leaving an estate having a gross value of four thousand dollars, according to a report made to the Commissioners of Probate, May 2, 1829. The heirs agreed that this gross estate should remain undivided in the sole possession of Captain Norton's widow, Luman proudly undertaking personal responsibility for all his father's debts. So after his death, as during his lifetime, no debt of honest old 'Potter Norton' went unpaid. The father's honor was safe in the son's keeping.

LUMAN NORTON

Next among those who worked at the original pottery to claim our attention is Luman Norton, known to his neighbors and friends at an early date as 'Major Norton' and to those of a later period of his life as 'Judge Norton.' To record the simple fact that he was universally held to be in all respects the equal of his father, and worthy of him, is to accord to his name and memory a tribute of which his descendants may justly be proud. He was born at Williamstown, Massachusetts, February 9, 1785. Brought to Bennington as an infant less than six months old, he was regarded as a native of the town in which all his life was spent, and so he regarded himself.

While Captain John Norton was himself a man of far more education than the average, and was keenly interested in giving his children every possible educational facility and advantage,* the circumstances of time and place conspired narrowly to limit the schooling of his oldest son. As soon as the lad was old enough to help on the farm, his services were too important, and too urgently needed, to be readily dispensed with. When the pottery was started by his father, in 1793, young Luman was nearing the age at which he could be very useful, both on the farm and in and around the pottery. In 1796, when Luman was eleven, Captain Norton brought to Bennington from his old home in Goshen, Connecticut, a young nephew of his, named Norman Judd, just past fourteen years of age, to be an apprentice in the pottery. Living in the family with Luman and his brother John and their younger brothers and sisters, the young apprentice and the oldest of his cousins naturally became close companions. It was quite natural, therefore, that Luman should also become a potter.

As early as 1765, according to Bancroft, there were in Bennington 'three several public schools.' † In 1780 the first incorporated academy in the State was incorporated — Clio Hall. The fine old church in the village now known as Old Bennington stands upon ground which includes the site of this famous academy, which, from about 1781 until 1803, when it was destroyed by fire, held a high place among the educational institutions of New England. Whether or not Luman Norton ever attended Clio Hall as an enrolled scholar is uncertain. He was eighteen years of age at the time of the destruction of that institution, and it is probable that he attended it for at least some portions of a year or two. The greater part of such formal education as he received was, however, in the district school. It must be remembered in this connection that the district schools were not in

* It is worthy of note that his oldest daughter, Clarissa, born 1789, was educated at Middlebury College — the first college-trained woman in the town.
† Bancroft, quoted by Jennings: *Memorials of a Century*, p. 337.

session during the months when everything on the farm called for the hands of strong boys and girls. They were conducted during the long winter months, when the boys and girls could best be spared.

With his cousin, Norman L. Judd, and those of his brothers and sisters who were old enough to go, young Luman attended the district school, in the support and supervision of which his father was most active. From numerous references in the Harwood diaries to conversations with Luman Norton, Judd, and others, we know that, as early as from 1794 to 1798, the two cousins had for schoolmaster one N. Brush, Jr. Long afterward, when he was a substantial citizen and a grandfather, Judge Luman Norton would frequently talk of his old schoolmasters, and would display with pride his old 'cyphering books,' which he had carefully saved. It seems certain that he was a fairly steady attendant at the village schools from 1794 to 1804. One of his schoolmasters was H. A. Fay, a man of rare character and understanding.

Beyond the rudimentary education so acquired, Luman Norton was self-taught. In his maturity he enjoyed considerable local reputation as a man of exceptional erudition and culture, and there is abundant evidence to show that this reputation was not undeserved. Throughout his life he was a constant reader, and he read with discrimination and to good purpose. A list of the books and papers recorded as having been read and discussed by him would astonish the average business man of to-day. He read the *New York Spectator* with great regularity, and it was his custom to discuss the principal articles in that paper with his friends and associates. He was keenly interested in politics and took great pains to inform himself concerning international affairs. Neighbors sought his opinion as that of a man who knew far more than they, and it was his habit to read aloud, to such as cared to listen, the foreign news, important political speeches delivered in Congress and elsewhere, state papers and similar documents. Scattered through the Harwood diaries during a period of thirty years are numerous entries of which the following are fair examples:

... visited L. N. — found him engaged with the 2d. Vol. of State Papers, U. S. — *July* 11, 1824.

... having been to church, I walked with him (Mr. Southworth) across lots to within a short distance of Maj. L. Norton's where I spent the evening — S. Loomis, Newt. Bates & others being present. Talked of roads — Looked at the Road Act for 1827 — heard my friend read Cooper's Hist. of America. — *February* 24, 1828.

... walked direct for Major Luman's shop... The Major held me sometime in social chat concerning Randolph's speeches in 1826 — his mission to Russia — Correspondence of Jackson & Calhoun, &c &c. — *February* 28, 1831.

In the evening visited Major L. Norton's.... Made inquiry of the Major as to foreign news and our Cabinet — Poles wonderfully successful — Old Cabinet friends coming out against one another, &c &c. — *May* 27, 1831.

Called at Maj. L. Nort's. ... Major read some paragraphs of Pres. Proclamation of which he was a great admirer — that is, read it to me. His daugh. Louisa and others were engaged on bedquilts. — *December* 18, 1832.

... Evening accomp^d by cous. G. visited major Luman Norton whose children were all at home. He immediately employed me in reading the very fine Remarks of Mr. Webster on introducing the Resolutions of the late Boston Meeting on the alarming state of Public Affrs. in the Senate of the U. S. — His suggestions were more to the point than anything I have seen during the past session. — Also read another Letter from Jack Downing * in which he sustained himself nobly. — *February* 1, 1834.

He read English and French history and biography with keen

* Pseudonym of a political writer, contributor to the *New York Spectator*.

interest and was never happier than when he could gather his children and a friend or two together and read aloud from Hume and similar writers, always discussing what was read. The whole of Hume's *History* was covered in this manner. In the same way he set about going through the whole of the historical and biographical material in Reel's *Cyclopedia*, taking the articles alphabetically! His favorite authors were Homer, Shakespeare, Milton, and Pope — Homer above all. He had an astonishing memory for poetry, and to his children and grandchildren he would recite long passages from the *Iliad* and the *Odyssey*, from various plays by Shakespeare, from Milton's *Paradise Lost*, and from Pope's *Essay on Man*. Pope's translation of Homer was his daily companion. He carried it in his pocket and frequently read it as he walked across the fields or through the streets of the village.

It is evident from this list of his favorite authors that he had a liking for the 'grand manner' in literature, as have most people who are much given to reading aloud.

Evidently there was a romantic streak in Luman's character, for it is said that he enjoyed thunder-storms immensely. It fascinated him to listen to the crashing of the thunder among the hills and to watch the lightning. He never lost an opportunity to watch an electrical storm, and his children used to tell how he would gather them together on the porch, whenever there was such a storm, and, mid the crashing of thunder and the flashing of lightning, read to them from Homer!

He found time, likewise, for reading upon subjects related to his craft — chemistry, making glass, porcelain manufacture, and so forth * — and, in his conversations with his friend and neighbor, Governor Isaac Tichenor, he manifested as keen an interest in 'the

* Harwood Diary, August 4, 1833.

Parian Marbles brought to England in 1814,' * as in crops, politics, 'McAdam roads,' books, or whist.

When he was twenty-three years old, in 1808, Luman Norton married Lydia Loomis, by whom he had three children — Julius, born 1809; Louisa, born 1811; and Laura, born 1815. His family life was as happy and attractive as that of his father. Like the father, the son loved to be surrounded with young people and to share their pleasures and amusements. His children and their friends made the house merry with music and dancing. While Luman Norton was never such an accomplished flautist as his son Julius later became, he was a tolerably good performer upon flute and fife and was extremely fond of playing. At the pottery the intervals of waiting upon the kiln were often beguiled with the music of flute and fife and fiddle and snatches of song. The following notes by Hiram Harwood are quite typical:

In the evening visited Major L. Norton's — Burning stoneware — L. himself throwing in wood. Bates, O. W. Daniels, N. J. Norton and Leger Hoyt present, fiddle, flute and fife in the bargain. Something was done in music. — *May* 27, 1831.

I visited the house & shop of Maj. Luman Norton — selected a large 6 G. pot which we wanted to use in potting cheese — would not bring it home on account of being there on foot. Heard Julius play the flute and saw his new collection of Music in which there were a great many very fine pieces. — *June* 9, 1831.

Went to Maj. L's shop — tried to sell beef to Bates & Morton effected no bargain — heard Julius N. perform several pieces on the flute — tried a few pieces myself — Came out & pursued course directly for home. — *Dec.* 22, 1831.

Although he was never a scholar in the narrow sense of that word, Luman Norton was an exceedingly well-read man. He was *educated*,

* *Idem*, July 23, 1830.

in the largest and best sense of that much-misused term. Above all, he was a man of sterling character and notable refinement. The polished manners, the Old-World courtliness and dignified urbanity of 'Judge Luman' became a by-word in the town, and then a local tradition. Old Benningtonians to-day recall the stories told by their parents of the quaint charm of his ceremonial politeness. During many years he was known by his military title, by virtue of his commission as Major in what was locally known as 'Colonel Robinson's Regiment,' a militia company, the First Regiment, Second Brigade. He resigned his commission in 1821. Later he was made one of the Assistant Judges of Bennington County, and thenceforth unto the day of his death he bore the title of 'Judge.'

In some manner a legend grew up in the community where he lived and died concerning 'Judge Luman' — a legend which has been accepted as true, even by some of the Norton family. It is to the effect that he was a man almost wholly lacking in practical wisdom, especially in business matters; a dreamer, a visionary, charming but possessing little of the stern common sense essential to a successful business man. I venture to assert that this is a wholly mistaken and misleading view of Luman Norton. It does not accord at all with the evidence in my possession; it certainly was not the judgment of those who did business with the man and whose opportunities for judging him were best and most numerous.

Yet it is easy to account for the legend: from 1835 onward Luman progressively shifted the management of the business to his son Julius. Years before his retirement from the firm, in 1840, he had become little more than a figurehead, having transferred the responsibility to Julius. It is not surprising, therefore, that employees who came into the pottery after 1838 or thereabouts should have gained the impression that 'Judge Luman' was of no consequence so far as the business was concerned. From the time of his business retirement to his death, in 1853, he was not actively engaged in business; so he came to be known in the community as a man of books, an elderly gentleman of polished manners and courtly deportment, whose library and literary tastes were much talked of. The successful and enterprising business man of an earlier day was not remembered. Finally, his son Julius was a much more aggressive money-maker than he, himself, had ever been. Under the younger man's energetic management the business grew rapidly. Julius became a much richer man than his father had been, or had cared to be, perhaps, and people naturally spoke of him as the more 'successful' of the two.

There is, nevertheless, abundant evidence that an earlier generation held Luman Norton in high respect as a shrewd and capable man of business. There was no one in the village whose advice was more generally sought. He was one of the directors of the local bank. Year after year he was elected as one of the 'Listers' of the town; and all who are familiar with our New England form of local government will realize that, in the old days, men believed to be good judges of property values were usually chosen for this post. Certainly, it is most unlikely that a man commonly reputed to be a mere visionary and dreamer would be chosen by his fellow citizens to be a 'Lister.' Luman Norton was elected to the State Legislature in 1853. In the Harwood diaries there are records of many business deals in which he figured. It is possible to trace his negotiations for the purchase of real estate and other property, and the record shows him to have been as canny as any of the neighbors with whom he dealt. He was Selectman and School Trustee and Treasurer of the School Trustees — offices not high, truly, but indicating a local repute for being levelheaded and trustworthy.

More directly to the point at issue, perhaps, is a letter written by Hiram Harwood to his friend N. L. Judd in January, 1814, of which a synopsis is given in the diary. Harwood wrote to Judd 'of his friend Luman Norton's having purchased the Fisk Farm, which added to his other possessions & his habits of industry appeared to me to be a foundation on which he intended rearing a vast superstructure.'

Finally, there is the significant fact that, in the critical period of 1833 1834, when so many business men in Bennington and elsewhere failed, Luman Norton was one of those few who triumphantly weathered the storm, and, by his own account, was not seriously affected by it.

Like his father before him, Luman was a Freemason, devoted to that craft; but a large part of his lifetime after attaining maturity coincided with the anti-masonic movement, which was especially virulent in Vermont, and I have no means of measuring the extent of his masonic activities. That he was one of those who kept the organization alive, we know. Up to 1830 he was a faithful and active member of the congregation of the Church in the old village; later he became a communicant of Saint Peter's Episcopal Church. All in all, Luman Norton was a singularly attractive and lovable character; he lived justly and righteously, and, when he died, left behind him a reputation fragrant with honorable memories.

So much for the man and the citizen. As a potter he was a craftsman of the old school. Within the limits of the business as it was conducted during his lifetime he thoroughly mastered every branch of his craft. No ornamental wares were made by the firm until after his retirement from the business. So far as is known, all the work was of the 'thrown and turned' kind; that is, the clay was thrown upon the wheel and worked into shape by the hands of the potter. What are known as 'moulded and cast' wares were not produced until later. Luman Norton was a potter in the old sense of the word; he worked at the wheel, shaping the lumps of clay into vessels for use. That he was a good potter and that he loved his work and took pride in it, we know. By his fellow craftsmen he was held in high esteem as a workman of more than ordinary skill.

Norman L. Judd

Of the other potters who worked in the Norton Pottery prior to 1830, the most significant and notable was Norman L. Judd, to whom reference has been made in the preceding pages. Sufficient has been said of the boyhood and apprenticeship of this early Vermont potter, and it is necessary only to touch briefly upon his subsequent career. As apprentice and journeyman he remained with his uncle, Captain Norton, for about ten years — 1796–1806.

In the latter year he established a pottery at Burlington, Vermont, one of the first, if not the first, in that city. In 1809 his shop was burnt out, a common experience of our early potteries. It is probable, but not certain, that Judd never again started up in Burlington. When Hiram Harwood became a volunteer, in 1812, he was sent to Burlington for training. In a special journal recording his enlistment and his experience as a volunteer we find this entry concerning Judd:

Thursday, Sept. 24, 1812: On the left as we go down to the wharf [Burlington, Vermont] stands a brick building in the under part of which Mr. Norman Judd from Bennington once carried on a pottery — now occupied by a baker in the service of the U. S. I stepped in and entered into conversation with the old baker respecting the cause of Mr. J's leaving the place. He said he was universally respected — had more business than he could perform — did not owe so much but that he could soon have cleared out — and was steady and industrious. His — the baker's — opinion was that it was owing to his wife and mother-in-law that he left the place.

Upon leaving Burlington, Judd established himself at Rome, New York, where he started a new pottery and made common red ware. At the end of 1814 he wrote in a letter to Hiram Harwood:

ROME, ONEIDA,
STATE, N. Y., 28*th Decr.*

We make Earthen Ware fast — have burned 8 kilns since the 8th. of last May — amtg to $1500 — Ware is here ready cash. It is now 8 o'clock at night, I have just done turning bowls — I rest across my mould bench while writing — no wonder if I *do* make wild shots. remember me to my uncle's family. Tell John, if he labors for his saving, I want him to work with me — as he is some acquainted with this business, I can afford to pay him good wages. — I have been looking sometime for a line from Luman, but it does not come.

In his new location Judd prospered until the spring of 1817, when fire, the dread enemy of the potter, once more overtook him. Again he was burned out, shop, tools, materials, ware, and everything else being completely destroyed. To the unfortunate Judd it seemed that the only course was to leave Rome and seek employment as a journey-man. The people of Rome, however, had come to appreciate the advantages of having a pottery in their midst, and looked upon Judd's proposed removal as a public calamity. A popular subscription was taken up, and the pottery, quickly rebuilt upon a larger scale, was soon in operation again turning out stoneware as well as red ware. Judd seems to have prospered after this. The pottery was still in existence and apparently flourishing in 1837. How much longer it lasted I do not know.

RICHARD L. FENTON

Of the other workmen employed in the Nortons' pottery prior to 1833 only one needs to be more than mentioned. There are several reasons why special attention should be paid to the name of R. L.

Fenton. In the first place, it is important to remove, once and for all, the confusion of this man's identity with that of his more famous brother, Christopher Webber Fenton, which has found its way into numerous books and articles upon the subject of the Bennington potteries. In the second place, just as we considered N. L. Judd worthy of special consideration because he left Bennington and became connected with the industry elsewhere in Vermont, so R. L. Fenton merits attention because of his connection with the industry in another Vermont town — Dorset. Finally, he was apparently connected with the original Norton Pottery for a longer period than most of those of whom we have any record.

Let us begin with the first of the above-stated reasons: As an example of the confusion of identity referred to, we may quote Pitkin, who tells us that

No record has been found, showing the date when Mr. Fenton * went to Bennington. Had he done so as soon as he finished his apprenticement in Dorset, he might have worked for Capt. John Norton one year. At the end of which time, Captain John Norton died, in 1828. From the dates and ages given in the Norton Family Records, it is safe to assume that Mr. Fenton first associated himself with Mr. Luman Norton, Capt. John Norton's oldest son, succeeding Captain John Norton in the business.†

There is no evidence whatsoever upon which to base the suggestion that Christopher Webber Fenton may have worked for Captain John Norton; neither is there, in any known record of the Norton family, evidence that he 'first associated himself with Mr. Luman Norton,' nor anything else which gives us the right to assume anything of the sort. On the contrary, the Norton family records — in so far as they bear upon the matter at all — tend to show that Christopher Webber Fenton was never so associated with Luman Norton.

* Christopher Webber Fenton is here referred to.   † Pitkin, *op. cit.*, pp. 19-20.

As already noted, in his account of the death of Captain John Norton, Hiram Harwood calls attention to the fact that, among those who helped in 'laying out the corpse,' was a Mr. Fenton. This was *not* Christopher Webber Fenton, however, but an older brother of his, Richard L. Fenton, a potter at that time, and for some time afterward, in the employ of Luman Norton.

Richard L. Fenton was born in 1797. At the date of Captain Norton's death, therefore, he was thirty-one years old. He was then living in one of several farmhouses owned by Major Luman Norton, and was employed part of the time in caring for the farm and the rest of the time as a journeyman potter. The farmhouse which he occupied was nearer to Captain Norton's than was that of Major Luman, his employer, and it is perfectly natural that he should have been called upon for assistance. In proof that we are not mistaken in our identification of this Fenton may be cited an advertisement published in the *Vermont Gazette*, September 16, 1828, and a series of entries from the diaries of Hiram Harwood. The advertisement reads:

NOTICE

Broke into the enclosure of the subscriber on or about the 15th of August last a two year old Bull of a deep red color. The owner is desired to prove property, pay charges, and take him away.

RICHARD L. FENTON

Bennington, Sept. 13, 1828.

The diary entries, which are set down in their chronological order, will complete the chain of evidence:

1828. *Friday, August 22d:* . . . P. M. rec'd a visit from neighbor Fenton and his brother-in-law Allen from Dorset the latter was calculating to wait upon his sister, the late Teacher of our school, home — requested pay for her services — I had to ask some indulgence on this affair having made use of the public money left in my care — agreed to do the best I could. . . . Went to Fenton's & paid Miss Allen $5.00 towards school bill, leaving due of the public money $8.15. The whole of her demand amt'd to $14.75 — $1.60 to be collected of the District.

1828. *Tuesday, Sept. 23d:* . . . P. M. went to maj. Luman Norton's — Paid to Mr. Fenton to apply on debt due to Miss B. Allen for teaching school $8.13, public money — on my private or common school bill, 18 cts — this was paid by guess — next day made up the deficiency — 2 cts on each bill. Came up home with friend L. Norton and R. Carpenter who were bound to the Bk.

1830. *Monday, Mar. 22d:* . . . called on Mr. R. L. Fenton — rec'd but slight information about cows — had shoats to sell — was expecting teams to remove his family and effects to Dorset — had got tired of taking farms. Was himself going to remain in Maj. Luman's service. A Mr. Evans was coming into Norton's house after his departure.

1830. *Saturday, May 8th:* . . . Rec'd a note against Levi for his school rate including that of Mr. Cummings — due one day from date — to A. McKee or order — $4.17. In crossing out the names of Jewett & C. on the Bill committed a mistake & crossed out those of Fenton and I. Searls who had neither paid nor given notes which circumstance is entered on the back of the School Bill, that it may appear fairly   free from any suspicious trick.

1830. *Tuesday, Sept. 14:* . . . Made rather a long stop at Maj. L. Nort's conversed on European Politicks — borrowed two Nos. of N. Y. Spect — Spoke with *young Fenton* * to let him know that I had a small demand — 35cts. school tax — *against his brother* * of Dorset on which I had advanced the pay — S'd he would inform him of it.

1831. *Saturday, April* 16: Prepared and forwarded line to Asa Hill requesting payment of 36 cts. school rate. Had a similar communication intended for R. L. Fenton, Dorset, but afterwards saw him and asked favor of payment — only 35 cents paid last June to W. H. McKee for schooling — said he could not pay it now — referred me to Maj. L. Norton, with whom he

* Italics mine. — J. S.

said he had dealing. I put but slight dependence on this resource. Never *mind*, it is but small — let it go.

1831. *Monday, December* 12: ... Rec'd visit in the eve'g from E. Fay Jun who paid debt to Orr W. Daniels of $1.50 and to due me on Wight's School Bill 1/0 — I should pay s'd money over to the Dist. were it not for money which I advanced on McKee's bill for N. L.* Fenton — 35 cents for which I could never get a cent.

It is quite clear from the foregoing that the Fenton who was associated with Major Luman Norton from 1828 to 1831, as tenant and journeyman potter, was Richard L. Fenton, and not his brother who later on became the Major's son-in-law. The latter is the 'young Fenton' referred to under date of September 14, 1830, when he was told of his brother's debt. So far as is known, Christopher Webber Fenton never worked for Luman Norton, either before or after he married the Major's oldest daughter, Louisa, in 1832.

In the land records of the town of Dorset, in the Town Clerk's Office, there is a deed from Jonathan Fenton to Richard L. Fenton, dated December 9, 1826, which is doubly interesting in that it not only enables us definitely to locate the site of the Fenton Pottery in East Dorset, where Christopher Webber Fenton is supposed to have learned his trade, but also establishes once and for all the identity of the makers of the old jugs and jars that are occasionally found, marked *J. Fenton, East Dorset, Vt.* and *R. L. Fenton, East Dorset, Vt.*, respectively. The deed sets forth that Jonathan Fenton grants to R. L. Fenton certain land:

Beginning at a stake and stones eight rods North from the highway leading to Mt. Tabor & bounded on purkin brook & from said stake & stones ten rods west to a stone fence thence four rods North to a stake and stones & from thence East ten rods to purkin brook & from thence four rods down

* An obvious error — R. L. was intended.

purkin brook to the first mentioned bound containing one half acre more or less. It is further to be understood that the said Richard L. is entitled to one half of a water privilege on said purkin brook together with one half of a potters Factory being on said purkin brook.

Whether this pottery had been abandoned by 1828, when we find Richard L. Fenton working in Bennington, I do not know. Prolonged research has failed to uncover any information upon this point. Unless the pottery at East Dorset had been given up by that time, it is hard to understand why Richard L. Fenton, himself part owner of a pottery, should have been living with his family at Bennington, as a tenant of one of Luman Norton's farms, and working for the latter as a journeyman potter. Of course, there are other possible explanations: He may have been held in Bennington by a lease of some sort which he had entered into before he acquired a half-interest in his father's pottery; or he may have found it necessary, or profitable, to work at Bennington for a year or two in order to earn money for additional capital. It is not at all unlikely that his brother, Christopher Webber, was helping his father and that the little pottery could not support another potter. Whatever the reason may have been, the record speaks for itself. Richard did not live long after his return to Dorset, for a tombstone in the old cemetery on the highway leading to East Dorset records the fact that he died July 25, 1834, aged thirty-six years.

John and Norman Norton

Two of Luman Norton's brothers worked, more or less, at the old first pottery in Captain Norton's time — John, two years younger than Luman, and Norman, Captain Norton's youngest child, born in 1806. The former appears never to have learned the trade with anything like thoroughness, and to have been employed more or less as a handy man about the pottery. As already noted, when the firm of John Norton & Sons was dissolved, in 1823, he received a share in the pottery. But he did not care for the business, and the partnership of the two brothers was dissolved in 1827. John became a storekeeper in the lower village, East Bennington, as it was called. He was actively interested in politics and was twice a member of the State Legislature — in 1829 and 1834. Norman, the youngest brother, was apprenticed to his father and his oldest brother, and became a turner — that is, he worked at the lathe, finishing off the ware before glazing. It is from one of the references to his work in the pottery by Hiram Harwood that we learn that they made pails with 'button' ears to which were attached stout wire 'bail' handles, quite in the modern fashion. Norman did not care for the pottery business and left it to assist his father in the management of the distillery.

Early Employees

Of the other workmen employed at the old pottery from 1793 to 1833 the names of a few are known to us. Among them it is interesting to note the names of some whose sons and grandsons worked in the Norton Pottery almost to the end. The earliest of these potters of whom we have any record is Abel Wadsworth, already referred to, who was probably the first journeyman potter employed by Captain Norton. J. W. Winship * was a potter — that is, he worked at the wheel — for a number of years, starting in the early eighteen-twenties. F. Wickwire † also worked at the pottery in Captain Norton's day, working sometimes at the wheel and sometimes at other branches of the trade. J. Morton was employed about the same period, probably doing such work as grinding clay and attending to the kilns. At the

* There is some uncertainty as to the first name of Winship, and the initials may not be correct. —J. S.
† Idem.

time when Luman Norton and his brother John were still in partner-ship, S. Thayer * was a journeyman potter. Another employee at that time was Eben Gleason, though we do not know what branch of the work he pursued.

William Bates, of Pownal, worked at the pottery for many years, beginning when the business was conducted by Captain Norton and his sons, under the name of John Norton & Sons, and continuing until long after the removal of the pottery to the lower village — a period of sixty years or so. He seems to have been a general laborer or handy man in the old days, partly employed in farming and partly in the least skilled labor of the pottery. In the later period he used to set the kiln. J. Pitts Godfrey, clay grinder, Bliss Sibley, potter, and David Sibley, the nature of whose occupation is uncertain, were all employed in the pottery prior to 1833. Some of these names are almost as in-timately connected with the history of the industry in Bennington as the name Norton itself.

ITINERANT POTTERS

Wherever the materials available have made it possible to study intensively the history of early English and American potteries, we encounter the itinerant workman, tramping from town to town and working only a few days in any one place. In this and some other in-dustries 'tramp' workmen used to fill an important place. No disgrace or discredit was attached to them. Frequently — indeed, perhaps more often than not — they were above the average in skill, possibly because their wandering habits made them more adaptable and brought them into contact with methods and processes unfamiliar to most men of their calling. They brought news from the outside, and

* *Idem.*

were generally welcomed on that account. The itinerant workman is almost invariably a gossip and a highly sociable fellow. It is probably to some such temporary sojourners at the Bennington pottery that Hiram Harwood refers in the following entry, dated November 22, 1825:

... drove till arrived at L. Nort's — halted entered the shop and talked awhile with friends L. & John. — There was present a well-dressed good-looking young man — a journeyman potter who first informed us of the failure of the Eagle Bk, N. Haven — Middletown bk. & the Derby Bk &c.

Finally, there are two entries which present another type of traveling workman — the man working his way to a given place where he expects to settle down, but making the journey by easy stages, stopping to work at potteries along the route, a few days at each place, and so earning the cost of transportation for himself and family. The entries are of added interest on account of the mention of a 'gentleman Potter' at Fairfax, Vermont.

April 19, 1831: On Monday evening rec'd for boarder Jason Merrill — young married man nearly 25 years of age — potter by occupation — wanted to stay 5 days while he performed journey-work for Maj. L. Norton.

April 23rd, 1831: Mr. J. merrills took leave after paying $1.25 'board bill' — Calculated on going with his wife & child to Fairfax, Vt. to work for a gentleman potter of that place.

III

EXPANSION AND PROGRESS — 1833-1861

The New Pottery of 1833

MANY of those who have written about the Bennington potteries have demonstrated an incapacity for historical research that is almost incredible. Even those writers who have made the most ambitious attempts to write the history of these potteries not only have failed to establish the most simple facts, but have given wide currency to errors which might well have been avoided. Some facts have been far from easy to obtain, it is true; but in this respect the history of the Bennington potteries offers no more difficulties than history in general.

Thus we find so widely accepted an authority as Barber actually confounding the modern brick building in the lower village, which was built in 1874, with the original wooden structure built by Captain John Norton, in 1793.* Another widely accepted authority first gives erroneously the date of the removal of the Norton Pottery to the lower, or East, village as 1831,† then, a page or two farther on, intimates that the event occurred some time after 1839, which is equally erroneous. He adds that at the same time Christopher Webber Fenton entered into partnership with Judge Norton, ‡ which is quite without any basis in fact.

In the papers of that tireless local antiquarian, my veteran friend, the late Dr. H. A. Day, it is recorded that the pottery was removed

* Barber: *The Pottery and Porcelain of the United States*, p. 165.
† Pitkin, *op. cit.*, p 17.
‡ *Op. cit.*, pp. 18-19.

to the lower village, at that time called East Bennington, in 1833, Judge Norton and his son Julius then being partners, and the firm name being L. Norton & Son.* The *Bennington Banner*, March 23, 1874, says that the pottery was removed to the lower village by Norton & Son in 1833. Aldrich's *History of Bennington County* says the removal to the lower village took place in 1833.† That this date is correct there can be no sensible doubt. It is borne out by the testimony of the Harwood diaries for the years 1832–1834. Throughout the whole of 1832, as the diary for that year shows, the pottery stood in the upper village, on the site where it had been erected in 1823. At that time John Norton, the second son of Captain John, had established a shop in the lower village, where he was a resident. This shop was immediately adjacent to the site upon which the pottery was subsequently erected, the land and certain water rights and privileges being owned by the Nortons. In 1877, during a chancery suit over water rights, in which the members of the firm of E. & L. P. Norton were among the defendants, it was testified that the Norton privilege 'was first improved about 1830,' and this has been held to indicate that the pottery must have been built there in 1830 or 1831.‡

No such inference may be drawn from the facts presented to the Court in this case. The statement made in 1877 that the Nortons owned the water privilege and improved it 'about 1830' may be fairly regarded as elastic enough to cover the year 1833. And, in any event, even if that were not the case, the 'improvement' of the privilege did not require the building of the *pottery* at that time. A water privilege

* Papers in the Day Collection (Bennington Battle Monument and Historical Association), M. 117–18.
† Page 299.
‡ See *Brief for Defendants Valentine, Nortons and Putnam in the case of Enos Adams et als. v. Olin Scott, Alonzo B. Valentine, E. & L. P. Norton, and Henry W. Putnam, Chas. N. Davenport and A. P. Lyman, Counsel.* Printed at Brattleboro, Vermont, 1877.

might be 'improved' by making any sort of temporary use of the water, or provision for its use — a dam, for example. The members of the Norton family who, at or near the site, were carrying on a blacksmith or wagon-repairing shop may well have improved the privilege, either for actual use or to establish their rights. Be that as it may, up to the end of 1832 the pottery had not been moved downtown. The entry made in his diary by Hiram Harwood on December 18, 1832, indicates that there had been no recent change. On February 5, 1833, he notes that alterations had been made in the arrangement of the shop, but it is clear that there had been no removal to the lower village:

> . . . I assisted at loading besides sawing wood with father & procuring N. Y. Spect. of Jan. 24, 28 at maj. Luman's — where first noticed alteration of shop — the turning apartment now occupying the whole area of the building as it was previous to removal from the ground it occupied N. of his father's house — David Sibley — the only workman present.

In May, 1833, Judge Norton purchased a piece of property, then known as the 'Chatfield property,' a parcel of land that had been part of the original farm of Peter Harwood, deeded by the latter to his son Asa in 1796. In the course of negotiations for the purchase of this property, the Judge expressed grave uncertainty and doubt because his son Julius was seriously talking of going to Portland, Maine, and setting up in the pottery business for himself.* It is a fair presumption that it was at or about this time that the copartnership of father and son was effected, the latter agreeing to give up his plan of going into business on his own account at Portland, and to remain with his father, and being taken into partnership in return for this consideration. Child's *Bennington County Directory of 1880*, highly esteemed as a reliable authority, says that Luman and Julius entered into partner-

* Diary, March 29, 1833.

ship and moved the business to the lower village, to the location later known as Pottery Street, in 1833.* By the latter part of the year the removal had taken place, for on December 10, 1833, Hiram Harwood wrote in his diary:

> ... Strayed down to Maj. L. Norton's new pottery — saw everything going on well inside. Spoke to Norton — saw young Sibley at the wheel — Found the majr piling wood near the N. W. corner of his kiln house — appeared very lively & Agreeable — conversed with him a short time.

It was at this time, apparently, that clay from New Jersey was first used. The object of using this clay was twofold: the native clay when mixed with that from New Jersey was easier to work than when used by itself, and the stoneware produced from it was of a better quality. The wares made at this time are decidedly superior to those made earlier. It is probable, judging by casual remarks in some of his letters, that the advice of Norman Judd was responsible, in part if not altogether, for the decision to use the New Jersey clay. Judge Luman Norton had great respect for the opinion of his cousin upon all matters connected with the technical side of the business.

Although the new pottery was in operation, or partial operation, at the end of 1833, it was not completed until the spring of 1834. The new building was of wood, and was a good deal larger than the old one. Whereas in the latter, as late as 1831, the total number of workmen employed was twelve, by the middle of 1835 twice that number of hands were employed. It does not appear, however, that there was any material extension of the range of articles manufactured. So far as can be learned from the records and specimens that are known to exist, the only change of importance was in the quality of the wares, not in their variety. There was, of course, a great increase in the quantity pro-

* Child's *Bennington County Directory of 1880*, p. 87.

duced. The pottery manufactured at this time was salt-glazed and marked *L. Norton & Son, Bennington, Vt.* Much of it was decorated with neat floral designs sometimes in cobalt blue and sometimes in raw umber.

The new buildings were somewhat enlarged during the winter of 1834–1835; and, on March 14th of the latter year, Hiram Harwood duly recorded that his old friend and neighbor, the Judge, left off watching the stoneware kiln long enough to show him over the works, 'which appeared very extensive as well as permanent & convenient.' From this point onward the actual direction and superintendence of the factory appears to have been largely left to Julius. The father is rarely mentioned in connection with the actual operation of the pottery after 1835. He is generally referred to by Hiram Harwood as being in the 'counting room'; as, for example, in the record of a visit made to the works in June, 1836. This confirms the family tradition that, from 1835 onward, Julius was the actual head of the business.

In 1838 Judge Norton built the double house on Pleasant Street, a fine old brick mansion in which he spent the last twenty years of his life. He did not find it convenient to continue residing in the upper village, so far from the works. Moreover, the migration from the upper village to the lower was in full swing, and the latter community was fast becoming the real center of life in the town. The Judge was, above everything, a sociable man. He wanted to be near his friends, and, more especially, his children. To enjoy the company of these it was necessary that he move down to East Bennington: the much-derided and despised 'Algiers' was becoming highly respectable. Close to the pottery lived his brother John. When Julius married, early in 1837, the Judge felt keenly the separation from his family. Such a man as the Judge would. The last of the three children had now left the parental roof. Louisa, the elder of his two daughters and his second child, had married Christopher Webber Fenton — described, it is interesting to note, as a 'merchant' of Dorset — in 1832. Laura, the youngest of the three children, had married Albert Walker, a merchant of Manchester, Vermont, in 1836. Julius and his bride lived not far from the pottery, and so did Laura and her husband.

CHRISTOPHER WEBBER FENTON'S ADVENT

The Judge wanted his elder daughter to be settled near him in Bennington. For this wish there may well have been another reason, even more powerful than his longing for the constant association with all his family, namely, the desire to protect his daughter. All was not well with Fenton, and the Judge was anxious for the future of his child. So the fine double house on Pleasant Street was built in order that his daughter might be near him. Until his death, in 1858, Judge Norton and his wife lived in the western half of the house; while their daughter and her husband, Christopher Webber Fenton, occupied the eastern half.

Leaving to another section of this book the task of describing the personality and work of Christopher Webber Fenton,* it is necessary here to take notice of another Bennington legend which has been incorporated in numerous books and magazine articles and almost universally accepted as true. We may take this legend as we find it in Pitkin's account:

In 1839 Judge Norton took his son-in-law Christopher Webber Fenton, of Dorset, Vermont, into business with him. . . . In 1846, Mr. Fenton wished to go into a more decorative line of ware, and Judge Norton did not care to, but he offered no objections to the younger men making the venture, and in the north wing of the Norton Pottery, Mr. Fenton, Julius Norton, and

* See Part II — The Fenton Potteries.

Henry Hall started the manufacture of Parian Ware. . . . They brought
John Harrison from England to do their first modelling. . . . Their partnership lasted but a few years.*

So runs the legend. Now, as a matter of sober history, it is necessary
to set forth that (*a*) Judge Norton never took his son-in-law into par-
nership with him; (*b*) there never was such an arrangement between
the Judge and the 'younger men' of the firm; (*c*) Judge Norton was out
of the firm long before 1846; (*d*) Julius Norton was never associated
with Henry Hall as a partner, at any time. The story of the young
genius, Fenton, ambitious to go into the manufacture of 'a more
decorative line of ware,' and the cautious and conservative old gentleman declining to venture the experiment, but indulgently giving his
son and his son-in-law permission to risk their own capital in a small
way, and to let them use a little space for this enterprise makes excellent reading, no doubt; but it is pure fiction. The facts are more
prosaic, doubtless, but facts alone concern the historian.

It is quite possible that Fenton became 'associated with the Norton
Pottery' as early as 1839, or even earlier; but, if so, it was as an employee and not as a *partner* in the firm. At that time, Judge Luman
Norton had practically retired from active participation in the management of the business. He had already become the leisurely gentleman so well and so affectionately remembered by old Benningtonians.
In an article published in the *State Banner*, March 28, 1856, which
Fenton either wrote or personally inspired, it is said that 'Some twenty
years ago Mr. Fenton engaged in the manufacture of Stone Ware in
our village,' and the context makes it clear that his connection with
the Norton Pottery is referred to.† The words 'some twenty years ago'
would, if narrowly interpreted, place the date of Fenton's first con-

* Pitkin, *op. cit.*, pp. 18–19, 20.   † See p. 73.

nection with the Norton Pottery earlier than 1839 — say in 1836 or 1837. The reasons for believing that this connection did not begin until later are as follows: (1) Hiram Harwood kept his diary until October 23, 1837. Although he notes various visits to his friend Judge Norton during the last two or three years, mentions the works and gives the names of those whom he saw there, and records numerous items of news and gossip relating to different members of the Norton family, he apparently* makes no mention of Fenton or of his being in any manner associated with the pottery. The fact that he knew Fenton makes this omission all the more significant. (2) The house on Pleasant Street was built for the purpose of bringing the daughter — Mrs. Fenton — to reside near her father. There is no record that the Fentons were living in Bennington prior to their occupation of this house. (3) The tradition in the family is that Fenton in some way became associated with the pottery 'somewhere about 1840.'

FIRE-BRICK INTRODUCED

In 1837 the manufacture of fire-bricks was undertaken as an addition to the business. Just above the stoneware pottery a building for this new departure was erected. The faithful Hiram Harwood wrote in his diary for May 23, 1837, 'Visited works of Judge L. Norton — Large low building in forwardness for drying newly invented fire-bricks — erected N. old works.' We do not know a great deal about this branch of the business, except that it was carried on for a number of years and seems to have attained considerable importance by 1840. As will be seen later, it was flourishing when Julius Norton became sole proprietor on the retirement of his father. In 1841, for instance, he

---

* The reader will note that I say 'apparently' — it is quite possible that in looking over some thousands of pages of writing I have missed some reference to Fenton.

was advertising 'Patented Firebrick (The best in the world) at $50. per thousand.' The brick-making plant was operated until some time after the pottery was burned down, in 1845; and it is said that the brick used in the kilns of the new pottery was made there. From the *First Annual Report on the Geology of Vermont, 1845,* by C. B. Adams, we obtain some definite information concerning this 'Patented Firebrick.' This authoritative account says:

> Bennington. — Half a mile northeast of the village is a deposit of excellent kaolin, which supplies the manufactory of Norton & Fenton in the village . . .
> For fire-bricks, the kaolin is made into paste with water, from which bricks are formed and burnt. These bricks, retaining the whiteness of the kaolin, and becoming very hard, are called 'clay bricks.' They are next broken up by a mill and sifted, so as to be of the coarseness of fine gravel. This is mixed with unburnt kaolin and arenaceous quartz, pressed in molds of the required form and size and burnt in the same manner as before. These fire-bricks are very white and hard, and when fractured shew their composition of broken clay-brick and kaolin.*

In my collection there is a large fire-brick which quite conforms to the foregoing description. It is impressed with the mark *Fenton's NO. 1, Bennington, Vt.* It would appear, however, to belong to a somewhat later date — about 1850. Upon what was known as the 'A. P. Lyman Privilege,' where Lyman and others had conducted a wadding mill, the manufacture of patent fire-brick was carried on. Aldrich's *History of Bennington County,* says that this was 'about 1853,'† but in the *State Banner,* December 14, 1850, there is a letter which refers to the manufacture of 'patent fire-brick' at Bennington. This is almost certainly the same works. W. G. Leake, one of the old potters, long ago told the present writer that he remembered the

---

* *First Annual Report on the Geology of Vermont, 1845,* p. 52.
† Aldrich, *op. cit.,* p. 331.

manufacture of the patent fire-brick at the time of the United States Pottery, as late as 1855–1856.

Although no document establishing the *exact* date of Judge Luman Norton's withdrawal from the business has been discovered, it is not difficult to determine the *approximate* date with reasonable certainty. At the beginning of 1841, Julius Norton first began to advertise the business under his own name. Prior to that time the name of L. Norton & Son was used. We are fairly safe, therefore, in saying that the Judge withdrew at the end of 1840. The *State Banner*, in its issue of February 27, 1841, published this advertisement:

BENNINGTON STONE WARE FACTORY

Julius Norton Manufactures and keeps constantly for sale at his factory in Bennington East Village, Vt., a large assortment of STONE WARE, consisting of Butter, Cake, Pickle, Preserve and Oyster Pots, Jugs, Churns, Beer & Blacking Bottles, Jars, Plain and Fancy Pitchers, Ink Stands, Earthen Milkpans, Stove Tubes, Kegs, Mugs, Flower Pots, &c. &c.

Also Patented Firebrick (The best in the world) at $50. per thousand.

Orders from Merchants faithfully executed and ware forwarded on the shortest notice.

Bennington, E. Village, Feb. 27, 1841.

A PARTNERSHIP AND A FIRE

It will be observed that there is no mention of Christopher Webber Fenton as partner at this time. Julius Norton speaks as sole proprietor. In the *State Banner*, April 26, 1842, and the *Vermont Gazette*, May 3, 1842, are to be found advertisements which seem to prove that Fenton could not have been a partner at that time. In these advertisements notice is given that Christopher W. Fenton, of Bennington, described as a 'laborer,' has petitioned for the benefit of the Bankrupt Act, asking to be declared a bankrupt at the hearing to be held at Windsor, May 24, 1842. Thus Fenton's entrance into the firm as a partner must have been at some later date. That he was already employed at the pottery is probable.

On Sunday morning, June 6, 1845, the pottery was burned to the ground. The cause of the fire was the usual one which took such a heavy toll from potteries at that period. To hold the kilns in place, and to prevent their being burst by expansion when in operation, a framework of heavy timbers was built around each kiln. So constructed as to allow for the necessary and inevitable expansion due to the great heat, these frames were designed to take the strain thus imposed upon the brick walls of the kilns and to provide the necessary resistance. The charring of the timbers in immediate contact with the sides of the kilns was virtually inevitable and was a commonplace occurrence to which no attention was paid. The manner in which the timbers were wedged against the hot brickwork, while it permitted a slow charring process, yet, because of the total absence of draught channels between timbers and brickwork, precluded flame. As a practical matter, therefore, little alarm was ever caused by the slow smouldering of the timbers next the brickwork. There was, however, always the danger that a strong wind might fan the smouldering fire into flame at some point of the structure; and, for that reason, it was the general practice for kilns to be watched at night while the firing operation was going on. Despite this precaution, however, destructive fires were of frequent occurrence. The value of the annual production of the pottery and fire-brick manufacture at this time was about $20,000.

At the time of the fire, Christopher W. Fenton was in partnership with Julius Norton, the firm name being Norton & Fenton. I have not been able to discover any documentary evidence which would definitely fix the exact date at which this partnership began; but, after a most exhaustive study of all the available data, including every scrap of information concerning Fenton that could be found, I am led to the conclusion that the event took place not earlier than July, 1844, or not later than January, 1845. As already noted, it is probable that Fenton had been employed by his brother-in-law at the pottery for some time. Having regard to the fact that there appears to have been no publication of the firm name before 1845, and to the further fact that all references to the pottery in the local newspapers between 1841 and 1845 refer to it as Julius Norton's, we are justified in settling upon the dates given as marking with approximate correctness the beginning of the partnership. When we take into account Fenton's bankruptcy, already referred to, and the time required for the settlement of his affairs and for his discharge from bankruptcy, this conclusion is fortified. That the partnership was in effect at the time of the fire is proved by a signed advertisement published in the *Vermont Gazette*, June 10, 1845:

A CARD

Messrs. Norton & Fenton return their most grateful thanks to their neighbors and friends for their prompt and active exertions to preserve their property from destruction by fire, on Sunday morning last. This acknowledgement is not only due to the inhabitants and Fire Company of this village and especially to the Fire Company of that village, which was on the ground with great promptness and whose exertions were extraordinary and efficient.

June 9.

Julius Norton

Julius Norton was born in the old village, September 23, 1809. At that time and for some years thereafter, his parents lived in part of the house owned and occupied by Captain John Norton. The latter with his wife and family lived in the upper part of the house, Luman, his wife, and their child occupying the lower part until 1813 or 1814. Prior to that time the references to the Nortons in the Harwood diaries frequently mention the joint occupancy of the Norton house as above described.

As a lad Julius attended the ordinary district school, thence graduating into the Bennington Academy, where he completed his education. The Academy was a notable institution in those days and enjoyed a high reputation, ranking among the best schools of New England. Such records of the Academy as have been preserved do not indicate that Julius Norton was in any way distinguished. His name is to be found neither among those who shone on special occasions, as at the annual 'exhibitions,' nor among those who attracted attention by less admirable qualities. By all accounts he was rather a shy youth, quiet and reserved in his manner, with few intimate associates. In the family circle and among the neighbors and friends of the family, his passion for music occasioned much comment. Like his father and his grandfather before him, he was extremely fond of the flute. From his father he received his first instruction in playing that instrument, but soon surpassed his instructor in skill. To the end of his life he was devoted to the flute and was generally esteemed the most expert flautist in the county. He was an accomplished violinist and was fairly proficient at the piano. By members of the Norton family in general he is regarded as the most artistic of all the Nortons.

He first married Maria Spooner, a school teacher, in 1836. She was a lineal descendant of William C. Spooner, one of the signers of the Declaration of Independence. She died May 22, 1837, two months after the birth of her only child — Luman Preston Norton. In 1842, five years after the death of his first wife, Julius Norton married Sophia B. Olin. Of this union two daughters were born — Eliza, born in 1843, and Alice, born in 1848.

Julius Norton learned his trade as a potter in the old pottery on the Pownal Road, under the direction of his father. He loved his work and took a keen pride in it, and by his fellow craftsmen was regarded as an exceptionally good potter. Though universally respected, and honored as an upright man and a good citizen, he never endeared himself to the community as did his father. There was about him a cold and austere reserve, possibly a manifestation of shyness, which few could penetrate. He had little or none of the hearty geniality which characterized his father. When old potters speak of him they dwell most upon his quiet demeanor and his unfailing sense of justice and fair-mindedness. Those who came into intimate relation with him in his family circle speak most of his aloofness and his absorption in his music. As a business man he was keen, energetic, resourceful, and highly successful. Possessing the artistic temperament in greater measure than any other member of his family, he is remembered as the one 'money-maker' of them all. He possessed a *flair* for money-making not usually associated with artistic temperament.

Such was the man who, upon the withdrawal of his father in 1841, became the sole proprietor of the Bennington Stone Ware Factory, and who, at the opening of 1845, as already noted, entered into partnership with his brother-in-law, Christopher Webber Fenton. It was a co-partnership that was foredoomed to inevitable failure. A more ill-matched pair it would have been difficult if not impossible to find.

Norton was unassuming and modest, Fenton was always inclined to be arrogant and boastful; Norton was the embodiment of steady concentration, Fenton was flighty and erratic; Norton was the most abstemious of men, Fenton was frequently intemperate; Norton's ways were those of a careful investor, Fenton's those of the daring speculator.

THE PARTNERSHIP EXPLAINED

The real reasons for this strange and hopeless partnership can only be inferred from the general information we have concerning the firm. Most of the documents illustrative of the business relations of the two men have long since disappeared. Local traditions in which fact and legend are inextricably mingled, our knowledge of the men, scanty family records, scattered notices in contemporary newspapers, and local gossip more or less dimly remembered are virtually the only materials from which any theory may be deduced. That his devotion to his favorite sister, Mrs. Fenton, influenced Julius in this matter is not unlikely. It was already apparent that Fenton's greatest weakness was increasing, and it may well have been thought — by himself not less than by others — that the responsibility of such a partnership would exert a steadying influence.

Fenton possessed a mind of unusual fertility; he was quick to grasp facts and ideas and ingenious in devising adaptations. He possessed, too, a mechanical ingenuity characteristic of some generations of ancestors. It is quite easy to understand how a man of his type could deeply impress even those who were superior to him in many ways. Certainly it is easy to believe the story that of all the Nortons it was Julius who best liked his brother-in-law and defended him when he was subjected to harsh criticism.

Julius Norton was determined to make money. He looked upon wealth from a point of view quite different from that of his father and his grandfather. If the truth must be told, he had little respect for their modest standards. He was a child of his age. He frankly wanted to be rich, and not merely comfortably well-to-do. To see the business grow vast, to be himself an important figure in the world of finance and industry — such were the dreams in which he indulged. This attitude brought Julius into the sphere of his brother-in-law's influence. Here was the one characteristic they owned in common. Fenton also wanted to make money, to be rich. He was only three years older than Julius, was a plausible talker, gifted with an almost unbounded imagination. He was full of schemes which promised to bring large and rapid fortune. He was one of those men who are forever hatching out plans for the quick acquisition of 'big money.' In fact, he was always devising and developing plans for great things, some of them good plans, too. His talent for starting things was far in excess of his power of persistence in keeping them going. It is not at all surprising that Julius Norton should have believed that it would help him to have Fenton for a partner.

FENTON'S QUALIFICATIONS

The foregoing interpretation of the causes which led Julius Norton into an association so unsuited to him, and so hopeless, may be mistaken in some of its details, but there is ample warrant for holding it to be true as a whole. Certain it is that it was not any special skill or merit of Fenton as a practical potter that brought about the partnership. Without any disparagement of Fenton's undoubted qualities, which amounted almost to genius, he was not a Palissy or a Wedgwood, assiduously cultivated legends to the contrary notwithstanding. Pitkin tells us that 'We must infer, that Mr. Fenton was a practical potter, of extraordinary skill, well-nigh a genius at his trade, artistic in his tastes, a naturalist, something of a chemist, a profound student, probably erratic and perhaps visionary.' * For this eulogium there is not a shred of supporting evidence. There is nothing in any record of the man to warrant the suggestion that he was 'a naturalist'; not a scrap of testimony or evidence can be cited to prove that he was in any manner or degree interested in anything which would give him even the least claim to the title.

Nor is there any more evidence to sustain the verdict that he was 'a practical potter, of extraordinary skill, well-nigh a genius at his trade.' What evidence there is, clearly and unmistakably points to a conclusion diametrically opposite to Pitkin's rhapsody. Counting myself among the admirers of Fenton's real contribution to American pottery, I cannot by silence appear to acquiesce in a verdict so contrary to all the known facts.

During the past sixteen or seventeen years, it has been my privilege to hold many conversations with surviving potters in Bennington, who had known Fenton and had worked with him. I have likewise talked with old potters living elsewhere who remembered having worked with him or under him. Not one of these men has ever suggested that Christopher Webber Fenton was specially skilled as a practical potter. Were such the case, it would be strange indeed that no trace of a legend or tradition of his skill has remained. There are stories and echoes of stories concerning the skill of Luman Norton, of Decius W. Clark, of Enoch Barber, of Daniel Greatbach, of William Leake, and of many others — stories such as old potters in their reminiscent moods love to tell but no such tales are ever heard concerning Fenton.

* Pitkin, *op. cit.*, p. 24. The punctuation is Pitkin's.

When he is talked about, the themes never dwell upon his skill as a potter, but upon his habits, his personality, his business methods, his relations with Decius W. Clark, and so forth.

Finally, there are no treasured examples of his handiwork, no remarkable pieces made by him and prized on that account. This is something that can be said of no single one of the Bennington potters whose skill was sufficiently marked to be the subject of comment. I can personally account for pieces made by upward of a dozen of the old Bennington potters; but, in a careful study of the subject extending over many years, and an extensive experience as a fairly successful collector, knowing many other collections almost as well as I know my own, I have never seen or heard of a single treasured specimen of Fenton's handiwork.

Neither at the time of forming the partnership with Julius Norton, nor at any time thereafter, was Christopher Webber Fenton counted 'a practical potter of extraordinary skill.' In this respect he was far inferior to his partner, who was a practical potter of recognized ability. The mistake into which Pitkin has fallen — in which he is slavishly followed by others — is that of attributing to Fenton the merits and achievements of a man who was truly a remarkable potter, and a serious student of the chemistry of ceramics, Decius W. Clark.

When he joined Julius Norton in 1845, Fenton had enjoyed only a limited experience as a potter. He is supposed to have learned his trade at East Dorset, in the pottery of his father, Jonathan Fenton. Pitkin says that he was 'a common red-ware potter.' * Possibly so, though that statement hardly lends support or credence to the assertions that we have been discussing. It is hard to believe that a potter could have developed into a genius such as Pitkin believed Fenton to

* Pitkin, *op. cit.*, p. 9.

have become, without more experience in the finer branches of the art than a common red-ware pottery affords.

My examinations of the site of the old Fenton Pottery at East Dorset have, however, disclosed the fact that more than 'common red ware' was made there. I have found an abundance of fragments of red ware covered with 'slip' on the inside and plain on the outside; red ware, lead-glazed inside; red ware covered with 'slip' inside and lead-glazed without; stoneware salt-glazed, both undecorated and decorated. In a word, the pottery did a general business. Thus Christopher Webber Fenton had a training rather more extensive than is implied by the phrase, 'a common red-ware potter.' It is certain, however, that there was nothing in the kind of work done at the East Dorset pottery to develop a potter of such extraordinary skill as Pitkin imagined. Prior to his coming to the Norton Pottery Fenton had no experience, so far as there is any evidence, outside of the manufacture of coarse earthenware and stoneware. Whatever else he knew when, later, he set up in business at Bennington on his own account, he had learned at the Norton Pottery.

In view of this fact, it is rather amusing to find Fenton claiming for himself full credit for the high reputation of the wares made at the Norton Pottery. Notwithstanding that the Nortons were manufacturing wares which had a deservedly high reputation before he was born, and that, when he was yet a mere child, the stoneware products of the Norton Pottery were so highly esteemed that the market for them extended to several States, he could yet write, or cause to be written, in 1856, that 'that pottery, now owned by the Messrs. Norton, continues to enjoy the high reputation established for it by Mr. Fenton, while connected with that business.'* This ungracious boast-

* *State Banner*, March 28, 1856.

ing was as silly as it was offensive to those by whom he had been be-friended. It was characteristic of the man, whose habit of self-adula-tion was so marked that it frequently obscured his more admirable qualities, and made association with him over any long period difficult for most men.

The Pottery of 1845

The reconstruction of the pottery after the fire of 1845 afforded Christopher Webber Fenton his first opportunity to exert anything like a profound or important influence upon the industry itself or upon the policy of the firm. The works were rebuilt — this time more sub-stantially, the building being of brick instead of wood as formerly. The new structure was much larger than the old one. It formed a hollow square 114 feet by 92 feet,* with an open court or yard in the center. It was designed to be, and believed to be, fireproof, and in the construction of the building itself, and the arrangement of machinery, benches, racks, storage, and so forth, every known improvement was introduced. The same may be said of the kilns, of which there were three, above the average in size, situated in the western or rear portion of the building. Fenton used to claim that he designed the kilns and introduced some new features into their construction, and there is good reason to believe that this claim was well founded. Not only so, but, throughout the whole reconstruction of the plant, his fertile and ingenious mind effected many innovations and improvements.

Whether and to what degree his mind actually originated these improvements, or whether it simply developed suggestions received from others, cannot be authoritatively told, of course. Whoever has studied the history of the Bennington potteries with any approach to

* *Vide* Letter of Fenton to C. B. Adams, dated September 15, 1845.

thoroughness will be inclined to believe that the latter supposition is the correct one, I think. Fenton had already entered upon that friendship with Decius W. Clark, and that dependence upon him, which were to last to the end of his life.

Clark joined the Norton Pottery late in 1840, having been brought there by Julius Norton. A workman of much more than average skill, he was also a serious student of everything pertaining to the manufacture of ceramics. It is not too much to say that he was one of the most extraordinary men that the pottery industry in this country has produced. When the story of the United States Pottery is reached in the course of our narrative, it will be seen that he was its one creative force. That he worked through and with Fenton is certain, and there is good reason to believe that he had already begun to do so in 1845, and that Fenton's contributions to the improvement of the building, the kilns, and the machinery were actually the outcome of Clark's creative thought.

To say this is not to lessen the importance of Fenton, let me hasten to observe at this point, to prevent misunderstanding. There is no more useful genius than he who gives living reality to the thoughts and dreams of others. To take the thought of another, grasp its significance, develop its possibilities, perceive its value, translate it into terms of actual achievement, when, without such appropriation, the thought would die barren, is creative work of the highest order and utmost value. And that is precisely what Christopher Webber Fenton accomplished.

It took virtually all of the remaining months of 1845 to complete the new pottery and get into operation again. As early as 1843 Julius Norton had considered adding the manufacture of porcelain to the business, and had sent to England for an expert modeller with that end in view. At the time Fenton joined his brother-in-law in partnership, experiments in porcelain-making were being carried on, and when the fire took place, making the construction of a new building necessary, it was decided to set aside one wing of the building for the manufacture of porcelain. The north wing was accordingly devoted to that special purpose. Here, then, is the little grain of truth in a familiar legend which we have already examined at some length. It appears, however, that before the new building was finished, Julius Norton had reached the conclusion that it would be unwise to continue the experiments in porcelain-making — for it had not progressed beyond the experimental stage. Whether that decision reflected anything more than characteristic caution on the part of Julius Norton is not known. It should be said that, contrary to a widely prevalent belief, Julius Norton was every bit as progressive as his brother-in-law. In the advertisement which we have quoted earlier in this chapter from the *State Banner* of February 27, 1841, appears a list which indicates quite clearly that, years before Fenton became his partner, Julius Norton was reaching out far beyond anything that had been attempted under his father's management.

One of the 'Ink Stands' referred to in that advertisement was formerly owned by Edward Norton, and is now in my collection, a gift from his widow, Mrs. Edward Norton, of Bennington. It is made of gray stoneware, similar to that used for jugs, churns, and other articles, and is decorated with cobalt blue. The stand itself is rather elaborately ornamented with scrollwork, and is characteristic of the period in its ugliness. The dog, however, is splendidly modeled and executed. The combination of blue and gray is well managed and exceedingly effective. This inkstand and the announcement in the advertisement that he was manufacturing 'Plain and Fancy Pitchers' show that Julius Norton was advancing his standards before Fenton became his partner. Not less than the latter was he influenced by that urge for progress which was stirring the industry in America at that time.   [See Plate VII]

EXPERIMENTS WITH PORCELAIN

There had recently been a great deal of improvement made in the manufacture of porcelain in England. Importations of this English ware had greatly increased. In the large shops of the principal cities the goods of the best English manufacturers were carried, and they found their way into the homes of the people. There was a stirring of interest in the principal potteries of New England, New York, and New Jersey. The keenest interest of all was aroused by the appearance upon the American market of a new type of porcelain, sometimes called Statuary Porcelain and sometimes Parian Ware. The names themselves indicate the character of this new material: because its texture and finish closely resembled Parian marble, Parian was the name generally given to it within the trade, and because — on account of the peculiar quality mentioned — it was successfully used for the reproduction of sculpture, and was at first used mainly for making small ornamental figures which bore a close resemblance to sculptured marble, the name Statuary Ware or Statuary Porcelain was featured commercially.

This new type of porcelain had been introduced to the English and American markets in 1843. Although there has been a good deal of controversy upon the subject — too extensive and voluminous to be entered upon in this history — there is no doubt in my mind that the credit of having originated Parian porcelain belongs to Copeland, of Stoke-on-Trent, who made some splendid examples early in 1842.

Minton, Wedgwood, Moore Brothers, of London, The Worcester Royal Porcelain Company, and other noted English makers were soon in the field, some with exceedingly beautiful productions. Not in a generation had the introduction of any new or improved ware awakened such widespread interest.

When Julius Norton decided to send to England for the modeler, John Harrison, his intention was to experiment with the manufacture of porcelain from local materials. That he was urged to do this by Fenton we may take for granted. It is extremely likely that both men, together with such men as Decius W. Clark, were keenly interested in the new Statuary Ware. It is not probable, however, that Norton had any definite plan of becoming the first American manufacturer to introduce the new ware. Neither he nor Fenton could have known enough about its manufacture to warrant a man like Julius Norton in so far committing himself. It was to institute the manufacture of porcelain in general, and not the Parian Ware in particular, that John Harrison was sent for. Believing that excellent porcelain could be manufactured from local materials, which could be had as easily and cheaply as English manufacturers obtained theirs, Fenton had urged that the manufacture of porcelain should be tried, upon a small scale at first, and Norton had agreed to attempt the experiment. One end of the pottery was set aside for this purpose.

Little is known of John Harrison. Beyond the tradition that he had previously worked for Copeland at Stoke-on-Trent, we have no information about him. He is believed to have arrived at Bennington toward the end of 1843, and to have brought with him many designs, models, and finished pieces, some of which had not yet been placed upon the market, even in England. One of the earliest pieces modeled by Harrison after his arrival here is in my collection. Its sentimental associations are not less interesting than the historical one just noted. The first child of Julius Norton, Eliza, was born November 23, 1843. Harrison appears to have decided that his first successful demonstration should be a gift to the wife of his employer, in honor of the birth of the baby. When she presented this piece to a member of the Norton family, many years later, Mrs. Norton said that it was made and presented to her on the occasion of the birth of her first child. It is extremely unlikely, of course, that it was ready for the event, or that it was given to her until she was able to receive visitors. It is equally unlikely that the presentation took place more than a few weeks after the date abovenamed.

The piece is a small elliptical basket in which reposes a sleeping child surrounded with flowers and fruit. It is about three and one half inches long by two and one quarter inches wide and one inch in height. The basket is a deep blue gray, unglazed, ornamented on the bottom and around the sides with a conventional acanthus-leaf design. The top is white. In a bed of finely shredded moss lies the nude child, well modeled, with fruit and blossoms — the latter especially in bold relief.

In 1861, after the death of her husband, and prior to her removal from Bennington, Mrs. Norton gave the little piece to a relative, Mrs. Daniel McEowen, granddaughter of Captain John Norton; she, in turn, gave it to another relative, Miss Luther, a young girl, a great-great-granddaughter of Captain John Norton. The existence of this little piece and its sentimental history were well known to members of the Norton family in Bennington long before I acquired it, and they have been gratified by its return to Bennington. Of its authenticity there is not the least shadow of doubt. It may fairly be accepted as the first piece of porcelain made at the Bennington pottery. It is not impossible, or even unlikely, that it was made of English materials brought by Harrison for experimental work, but that, of course, cannot be determined. Crude and naïve in design, this tiny porcelain sculpture is exquisitely wrought, and I have felt that its resemblance to some of the early Copeland Parian pieces is not to be mistaken. A companion piece, in pure white, having the fruit and flowers, but no baby, was made at the same time and presented to a young lady, Miss Park. Possibly the pure white and the omission of the baby were a tribute to virginity.*

In a letter which Fenton wrote to C. B. Adams, dated September 15, 1845, he refers to the fire and the rebuilding of the pottery as having 'suspended all my experiments in the manufacture of porcelain, to an indefinite period.' John Harrison is believed to have returned to England soon after the fire, and it is not unlikely that the decision of the firm that it would be necessary to give up the plan to manufacture porcelain was responsible for his return to his native land. If the gossip of later days is to be relied upon, Harrison left behind him one example of his craftsmanship that was destined to become famous and much sought after — but of that more anon. Norton & Fenton appear to have resumed experimentation in the manufacture of porcelain, in a small way, but they never manufactured it on a commercial scale.

NORTON & FENTON DISSOLVE PARTNERSHIP

By the beginning of 1846 the new pottery was in full swing. It is noteworthy that none of the advertisements published during that year make any reference to porcelain, nor is any mention made of it in the local press. Whatever experimental work was carried on in the north wing of the pottery, was tentative and had not developed to the point of commercial practicability. By means of the published ad-

* This piece is also in my collection.

vertisements we are in a position to follow the whole course of the story of the firm of Norton & Fenton. The first advertisement is from the *State Banner*, a paper published in the lower village, commonly called East Bennington at that time:

NORTON & FENTON
Manufacturers of Every Description of
STONE WARE
East Bennington, Vt.

Beginning with March 16, 1846, and continuing every week, the advertisement ran in this form, unchanged, until Monday, April 19, 1847. In the next issue, and thereafter to November 15, 1847, it ran with a slight change. The body of the advertisement was not altered, but the name East Bennington was dropped and Bennington was used instead. Mark that, in this paper, East Bennington was used prior to April 19, 1847, and Bennington from that time to the middle of November. Now, let us turn to another local paper, the *Vermont Gazette*. As there were two papers published with that title, one in the upper village and one in the lower, it is necessary to make clear which of the two is meant. The following advertisement, then, is from the *Vermont Gazette* published in the lower village, by J. C. Haswell, and the date is March 17, 1847:

NORTON & FENTON
Manufacturers of Every Description of
STONE WARE
Bennington, Vt.

This advertisement ran regularly through successive issues up to December 1, 1847. On that date the paper carried two other advertisements from which we learn much. The first of these supplies the exact date of the dissolution of the Norton and Fenton co-partnership:

The Co-partnership heretofore existing between the subscribers was dissolved by mutual consent, June 25, 1847.

JULIUS NORTON
C. W. FENTON

November 23, 1847.

The business of the late firm is continued by the subscriber at the old stand.

JULIUS NORTON

November 23, 1847.

This appears to have been the first formal announcement of the dissolution of the firm of Norton & Fenton. At the same time appeared the first announcement that Fenton had started in business upon his own account:

C. W. FENTON

Manufacturer of Yellow Fire Proof Ware, Dark Lustre or Rockingham Ware, White Flint Ware, Earthen and China.
Bennington, Vt.

As already noted, the *State Banner* published the Norton & Fenton advertisement from March 16, 1846, to November 15, 1847. One week later the advertisement of Julius Norton took its place, and was regularly published to the end of March, 1848.

These announcements are of the highest importance for the reason that they enable us to clear up a number of points concerning which

there has been much confusion.   We are now able to assert with certainty that (*a*) the partnership of Julius Norton and Christopher
Webber Fenton, which was entered into between June 30, 1844, and
January 1, 1845, was terminated June 25, 1847; (*b*) there were only two
partners, neither Henry Hall nor any other third person being associated with them; (*c*) all pottery marked *Norton & Fenton* belongs
to the brief period of the partnership, three years, or less, 1844–1847;
(*d*) Christopher W. Fenton began manufacturing on his own account
sometime between June 25 and November 23, 1847. Upon each of
these points there has been a great deal of uncertainty and almost
unlimited speculation, which, by virtue of these authentic announcements, may now be finally dismissed.

It is worthy of note that the advertisements of Norton & Fenton,
of Julius Norton and C. W. Fenton, covering the period from February, 1846, to November, 1847, inclusive, are all equally free from any
mention of Parian or any other kind of porcelain. In the absence of
any positive evidence to the contrary, we are not merely justified in
believing that none had been produced on a commercial scale up to
that time, but are *compelled* so to believe. Refusal by Norton to go on
with the manufacture of porcelain may well have been among the
causes of the separation, and it is quite likely that Judge Luman
Norton, though no longer in the firm, advised his son, Julius Norton,
to stick to the old and well-established lines. This is probably the
germ of fact which became enshrouded in the romantic legend already
noted at the opening of this chapter.

To conclude our historical survey of the brief connection of Fenton
with the Norton Pottery, as a part proprietor, it may be well to summarize another episode brought forth from searchings in the advertising columns of contemporary newspapers. It has never been men-

tioned by any other writer, and was wholly unknown to members of the Norton family now living and to the daughter of Albert Walker. It throws new light upon the career of Fenton and suggests that, in addition to the reasons already given for the dissolution of the partnership between him and Julius Norton, there was another strong and compelling reason. The following advertisement first appeared in the *State Banner*, April 3, 1848.* With trifling changes in the wording (the change of the date to March 10, 1849, and the substitution of 'two years ago' for 'one year ago': it was regularly published until March 1, 1851, and possibly after that date:

NOTICE

The late firm of 'A. Walker & Co.,' manufacturers of Gun and Blasting POWDER, was dissolved about one year since, Mr. Walker having retired from the business.

The firm has since that time been 'LYMAN, FENTON & Co.,' to whom all communications and orders for Powder should be addressed.

Our mills were built with great expense with the intention of making a better article than is made at any other mill in the country. We make nothing but the best of Wheel Powder, and are determined at all times to give satisfaction in quality as well as price.

LYMAN, FENTON & Co.

East Bennington, March 14, 1848.

This advertisement shows that, up to March, 1847, or thereabouts, Fenton had been a partner in another business quite unrelated to the manufacture of pottery. That Julius Norton should have become dissatisfied by reason of his partner's divided interest and attention at

* From April 5, 1848, to the end of the year this advertisement was also published in the *Vermont Gazette*, the East village paper of that name.

the time when the extension of the business was engrossing all his own time, is a reasonable conjecture. Moreover, the dissolution of the firm of A. Walker & Co. involved an unpleasant family entanglement. Like Fenton, Albert Walker was Julius Norton's brother-in-law. Christopher W. Fenton was the junior member of the powder manufacturing firm, Albert Walker being the senior member. In some manner not now known, Walker was edged out and the firm became Lyman & Fenton. A good deal of unpleasant feeling resulted from this development. Mr. Walker and a partner named Harrington started another powder manufactory in another part of the town, being assisted, it is believed, by the former's father-in-law, Judge Luman Norton. That the episode adversely affected the partnership of Julius Norton and Christopher W. Fenton is practically certain. The advertisement is of further interest because it shows that the firm of Lyman & Fenton, which for some years was engaged in the manufacture of pottery, and whose trade-mark is so familiar to all collectors of Bennington ware, was originally formed for quite another kind of business.

NORTON & FENTON PRODUCTS

So much for the history of the business side of the firm of Norton & Fenton. Of greater interest to the student of our ceramic history is the firm's contribution to the development of the pottery industry in this country. We have already observed that Julius Norton had already begun to increase the variety and improve the quality of his wares before Fenton joined the firm. We have described in some detail the preparatory steps taken toward the manufacture of porcelain, steps which had no commercial result up to the time of the dissolution of the partnership. It remains now only to make a rapid survey of the various lines of manufacture followed while the partnership was in force, and, later, by Julius Norton himself.

Pitkin is in error when he says that the firm of Norton & Fenton made 'nothing but stoneware and brown-glazed pottery.'* In the north wing of the pottery, where the experiments in porcelain-making were carried on, several kinds of ware other than 'stoneware and brown-glazed pottery' were made. Cheap white ware for table use, known to the trade as Common White, was made in large quantity. About two miles away, in what is locally known as the Lyons District, was a plentiful supply of white clay of good average color, exceedingly plastic, and therefore admirably adapted for use as Ball Clay. Highly vitreous when fired, when mixed with china clay and a small percentage of feldspar it produced a body that was durable and fairly fine. Given a glaze compounded of certain proportions of white lead — or even litharge — feldspar, flint, whiting, and china clay, the result was an excellent white ware for ordinary table use, at a price not higher than that asked for the inferior ware of the same general type then sold.

A cheap grade of Common Yellow was made in much the same way. The mixture of the body differed only slightly, and the glaze mainly in that about twenty-five per cent less lead was used, about half the quantities of feldspar and flint, and no whiting. In this ware the coarser and heavier domestic utensils were made — milkpans, pitchers, mixing-bowls, baking-dishes, and the like. Neither the white nor the yellow ware made at this time was marked in any manner, and its identification is absolutely impossible. A great deal of both kinds of ware is found locally, particularly in old houses, but as their manufacture was continued by C. W. Fenton after the dissolution of

* Pitkin, *op. cit.*, p. 24.

Norton & Fenton, and then by the firms he later organized — the whole covering a period of fifteen years — there is no method whereby wares of these two groups made by Norton & Fenton in 1845–1847 may be distinguished from those of the same types made later, from 1847 to 1860. Not merely so, but wares of identical appearance, and of quality indistinguishable from those made by Norton & Fenton, have been made in hundreds of potteries, over a long period of years, and there is no method known whereby the most expert can distinguish between many of these and the Norton & Fenton products.

At the same time was begun the manufacture of the familiar brown-glazed ware, generally known — in this country, at least — as Rockingham. When first introduced it was frequently called Dark Lustre, the name Fenton preferred and strove hard to popularize. As the known examples of this ware made by Norton & Fenton are all marked, we are able to identify them, and, what is even more important from some points of view, to tell wherein their manufacture differed from wares of the same name made later on at the United States Pottery. This Rockingham has been defined as 'a yellow ware, spattered before firing, with a brown clay, which gives it the mottled appearance.' * That is not a correct description of ninety-five per cent of the Rockingham made at Bennington during the fifteen years of its manufacture; it is wholly misleading as a description of the Rockingham Ware made by Norton & Fenton. Leaving for later consideration the improvements made in the Rockingham Ware by Lyman, Fenton & Co., and by the United States Pottery Company, and considering now only the Norton & Fenton product, it is perhaps sufficient to say that at this period the body of the Rockingham Ware was identical with that of the Common Yellow; that it was burned, and, when in

* Pitkin, op. cit., p. 18.

the 'biscuit' stage, was glazed. It was not 'spattered with brown clay,' but dipped into a glaze compounded of red lead, clay, ground feldspar, and flint, with some manganese added. From the latter was derived the brown color. With the precise formula we are not here and now concerned: it is enough to note the component parts of the glaze and to remark that, in view of the fact that clay constituted less than one ninth of the whole, it is incorrect to refer to it as 'brown clay.' There is a difference between *clay* and *glaze*.

JULIUS NORTON RESUMES

After separating himself from Fenton, Julius Norton carried on the business alone. He did not continue to make either the Common White or the Common Yellow. By agreement, this branch of the industry was left for exploitation by Fenton. The manufacture of Rockingham was likewise left to Fenton, Julius Norton confining himself to the production of stoneware. It is true that, in later years, the manufacture of Rockingham was resumed by the latter, but with that we have no present concern. Julius Norton once more marked his stoneware with his name, as he had done from 1841 to 1844. All pottery so marked, therefore, belongs to one of these periods, 1841–1844 and 1847–1850.

J. & E. NORTON, 1850–1859

In 1850 Edward Norton, cousin of Julius, was taken into partnership and the firm name became J. & E. Norton. All pottery so marked belongs to the period 1850–1859. Edward Norton was the son of John Norton, who was the second son of Captain John Norton, the founder of the business. Born in 1815, he spent his childhood in the old Norton home. He was educated in the district school and at the

Bennington Academy, in the old village. As a youth he 'clerked' in his father's store, and subsequently became a part proprietor, his partner being one Abel Wills.

On joining the pottery firm as his cousin's partner, Edward Norton devoted himself largely to salesmanship and to the management of the considerable out-of-town trade. At that time the ware was conveyed to all parts of New York and New England in huge wagons, and Edward Norton frequently accompanied these, taking orders, settling accounts, and so forth. He appears to have had a limited partnership at first, sharing in the earnings but not in the ownership of the properties. Paying a large part of his share of the profits to his partner, by April, 1861, he had acquired a one-third share in the property. By 1865 he had acquired one half.

Like so many members of his family, Edward Norton was an ardent and active member of the Masonic fraternity. For many years he was the treasurer of Mount Anthony Lodge, F. & A.M., and was greatly honored and beloved by his brethren. To this day his memory is cherished by many of the older members of the fraternity. He was respected as one of Bennington's finest citizens.

J. & E. NORTON & Co., 1859 1861

In 1859 the firm was enlarged by the admission of Luman Preston Norton, the only son of Julius Norton, the senior partner. The young man was then twenty-two years of age, and had just graduated from Union College, Schenectady. The firm name was again changed — this time to J. & E. Norton & Co. This was the mark used upon the stoneware from 1859 to 1861, when the death of Julius Norton made another change necessary. Julius Norton died October 5, 1861. The local newspaper recorded his death in the following paragraph:

SUSTAINED A LOSS. — Bennington has sustained a great loss in the death of one of its oldest, most enterprising citizens. MR. JULIUS NORTON expired at his residence in this village last Saturday night. His disease was apoplexy, with other ailings combined, and he has been quite low for some weeks. MR. NORTON has long been a resident of this place. He was the senior member of the firm of J. & E. NORTON & Co., in the Stone Ware manufactory and has always been known for his uprightness in business dealings. His energy was great; for affability not less so. His friends were numerous, and his death has occasioned deep felt regret. His age was 52 years.

THE PERIOD REVIEWED

At this point we may well suspend the chronological record and, regarding the death of Julius Norton as marking the close of an important chapter in the enterprise, make a brief review of the progress and growth of the business from the time of its removal to the lower village, in 1833, to the death of Julius, in 1861. By the middle of 1835 there were about twenty-five hands employed, which was double the number employed at the end of 1830. By 1850 the number had increased to about forty. In the *Vermont State Banner*, November 23, 1850, an anonymous writer, in an article principally dealing with the establishment of Lyman, Fenton & Co., and signed 'A Visitor,' wrote:

Not far from these works is the Stone Ware Factory of Mr. Julius Norton, a descendant of a family of the same name, who have carried on the business in Bennington for upwards of 80 years. It is the largest establishment of its kind in the Union; and it is conceded on all hands, I believe, that he sends to all parts of New England and New York, the best quality and best manufactured ware in the country. The building is of brick with slated roof, about one hundred feet square, aside from the sheds and kilns adjoining. Bennington, it would seem, bids fair to become the great central position for the manufacture of different kinds of Pottery Ware in the United States.

In an account of Bennington Village, contributed by N. B. Hall to the *Vermont Historical Magazine*, written in 1859 and published in the following year, it is said that at that time the Stone Ware Pottery employed 'about 30 hands.' This is either a misprint or an error on the writer's part, for at that time the Stone Ware Pottery was at or near its zenith, and the number of its employees was nearer fifty than thirty. As to whether or not it was 'the largest establishment of its kind in the Union,' as stated by the anonymous writer already quoted, I have not investigated, but it is improbable.

This chapter would be incomplete if no mention were made of the spirit which pervaded the pottery during these years, the ties of friendship and fellowship which bound employers and employed into a sort of brotherhood. This was characteristic of the old Norton Pottery, first under Captain John Norton and then under his sons. It was continued by Julius, and became traditional. To this day, old potters who worked under the latter are fond of recalling the fraternal spirit which prevailed in the works under his management. Something of the spirit of the ancient guilds prevailed among these potters here in old Vermont in the middle of the nineteenth century. During one hundred and one years there was never an industrial dispute of any kind in the Norton Potteries.

IV

THE LAST PHASE

E. & L. P. NORTON, 1861–1881

UPON the death of Julius Norton, in 1861, the business was carried on by the two remaining members of the firm, Edward and Luman * Preston Norton, under the firm name of E. & L. P. Norton, which is found impressed upon a greater number of pieces of stoneware — and upon a greater variety of articles — than any other of the many marks used during the long history of the Norton Potteries, extending over a full century — 1793–1894. Pieces bearing this mark are extremely common, a circumstance which is not surprising when we remember that the partnership of Edward and Luman Preston Norton lasted just twenty years, from 1861 to 1881 — a longer period than that covered by any other of the numerous partnerships in the long history of the business.

Luman Preston Norton was a man of marked ability and sterling character, worthily maintaining the high standards of his family. He was the business manager of the firm, his partner caring for the industrial end of the concern. No business man in the community was more highly respected, alike on account of his sterling character and his business sagacity. When, in 1882, the Village of Bennington acquired a new charter, he was elected President of the village. He was also the first president of the Bennington County Savings Bank. Like so many of his family, he was keenly interested in Masonic affairs and passed through all the chairs of the local Lodge.

The Civil War period was a severe test for this and for all other

* Pitkin erroneously gives the name as *Lyman.*

similar enterprises. The firm of E. & L. P. Norton passed through the ordeal of those difficult years, thanks to the high reputation of the Norton products, the splendid repute of the Norton name, and the sagacious management of the business by Luman P. Norton. For a decade there was little opportunity for expansion, and it is not at all surprising that there is so little to chronicle concerning the firm during that time. It weathered the Civil War and the critical post-war period of readjustment — 1866–1869 — and faced the future with confidence, notwithstanding the fact that the steady growth of potteries in the Middle West indicated a narrowing market and a sterner competition. Then came the disastrous fire of March 20, 1874.

THE FIRE OF 1874

The fire broke out in the night and spread with great rapidity. The cause of the outbreak was identical with that of the 1845 disaster — a smouldering fire in the framework of heavy timbers surrounding one of the kilns was fanned into flame by a strong wind. An account of the fire published in a local newspaper says that on Sunday afternoon one of the employees, Fred Godfrey, discovered that the storeroom of the pottery, in the upper part of the building, was filled with smoke. He notified L. P. Norton, one of the two proprietors, and together they poured water over the smouldering timbers, until they believed that by so doing they had averted all possible danger. Later, when it was too late, it was discovered that they had not extinguished the fire as they had supposed. When the timbers had dried, as they quickly did, the smouldering fire again burst into flame under the influence of a gale that developed during the night.

It was a severe blow to the firm. The building was completely gutted, though a considerable portion of the walls remained standing.

The tools and most of the machinery were completely destroyed, as was the large stock of finished ware on hand — the largest accumulation in the history of the business. One of the kilns was ruined and had to be completely rebuilt.

The loss was estimated at about thirty thousand dollars, for the most part uncovered by insurance. Mr. Edward Norton had permitted most of the insurance upon his half-interest to expire, holding at the time just one policy for five thousand dollars — of which one thousand dollars was on the wood supply in the yard, which was not destroyed, so that the total amount of insurance he held upon the building and contents was just four thousand dollars. The other member of the firm, Luman P. Norton, had permitted the insurance he had long carried upon his share to lapse some time before the fire.*

Notwithstanding the extent of their loss, and the fact that it had been apparent for some time that the competition of the potteries of the Middle West was growing in volume and intensity, the work of rebuilding, upon a larger scale than before, was immediately begun. Before the end of the summer the factory was once more in operation, and through the streets of the village passed the familiar wagons laden with wares for distant points.

THE POTTERY WAGONS

Concerning these famous 'pottery wagons,' each drawn by a fine team of four horses driven by a silk-hatted and white-frocked driver, so many writers have given inaccurate accounts that a brief statement concerning them may be worth while. To avoid repetition later on, it may be observed that what is said of the Norton wagons applies equally to the similar delivery teams of the United States Pottery.

* *Bennington Banner*, March 23, 1874.

It seems to be a prevalent belief that the ware carried in these wagons was peddled from door to door by the drivers. As a matter of fact, no such 'peddling' was done. When one recalls the character of the roads over which the teams had to travel — particularly the mountain roads — it may well be imagined that extraordinary care had to be used in packing the ware, especially in the case of the finer products of the United States Pottery. To stop at a farmhouse, un- pack enough ware to provide an assortment from which a prospective customer might choose, repack it, drive a mile or two and go through the same process would have been altogether too expensive in time and certain breakages. It would have taken an entire day to cover one village, in door-to-door visits.

The wagons were for delivering ware, not for peddling it. The firm had its agency in virtually every town and village. In most cases this was a general store. Orders were taken on one trip and filled at the next, the ware for each agent or customer being packed in 'tierces,' specially built for the purpose. In this manner ware was carried all over New England and up into Canada, as well as throughout New York and New Jersey.

E. Norton, 1881–1883

In 1881 Luman P. Norton retired from the firm and from the pot- tery business, selling his interest to his partner, Edward Norton, who became sole proprietor. From 1881 to 1883 the ware produced was marked *E. Norton, Bennington, Vt.*

Edward Norton & Company, 1883–1893

In July, 1883, Edward Norton sold a half-interest in the business to C. W. Thatcher, of Bennington. The firm name *Edward Norton &*

Company was stamped on all wares made from that time until 1886, and, more or less, to 1893. Until Mr. Thatcher came into the business through his purchase of the half-interest that had formerly been held by Luman P. Norton, only one person outside of the Norton family had ever participated in the ownership of the pottery. That was Christopher W. Fenton — and he was connected with the Norton family by marriage.

Two years after the entrance of C. W. Thatcher into the firm came the death of Edward Norton, on August 3, 1885. He was seventy years old when he died, having been born at the old homestead of Captain John Norton, by the original pottery, August 23, 1815. Of him it may be said that he was worthy of his race, the peer of a line of noted craftsmen, honored for their probity of character and their constant exemplification of the primal virtues. Edward Norton was held in high esteem and respect by his fellow citizens, among whom he walked uprightly, dealing justly with all, and bestowing compassion and aid upon the needy to the utmost of his power.

Edward Lincoln Norton

His place was taken by his son, Edward Lincoln Norton, then a young man of twenty, who, for some three years, had been employed as salesman for the firm. Upon succeeding to his father's interest, Edward L. Norton proposed a radical departure. It was obvious that the manufacture of stoneware could not be carried on profitably, except upon the smallest possible scale to serve the immediate local market. There was no hope of meeting the low prices of the potteries of the Middle West with their low manufacturing costs. That the Bennington ware was superior in quality to most of the product of Ohio and Illinois was freely conceded; but that was of small importance. Stoneware was stoneware, and the inferior goods from Ohio would serve every practical end just as well as the superior article from Bennington.

So Edward Lincoln Norton proposed that the firm, which was now known as The Edward Norton Company, should undertake wholesale dealing in glassware, china, and pottery of all kinds. The proposal was adopted, and the venture soon proved profitable. This departure from the old line of business is of especial interest to collectors for the reason that many pieces which are quite unlike anything known to have been made at Bennington, but which are vouched for by credible witnesses, who know that they were 'bought at the Bennington pottery,' are found on investigation to have been purchased at the time when the wholesale business was flourishing. I know of pieces of pottery of indubitable English make, some even bearing English makers' marks, which were bought at the pottery in Bennington at this period. Other pieces, unquestionably purchased at the Bennington establishment during this period, were as certainly made in Jersey City.

Steadily, year by year, the volume of this wholesale business grew, while the manufacture of stoneware was maintained upon a small scale. In 1893, when the firm celebrated the one hundredth anniversary of the founding of its business, its actual output of pottery was probably no larger than it had been at the end of Captain John Norton's first year of operation. Yet it was possible to say that the pottery business had been carried on for a full hundred years, almost exclusively by Nortons. Edward L. Norton was planning to revive the manufacturing end of the business, and was negotiating with potters, with a view to beginning the manufacture of different kinds of pottery, when, in 1894, he died, aged only twenty-nine years.

And the wheel of the potter was stilled forever.

A CHRONOLOGICAL LIST OF ALL MARKS USED BY THE NORTON POTTERIES

Note: As the marks used by the Norton Potteries consisted simply of stamped plain lettering, with no ornamentation or devices of any kind, it has been thought unnecessary to list minor variations in the arrangement of the same words, as, for example, when 'Bennington, Vt.' is printed on two lines instead of on one. As a general rule, the name and address occupy two lines. One line and three lines are uncommon arrangements. Where the mark takes the form of an arrangement of the words in a circle, the fact is here indicated. The principal value of this list to the collector is, of course, the fact that it provides a complete and convenient check-list by means of which any piece of stoneware bearing a Norton mark may be dated with virtual certainty.

L. NORTON & Co., BENNINGTON, VT.	1823–1828
L. NORTON, BENNINGTON, VT.	1828–1833
L. NORTON & SON, EAST BENNINGTON, VT. ⎫ L. NORTON & SON, BENNINGTON, VT. ⎬	1833–1840
JULIUS NORTON, EAST BENNINGTON, VT. ⎫ J. NORTON, EAST BENNINGTON, VT. ⎪ JULIUS NORTON, BENNINGTON, VT. ⎬ J. NORTON, BENNINGTON, VT. ⎭	1841–1844(5)
NORTON & FENTON, EAST BENNINGTON, VT. ⎫ * NORTON & FENTON, BENNINGTON, VT. ⎬	1844(5)–1847
JULIUS NORTON, BENNINGTON, VT. ⎫ J. NORTON, BENNINGTON, VT. ⎬	1847–1850
J. & E. NORTON, BENNINGTON, VT.	1850–1859
J. NORTON & Co., BENNINGTON. VT. ⎫ J. & E. NORTON & Co., BENNINGTON, VT. ⎬	1859–1861
E. & L. P. NORTON, BENNINGTON, VT.	1861–1881
E. NORTON, BENNINGTON, VT.	1881–1883
EDWARD NORTON, BENNINGTON, VT. ⎫ EDWARD NORTON & Co., BENNINGTON, VT. ⎪ E. NORTON & Co., BENNINGTON, VT. ⎬ EDWARD NORTON & COMPANY, BENNINGTON, VT. ⎭	1883–1894

(Sometimes the word 'Company' is spelled in full)

EDWARD NORTON COMPANY, BENNINGTON, VT.	1886–1894

(This last mark is uncommon).

BENNINGTON FACTORY

(This mark is exceedingly rare — I know of only one piece so marked — and the date of its use is unknown.)

* Sometimes arranged in a circle.

In his discussion of the marks found upon Bennington pottery, Pitkin directs attention to the elliptical mark formed of the words 'Norton & Fenton, Bennington, Vt.' which he designates as 'Mark 1,' and the mark composed of the words 'Norton & Fenton, East Bennington, Vt.,' in two straight lines, which he designates as 'Mark 2.' If by the numerical designations he intended to state the order of their use, giving priority to the first-named, he is almost certainly in error.

No Benningtonian who knows history would care to base any opinion upon the point solely on the basis of the use of the name 'East Bennington.' At the period we are here discussing, 'Bennington' and 'East Bennington' were in equally common use as the name of the lower village. It is not at all surprising that Norton & Fenton used both names with little discrimination or plan. This was the common practice. The *Vermont State Banner*, for example, used 'East Bennington' in its heading on Monday, April 19, 1847, as it had done for some weeks. On Monday, April 26, 1847, and for several weeks thereafter, it used 'Bennington.' The issue of the same paper for February 7th, 1848, is dated from 'Bennington,' but that of the 14th is dated from 'East Bennington.' It would be easy to multiply such examples, *ad infinitum*. My own opinion, that 'East Bennington' was used by Norton & Fenton somewhat earlier than 'Bennington,' is entirely based upon the usage adopted in the firm's advertisements. It is probable that their markings corresponded with their formal announcements in this particular.

Of the 'East Bennington' mark Pitkin observes, 'A brown glazed pitcher in the Pitkin collection bears this mark. This pitcher and a stoneware jug are the only pieces I have ever seen bearing this extremely rare mark.' This statement is wholly incomprehensible to me. I know of no collection of Bennington pottery of any considerable importance or size that does not have one or more of the Rockingham pitchers bearing this mark. Certainly, I can account for at least thirty of the hexagonal pitchers so marked.

As for the appearance of this mark on stoneware, I can only say that examples are not at all uncommon, let alone 'extremely rare.' First and last, I must have seen and handled well over a hundred fine examples of stoneware marked thus, and I have never experienced the slightest difficulty in obtaining them for a nominal sum. The mischief done by such a statement as the one quoted lies in the fact that it deceives both dealers and collectors, and that persons owning examples of stoneware bearing this mark are led by the statement to believe that they have something which must be of considerable value because 'extremely rare.'

PART TWO

THE FENTON POTTERIES

NOTE

THE following pages are devoted to a comprehensive historical and descriptive account of the various wares made at Bennington by Christopher Webber Fenton and his associates. The designation which I have chosen for this second part of my book, namely, 'The Fenton Potteries,' is open to criticism in that it ignores the fact that Fenton was always — with the exception of a few months — associated with others in the enterprise. In the chapters devoted to the subject, these various associates and the several organizations and partnerships formed by them will be found to be fully considered. Fenton had so many different partners and the changes of name and form of organization of the firm were so numerous that it has seemed to me the best, as well as the easiest, course to use this simple title for Part Two, leaving to my text the task of needful amplification.

PART TWO

THE FENTON POTTERIES

I

FENTON AND THE UNITED STATES POTTERY

THE FENTON GENEALOGY

FOR a long time all that could be learned of the early history of Christopher Webber Fenton was that he was reputed to have been born, in 1806, at Dorset, Vermont, though no record of the fact had been found; that he was supposed to have learned his trade as potter at Dorset, though no record or trace of a pottery could be discovered there; that he married Louisa, elder daughter of Luman Norton, the Bennington potter, at some unknown date; that he came to Bennington at some unspecified time in the early part of the nineteenth century, and there engaged in the pottery business — perhaps with Captain John Norton, but certainly with his son, Luman Norton. Altogether, that was scant information, and some of it was quite wrong, for we now know that Fenton never engaged in the pottery business with either Captain John Norton or his son Luman.

I well remember the disappointment with which Albert W. Pitkin returned to Bennington on several occasions after days spent in Dorset in a fruitless effort to discover something definite concerning Fenton's origin and early history. Long afterward it was my own lot to find myself experiencing the same sense of discouragement and disappointment over the same task. Even such a simple matter as the date of Fenton's marriage seemed utterly impossible of certain determination.

Of course, to the student of American ceramic history, interested in Fenton's contribution to the development of an important industry, and to the collector, interested in the products of the Bennington potteries with which Fenton was associated, the date of the man's marriage, or the question of whether or not he was married at all, is really of no consequence. One could write a fairly comprehensive account of the Bennington potteries without either knowing or caring anything about the ancestors of Fenton, or about the potteries of Dorset. So much is obvious. At the same time, I found it impossible to rid my mind of the realization that the facts mentioned, and similar ones, *might*, if they were known, illumine the whole history of the Bennington enterprise, and that to pass them over for no reason other than the unusual difficulty of finding authentic information concerning them was a poor way to begin writing a history. If one abandons the search for one group of facts, merely because the search is attended by unusual difficulties, the temptation to get rid of the next problem in the same easy manner will be strong and not easily resisted.

To find out all that could be found out concerning the origin of Fenton, his ancestry, parentage, early life, training, habits, talent, character, began as a diversion and speedily became an all-absorbing task. I think that I have made inquiries concerning the ancestry of hundreds of Fentons and 'Fintons' in all parts of the country, and I hesitate to say how many musty records I have searched. The result is a fuller and more authentic outline of the man and his career than has ever before been possible. That much may be claimed for it, whatever it may leave to be desired by the reader whose interest in the inanimate things described in these pages is accompanied by an equal, or perhaps greater, interest in the men responsible for their being.

In an elaborate, but poorly arranged, genealogical work entitled

The Fenton Family of America and Great Britain, published in 1912, the author, Thomas Astley Atkins, LL.B., notwithstanding the fact that the course of his research brought him to Vermont, made no reference to Christopher Webber Fenton, to any of the St. Johnsbury, Vermont, Fentons, or to any person bearing that name who appeared to be related to these foregoing members of the family.

Mr. Atkins, however, found that one William Fenton, who was born at Urney, County of Tyrone, Ireland, and whose son was born there in 1716, settled in Roxbury, Massachusetts, at some time before 1722, in which year he bought land at Rutland, Massachusetts. He seems to have written his name 'Ffenton,' but his father in Ireland signed his name 'John Fenton.' Mr. Atkins traces the Fentons of Urney, County of Tyrone, back to Staffordshire, England, to one James Fenton, a General in Queen Elizabeth's army, who died at his ancestral estate, Fenton Hall, City of Fenton, Staffordshire, England, in which place his descendants still reside. The grandson of this General James Fenton was the poet, Elijah Fenton, who collaborated with Alexander Pope in translating Homer's *Odyssey*, being responsible for four of the books, according to most authorities. This Elijah Fenton published, in 1717, a volume of verse, *Poems on Several Occasions*. He died in 1732. The only interest which this information possesses comes from the fact that, among my notes, I find one, written in 1917, to the effect that, according to Dr. Day, C. W. Fenton claimed that he was directly descended from a relative of the Fenton who was associated with Pope in the translation of the *Odyssey*. Unfortunately, there is nothing to indicate the original source of Dr. Day's authority. That Christopher Webber Fenton was of the same family, however, is fairly certain.*

* It is perhaps worthy of note that one of the few authenticated pieces (indeed, I know of no others) of the work of the English potter Twyford is a brown jug inscribed with the name of Thomas Fenton, brother of the poet, who is said to have owned Twyford's pottery at Shelton.

There was an earlier genealogy of the American Fentons, compiled by William L. Weaver, editor of the *Willimantic Journal*, and published at Willimantic, Connecticut, in 1867. Its title is *A Genealogy of the Fenton Family, Descendants of Robert Fenton, an Early Settler of Ancient Windham, Conn. (now Mansfield)*. In this I find that, in 1585, Captain Edward Fenton, of the British Royal Navy, in the reign of Queen Elizabeth, visited St. Augustine, Florida, as a member of the exploring expedition of the famous Sir Martin Frobisher. This Captain Edward Fenton was the eldest brother of the General James Fenton, of Staffordshire, above referred to.

More to our purpose is the following: In 1688 one Robert Fenton appears in Woburn, Massachusetts, as a taxpayer. His name is on the tax list for the years 1688, 1689, 1690, and 1691, and then disappears. In 1694, Robert Fenton appears in Windham (later Mansfield), Connecticut. This is, probably, the same Robert Fenton who had lived at Woburn. He appears to have been a carpenter. That he was a man of such qualities as would command the confidence of his fellows is indicated by his occupancy of responsible offices in the town.

This Robert Fenton had eight children. The seventh child was a son, Ebenezer, born at Windham (Mansfield) in 1710. This Ebenezer in turn had fifteen children by two successive wives. His first wife was Mehitable Tuttle; his second, Lydia Conant. His oldest son by the first wife was Jonathan, born 1740.

Jonathan Fenton served in the Revolutionary War, enlisting for two years from Mansfield, in 1779. He married one Mary Cary, a widow, in 1762. Jonathan Fenton had six children, three sons and

---

Twyford is best remembered as the man who, posing as an idiot, spied upon, and stole the secrets of, John P. Elers and his son — a notable chapter in English ceramic history. The fact that so many of the Fentons in America became potters, together with the Staffordshire ancestry, suggests a tradition of the craft in the family which helps to account for much.

three daughters. The second son was Jonathan, born July 18, 1766, and the third son — and fourth child — was Richard Webber, born September 4, 1771.

The Jonathan Fenton, son of Jonathan and Mary (Cary) Fenton, was a potter and the father of Christopher Webber Fenton. His brother, Richard Webber Fenton, also a potter, appears in St. Johnsbury, Vermont, in 1804, as one of a committee appointed 'to Expel dogs from the Meeting House on Sundays.' He was then thirty-three years old.

In the old cemetery at Dorset, I found the grave of Mary Fenton, who died in 1832, aged ninety-nine years, showing that the eldest son, Jonathan, had taken his mother with him when he migrated to Vermont. Her age as given on the tombstone would indicate that, although a widow when she married Jonathan Fenton, Sr. in 1762, she was, nevertheless, but twenty-nine years of age. Undoubtedly she was the 'Widow Fenton,' of whom two of the oldest living residents of Dorset, both octogenarians, had heard their parents talk about as a 'good, lively and cheerful old soul' and a 'wonderful old lady.'

We can trace the movements of Jonathan Fenton, Jr., father of Christopher Webber Fenton, by the records of the birth of his eight children. For assistance in obtaining these I am indebted to Miss Anna A. Sherlock, Town Clerk of Dorset, Vermont, and to Mr. Herbert Williams Denio, Librarian of the Vermont Historical Society. Jonathan Fenton and Rose Lyndia (or Lydia — both forms are given) had nine children, as follows: *Harriet*, born at New Haven, Connecticut, March 16, 1793; *Sally*, born at Boston, Massachusetts, September 26, 1794; *Melyndia*, born at Boston, Massachusetts, January 11, 1796; *Richard L.*, born at Walpole, New Hampshire, January 22, 1797; *Almira*, born at Windsor, Connecticut, November 12, 1799;

Maria, born at Dorset, Vermont, November 1, 1801; *Eliza*, born at Dorset, Vermont, April 12, 1803; *Clarecy*, born at Dorset, Vermont, August 27, 1804; *Christopher Webber*, born at Dorset, Vermont, January 30, 1806.

It is evident that Jonathan Fenton, for some years of his early married life, was much given to wandering from town to town. This, in all probability, was due to the exigencies of his employment, and to the precarious condition of many of the potteries that sprang up in all parts of New England. Be that as it may, he came to Dorset from Windsor, Connecticut, some time between November, 1799, and November, 1801. We can narrow that a little more closely: The United States Census for Vermont, taken in 1800 — of which there is a photostat copy in the library of the Vermont Historical Society — shows that there was no head of a family named Fenton in Dorset at the time of the census. Fenton and his family, therefore, must have settled in the village quite late in 1800 or else prior to November, 1801. It may be added that the same census indicates that there was no family by the name of Fenton in St. Johnsbury in 1800; General R. W. Fenton, brother of Jonathan, must therefore have come thither at some time between 1800 and 1804, when he was appointed to the 'Dog Committee.'

CHRISTOPHER WEBBER FENTON

Now we know all that is necessary or important concerning the ancestry and parentage of Christopher Webber Fenton. He was the youngest of nine children, six of whom were girls. He was born at Dorset, Vermont, January 30, 1806. His father was a potter, and so was his father's brother. There was a Jacob Fenton, a potter, in New Haven in 1800 who in 1801 moved to Burlington, New York, and established a pottery there. We may safely conclude that Christopher Webber Fenton belonged to what we may term an old potter family, and, judging by his career and his work, that he possessed a liking and an appetite for the trade. His father we know to have been a man of small fortune, a simple craftsman, who established and for some years operated a small pottery at East Dorset, where he made red earthenware and stoneware, the simple, homely pottery of which common domestic utensils were fashioned, differing in no notable particular from similar ware made at many other places in New England. That he was a good potter is evidenced by the excellent specimens of his work that have survived, and bear his mark. The son, Richard L.* Fenton, Christopher's brother, who acquired a half interest in the pottery in 1826,† was likewise a good potter, as the pieces bearing his name prove. The family was of good Anglo-American stock, as the brief genealogical sketch above given shows.

Fenton's Character and Attainments

What education Christopher Webber Fenton received I have not been able to ascertain. There is no evidence that he ever enjoyed the advantage of anything better than the instruction supplied by the district schools of his day. The old potters with whom I have discussed his character and attainments have invariably represented him as a man of just a little more education than the average potter, but inferior in that respect to some.

A composite of all their recollections would make a picture something like this: A man of rather more education than the average me-

* I have always understood that the 'L' stood for 'Leander' — the name of his cousin, Leander Fenton, of St. Johnsbury, who was also a potter, and worked for some time at Bennington with his cousin. Mrs. Ruth Howe Wood, a descendant, says, however, that the initial stood for 'Lucas.' (See *Antiques*, vol. VIII, No. 5, p. 152.)

† See p. 51.

chanic of his day, in no wise noted for exceptional learning or intellectual gifts; not much given to reading; rather good at figures, and with something of a natural talent for drawing, his readiness at making pencil sketches of designs and patterns being well remembered; a Whig in politics and fond of talking about politics, but with insufficient command of his temper, being easily angered in discussion; rather uncertain in his relations with men, changing from extreme affability and good-fellowship to sullen aloofness without apparent reason or cause; restless in manner, constantly altering plans and orders and introducing changes in the arrangements of the factory; fastidious in his dress; careful and precise in his speech; exceedingly formal in his manners, but given to boasting; addicted to constant dram-drinking, intensified by periodic 'sprees' followed by mental depression and despondency.

Such a composite of the recollections of men who knew Christopher Webber Fenton is not a complete portrait of the man, and it would be wrong to regard it as such. It is probable that a contemporary sketch, written by one who knew the man intimately, would be so different as to make my portrait at second hand appear as a mere caricature. Moreover, we must remember that this portrait is drawn from the last few years of Fenton's life, not one of the recollections upon which it is based going further back than 1855.

He learned his trade as a potter at the little pottery at East Dorset, owned and operated by his father and then by his father and elder brother in partnership. As pointed out elsewhere in this study, the opportunities which existed here for learning anything of the higher forms of ceramic manufacture were exceedingly limited. However interested in his craft the apprentice may have been, and however skilled as a workman, he could not have acquired at the East Dorset pottery any practical experience in the finer branches of the potter's art.

MARRIAGE AND CHILDREN

He was married to Louisa Norton, daughter of Luman Norton, at Bennington, October 29, 1832. It seems almost incredible, but years of steady and persistent searching were required to ascertain that date. Neither in the records of the Norton family nor in any of the accessible local church records could the date be found. A careful search of the files of the local newspapers of the period did not disclose it. Fenton's granddaughter, Mrs. Ralph White, of North Bennington, did not know it; neither did her father, Fenton's son-in-law, Mr. Henry D. Fillmore, of Bennington. It was found at last, among the unpublished vital records of the State, on file at Montpelier, by Mr. Herbert Williams Denio, Librarian of the Vermont Historical Society. Almost simultaneously, in the diary of our old friend Hiram Harwood, for the year 1832, I came across the following entry:

Married this morning by the Revd E. H. Hooker, Mr. —— Fenton, Merchant, of Dorset to Miss Louisa eldest daughter of Judge L. Norton of this town. The young couple started immediately for N. Y. City — had the misfortune to wreck their carriage in the Parson's Hollow — proceeded afterwards in the Judge's waggon. — *Monday, October 29, 1832.*[*]

Of this marriage four children were born, two sons and two daughters. The eldest daughter, Fanny, became the wife of Calvin Park. Frank, the second child, in his young manhood went west, worked as a potter in Peoria, Illinois, served in the Civil War, and, I believe, died in Chicago, leaving a small family. Augusta, the third child, died of smallpox, at Bennington, February 22, 1857. She was then in her sixteenth year. Fenton, it appears, contracted the disease in New

* Pitkin, *op. cit.*, p. 19, gives the date of the marriage as 'about 1828.'

York City, but recovered from it. The infection was communicated from father to child, with fatal results. Henry, the youngest child, died, I believe, in a western hospital for the insane.

The Beginning of the Fenton Business

All that is known concerning the brief co-partnership that existed between Fenton and his brother-in-law, Julius Norton, has been set forth in an earlier chapter in connection with the history of the Norton Potteries, and need not here be repeated. That partnership was dissolved June 25, 1847. Fenton thereupon began business upon his own account, devoting himself to the manufacture of Common White and Common Yellow and Rockingham wares as the foundation of the business, with porcelain as a side line still largely experimental in character.

If ever the terms of the dissolution of the partnership between Norton and Fenton were recorded in any formal instrument, certainly no trace of such a document has been found. But what appears to have occurred is this: By mutual agreement Fenton took over the lines of manufacture enumerated above, which had previously been carried on in the north wing of the factory, in a relatively small space. Because of the quantity of materials on hand, the transfer of which would have been quite expensive, Fenton continued the work in the north wing until the materials were exhausted. Meanwhile he paid rent to Julius Norton for the privilege. This arrangement continued to November, when the first public announcement of the dissolution was made, the occasion for it being Fenton's removal to a neighboring building owned by Alanson P. Lyman, with whom he was already in partnership in another enterprise — the powder factory referred to in an earlier chapter.

ASSOCIATION WITH HENRY D. HALL

While he was doing business upon his own account in the north wing of the Norton Pottery, Fenton secured the financial support of Henry D. Hall, son of the famous Governor and historian of the State, Hiland Hall. This arrangement accounts for the legend perpetuated by practically every writer who has dealt with the subject, that, when Julius Norton and Christopher Webber Fenton could not persuade their senior partner, Judge Luman Norton, to go into the manufacture of 'a more decorative line of ware,' they leased the north wing of the pottery and, taking Henry D. Hall into partnership with them, started to make Parian Ware.* Henry D. Hall was never in partnership with Julius Norton. He did, however, become the 'silent partner' of Fenton at the time stated. There was no public announcement of the partnership. The firm name was Fenton, Hall & Co., but it seems only to have been used where legal forms required it. So far as is known, it never appeared upon any of the company's wares. Mr. Hall withdrew from the firm and terminated his arrangement with it after a few months.

That the foregoing is an accurate account of the relations of Fenton and Hall there can be no sensible doubt. Mr. Hall's daughter, the late Mrs. H. T. Cushman, of North Bennington, remembered hearing her father say many times that he was Fenton's partner for a few months, and that the legal name of the firm was Fenton, Hall & Co. Mr. Henry D. Hall wrote with his own hand, at the request of the editor

* Barber, in his well-known book, *The Pottery and Porcelain of the United States*, p. 165, also states that Messrs. C. W. Fenton, Julius Norton, and Henry D. Hall were in partnership. The paragraph in which this is stated is a most extraordinary jumble of misinformation. It says: 'Christopher Webber Fenton, Henry D. Hall, and Julius Norton commenced making yellow, white, and Rockingham wares at Bennington, Vermont, about the year 1846, in the north wing of the old stoneware shop (which had been erected in 1793 by the Norton family), operated by Messrs. Norton and Fenton. The new firm brought from England one John Harrison, who did their first modeling. Mr. Hall did not long remain in the company and after he and Mr. Norton withdrew, the style was changed to Lyman & Fenton, by the admission to the firm of Mr. Alanson Potter Lyman ... and shortly after to Lyman, Fenton & Park.'

of the *Bennington Banner*, a short sketch of his life, which was published in that paper. In that sketch he gave the facts as they are here given. Finally, in the obituary of Mr. Hall, which was written by his son-in-law, Mr. Henry T. Cushman, the same account is given. Mr. Cushman observes, in the obituary notice referred to, 'In 1846 a partnership was formed under the name of Fenton, Hall & Company.' Of course, the date is wrongly given here. It should be 1847, instead of 1846. But the main fact, the partnership of Henry D. Hall with Christopher Webber Fenton, is established beyond question.

Fenton's Works, Bennington, Vermont, 1847–1848

For several months after the withdrawal of Henry D. Hall, Fenton was without a partner. It is not until September, 1848, that there is any evidence of his having found new partners *for his pottery business*. The reason for emphasis upon the closing words of the last sentence will presently be manifest. For the moment our sole concern is with the fact that the wares made by Fenton during the time when Hall was his silent partner, and after the withdrawal of the latter until the end of 1848, were marked *Fenton's Works, Bennington, Vermont*, the words being impressed in a raised ornamental panel. This mark, which was used from June, 1847, to the close of the following year — not 'about 1845,' as Pitkin asserts — has been found upon Rockingham Ware and upon quite a variety of porcelain pitchers. Pitkin says of this mark, 'It is found on Rockingham ware, Parian, and pottery of a yellow body.' In a subsequent paragraph he states that this mark is to be found upon a Parian pitcher in the Morgan Memorial at Hartford, Connecticut, upon an octagonal water-cooler in Rockingham, having 'a yellow body mottled in light brown.' *

* Pitkin, *op. cit.*, p. 24.

If Pitkin had lived to complete his book and supervise its publication, he would not have permitted such confusion to stand uncorrected. It can only perplex the reader to be told that the mark we are considering is to be found on 'Rockingham . . . and pottery of a yellow body,' when, as the context shows, the Rockingham water-cooler upon which the mark is found is 'of yellow body,' which, indeed, is true of virtually all Bennington Rockingham. I have a similar water-cooler in my own collection bearing this mark. To the average reader, it is to be feared, the passage quoted may convey the idea that the mark we are considering was used on the Yellow Ware. That, however, is not the case.*

The same mark is often found upon white porcelain pitchers, which are frequently, but erroneously, classified as 'Parian.' A case in point is the glazed white porcelain pitcher, No. 7 in Williamson's catalogue of the Pitkin Collection. To call such ware 'Parian' is to destroy the basis of intelligent classification. Leaving to a subsequent chapter the important task of defining Parian and indicating wherein it must be sharply differentiated from other types of porcelain, it is sufficient to state here that nearly all of the examples of white porcelain marked with the raised panel impressed with the words *Fenton's Works, Bennington, Vermont,* are *not* Parian, but ordinary hard porcelain.

Yet it would be incorrect to state that no Parian was made by Fenton at this time, or marked in the manner described. A small syrup pitcher, copied from a well-known Alcock design, and known to collectors as the *Bird Nest* pitcher, is most often found in what can hardly be classified as anything other than Parian. The nature of the design

* It is unfortunate that the classification of Bennington wares in Pitkin's book, and in the collection bearing his name at the Morgan Memorial, Hartford Athenæum, is extremely faulty and confusing.

itself, in this instance, is wholly unsuited to reproduction in marble, or in a substance intended to imitate that material. This tends to weaken the jug's resemblance to marble. Even the best specimens cannot be said successfully to effect the illusion which Parian should achieve. Far more successful is the little-known pitcher bearing the same mark, decorated with relief figures of mounted knights in conflict on one side, and of a lover and his lady upon the other. This design, originally made in England by Alcock, was known as *Love and War*. In the quality of the workmanship and of the material itself the pitcher is one of the finest examples ever made at the Bennington potteries, at any time. Although its mark indicates that it was produced during the experimental period, its excellence was rarely equaled at any time thereafter. It is an exquisite thing, and closely approximates the ideal Parian standard. (Plate XXI.) *

FENTON AS DRY-GOODS MERCHANT

In the early spring of 1848, Fenton somehow acquired a new interest and entered into a new partnership. This did not at first appear to be connected with the pottery business, and herein lies the explanation of the statement made earlier in this chapter, that it was not until September, 1848, that Fenton 'found new partners *for his pottery business.*' He was already in business as a potter upon his own account, while he was, at the same time, in the powder manufacturing business with A. P. Lyman as a member of the firm of Lyman, Fenton & Co. On April 19, 1848, he appeared in still another rôle. On that date the *Vermont Gazette*, published in the lower village, carried the advertisement shown at the top of page 117.

* Pitchers of this design, bearing the same mark, and obviously made from the same mould, but of a heavy brownish-yellow clay, quite highly glazed, are among the least attractive of all Fenton's works.

This advertisement of the firm of Lyman, Fenton & Park, dealers in dry goods, was neither preceded nor accompanied by any formal an-

---

APRIL 17, 1848
SPRING AND SUMMER GOODS

The subscribers this day received their Spring and Summer Goods, comprising a much larger assortment than has usually been brought into this part of the country.

They intend to offer goods as cheap as they can be had at any other store, and cheaper if they can afford it.

Ladies and Gentlemen are respectfully invited to call and examine their goods and prices.

LYMAN, FENTON & PARK

---

nouncement of a new partnership entered into by Fenton. It appears simply as an entirely new enterprise. The most careful search of the files of the contemporary local newspapers, and of all other known local records, has failed to reveal anything concerning this partnership

---

SPRING AND SUMMER
GOODS

Which cannot be beat in this town, either in quantity, quality, or prices.

Ladies and Gentlemen are respectfully invited to give them a call, and see.

LYMAN, FENTON & PARK

East Bennington, April 17, 1848.

---

other than appears upon the surface — that Fenton, either as an individual or as a member of the firm of Lyman & Fenton, powder manufacturers, had become associated with the dry-goods business.

It may or may not be significant that, about four weeks before the appearance of this advertisement in the *Vermont Gazette*, on April 19, 1848, the regular weekly advertisement of 'C. W. Fenton, Manufacturer,' ceased to appear, the last insertion being on March 15, 1848. The *State Banner*, in its issue of April 24, 1848, published a somewhat different advertisement of the dry-goods firm of Lyman, Fenton & Park, as given at the bottom of page 117.

CALVIN PARK A PARTNER

I make no pretense of explaining this strangely complicated chapter in the history of Christopher Webber Fenton and his work as a potter here in Bennington. In so far as I am aware, there is not a scrap of authentic history, or even of credible local tradition, which can be cited to throw any light upon it. The record must stand as it is, valuable for the information it imparts concerning the precarious existence of Fenton's cherished enterprise. It is evident that he was finding it difficult to finance his pottery; though just how that situation would be remedied by his joining a dry-goods firm is not readily manifest. In some manner, however, the move eventually brought into the pottery business Mr. Calvin Park, a local business man, who subsequently — much later — became Fenton's son-in-law.

Once more we find our way with the aid of the files of the contemporary local newspapers. On October 5, 1848, the *Vermont Gazette* — the paper of that name published in the lower village — contained an account of the Exhibition of the Bennington County Agricultural Society, which had been held at Shaftsbury during the preceding week. In the accompanying description of the exhibits appears the following:

Our neighbors, Lyman, Fenton & Park, presented specimens of their Crockery, which elicited much remark for its surpassing beauty and excellence. A large amount was sold to visitors. The manufactures of this Company have obtained a reputation in our principal cities as not only the best manufactured in this country, but superior to any imported.

In the list of prizes awarded, we find that one prize of fifty cents was awarded to the firm of Lyman, Fenton & Park, for an exhibit of door knobs, and another of two dollars for an 'exhibit of Crockery.' The same list was published in the uptown *Vermont Gazette*, October 3, 1848. It should be said, perhaps, that these exceedingly modest premiums were up to the general average for the whole Exhibition, and that the exhibits of Messrs. Lyman, Fenton & Park were the only ones in their respective classes. So far as I have been able to discover, this account of the Exhibition of the Bennington County Agricultural Society for 1848 constitutes the first public mention of the connection of the firm of Lyman, Fenton & Park with the pottery business. Some weeks later, in its issue of November 22, 1848, the same paper published for the first time the advertisement of this firm as pottery manufacturers. The advertisement appeared among the 'Business Cards,' immediately below that of Julius Norton, and read as follows:

LYMAN, FENTON & PARK

Manufacturers of Every Description of
Rockingham, White Flint and White Earthen
CROCKERY WARE
East Bennington, Vt.

It is worthy of note, in passing, that neither in the account of the Exhibition of Shaftsbury, nor in this or any other known advertisement, is there any mention of Parian Ware. This is certainly a remarkable fact. Fenton was too fond of publicity, I believe, to have missed the chance to persuade the local press to take notice of the fact that the new Statuary Ware, which had attracted so much attention, was being successfully made by him. It can hardly be doubted that some of the ware would have been displayed at the Exhibition, or that it would have been the subject of much local comment, if it was then being manufactured upon any considerable scale. At the same time the fact remains that many porcelain pitchers, including the best examples of Parian, bear the mark that was in use at this time. We are forced to believe that the manufacture of porcelain in general, and of Parian porcelain in particular, was still wholly experimental and entirely subordinate to the manufacture of the commoner types of ware. The fact that some of the porcelain pitchers bearing the mark *Fenton's Works* are found in such large numbers does not, of necessity, invalidate this theory. It is quite likely that the moulds made during this experimental period were continued in use for years afterward. It is also worthy of note that, from the date of the first appearance of the advertisement of Lyman, Fenton & Park as manufacturers of pottery products, the advertisement of dry goods by the same firm disappears. In the meantime, the firm of Lyman & Fenton, manufacturers of gun and blasting powder, maintain their separate identity and advertise regularly in the local newspapers.

Calvin Park Withdraws

Calvin Park withdrew from the concern on or about November 1, 1849. There is no known record of the dissolution of the firm. It appears that Park simply withdrew, leaving the business to the other two members, A. P. Lyman and C. W. Fenton. In the uptown *Vermont Gazette*, Thursday, September 27, 1849, appeared the advertisement of Lyman, Fenton & Park, as manufacturers of pottery products.

The advertisement was identical with that published regularly during the year by the rival paper of the same name, and already quoted in full. In the issue of the same uptown paper for October 11, 1849, appeared a list of the premiums awarded at the annual Exhibition of the Bennington County Agricultural Society for that year, held at Bennington, from which it appears that the firm of Lyman, Fenton & Park had entered an 'exhibit of six pieces of Crockery,' and had been awarded the first premium — $1.50. Shortly after that Park ceased to be connected with the firm, and the other two members sometimes styled themselves Lyman & Fenton and sometimes, Lyman, Fenton & Co.

FENTON'S PATENT PROCESS

It was at this time that Fenton secured the patent for his process of using metallic colors in connection with flint glaze. This patent, which was issued November 27, 1849, is the one referred to in the well-known elliptical mark found on so much of the Bennington ware, impressed into the ware and bearing the words *Fenton's Enamel Patented 1849*, in the center and surrounded by the name *Lyman, Fenton & Co., Bennington, Vt.* As Pitkin rightly pointed out, what Fenton secured a patent for was not flint glaze itself, nor the manner of applying it. The use of this glaze had been usual with most of the English potters for many years; it was the common property of the trade. In this country it had been used with success for a number of years. Neither was it the use of color in connection with flint glaze — which is correctly termed 'Flint Enamel' — that was covered by Fenton's patent. That had been used with success by other American potters, to say nothing of the great potters of England and Continental Europe. Palissy used metallic oxides with his glaze, achieving wonderful effects.

Still earlier, the unknown potters of Beauvaisie, at Lachapelle des Pots, used metallic oxides with glazes with marked success. As far back as the Sixth Dynasty (B.C. 3703) the Chinese used enamels made from oxides of tin and copper in the glazing of sepulchral figures.* The ancient Egyptians, and likewise the Assyrians, used siliceous glaze together with metallic oxide enamels, the colors used being blue, black, yellow, and red.† In the work of Whieldon, Dwight, and other Staffordshire potters of eminence, such metallic oxides as copper green, antimony, manganese, and zaffre were successfully used. Fenton's famous patent covered simply the manner of applying the metallic colors. In a subsequent chapter we shall discuss this subject more fully. It is mentioned here because the date of this patent coincided with the period under consideration, and, even though it involves some repetition, the belief that Christopher Webber Fenton 'patented Flint Enamel,' which persists in spite of all statements to the contrary, needs to be corrected.

THE FACTORY OF 1850

Early in the summer of 1850 the firm of Lyman, Fenton & Co. began the erection of a new factory upon the site now occupied by the Bennington Graded School. They had secured some new capital for the enterprise, and the new buildings and kilns embodied numerous improvements which Fenton and Decius W. Clark had devised, as well as many others which were copied from other potteries. The buildings were of wood, and there were three large double kilns. The cost of the undertaking is said to have been about fifteen thousand dollars. While the new plant was being constructed, work was carried on in the old

---

* See Samuel Birch, *History of Ancient Pottery*, for this.
† *Idem.* See also Sir Gardiner Wilkinson's *Ancient Egyptians*.

factory near by, and, even after the new plant was finished and in operation, the use of the old one was continued for a year or so.

The new establishment was completed by the beginning of November, 1850. Frank B. Norton, brother of Edward Norton, who later was associated with Frederick Hancock in the well-known pottery firm of Norton & Hancock, of Worcester, Massachusetts, wrote in his diary, under date of November 15, 1850: 'Lyman & Fenton drew their first kiln of ware today in their new shop. Very good for the first.' On the following day, November 16, 1850, the *State Banner* published the following article by an anonymous writer using the pseudonym 'A Visitor':

I visited while in your place the greatest 'curiosity shop' I ever witnessed, the Pottery Works of Messrs. Lyman & Fenton; and by the politeness of the proprietors was permitted to see all parts of the establishment. I could but remark the open and manly frankness of the proprietors in answer to questions, as we were going about the premises, it contrasting so much with the often repeated conduct of foreign manufacturers in reference to persons visiting their shops for information on the subject or art of Pottery. — The establishment is new, large and commodious, covering, I should judge, nearly an acre of ground, and presenting a grand appearance, with its high towering chimneys, or craters to the kilns, smoking and sending forth fire like so many volcanoes. A part of the business is now being carried on in the old establishment, as it is necessary to occupy all their apartments in order to fulfil their contracts. — In my humble estimation the Pottery business of itself will be sufficient to make your place one of the first in the country.

The new building and machinery cannot, I think, have cost less than from 12 to 15 thousand dollars, which, with the amount paid weekly to the great number of hands employed, induces me to consider the launching out of these proprietors in this business one of the great wonders of the age.

In the next issue of the same paper, November 23, 1850, the same anonymous writer gave a further description of the new establishment, which is interesting as a reflection of contemporary opinion and as an expression of the high hopes which the enterprise engendered:

I am aware that time will not permit me to say all that might be said of the extensive works of Messrs. Lyman & Fenton, in your place; and I am equally persuaded that the manner in which I should say it, would not be extremely interesting to your readers, but having in a previous letter said something of it, shall take the liberty to say on.

The greater proportion of the material from which the ware is made, I understand, is found near the establishment, which is a great advantage as respects the comparative profit to be realized in the vicinity where the goods are manufactured.

The number of different processes which the material has to undergo, and the great number of hands it passes through in its journeyings from the raw state, until it comes forth a 'perfect work of art,' would seem to the stranger to place a barrier in the way as to expense, which could not be overcome by the *length of purse* which, generally speaking, throughout the community (judging from my own experience) is not uncomfortably long. Articles too numerous to name of kind and form both for ornament and luxury as well as for every day use and convenience in the domestic circle, are produced with a beautiful polish. The enamel reflects a great variety of the richest hues, and defies the operation and action of fire or acids of any kind.

When this ware is known throughout the country, a limited supply only, can hinder every family from participating in the pleasures and comforts which the possession of it affords.

Not far from these works is the Stone Ware Factory of Mr. Julius Norton, a descendant of a family of the same name, who have carried on the business in Bennington for upwards of 80 years. It is the largest establishment of the kind in the Union; and it is conceded on all hands, I believe, that he sends to all parts of New England and New York, the best quality and best manufactured ware in the country. The building is of brick with slated roof, about one hundred feet square, aside from the sheds and kilns adjoining. Bennington, it would seem, bids fair to become the great central position for the manufacture of different kinds of Pottery Ware in the United States.

In March, 1851, the retailing of their products was started by Messrs. Lyman & Fenton. Prior to that time all their wares had been produced under contract for a wholesale house, and by the terms of the contract the manufacturers were prohibited from selling to other dealers, or to the retail trade. While positive proof is lacking, there is every reason to believe that the wholesale dealer with whom this contract was made was Oliver A. Gager, one of the best known men in the china and earthenware trade. It is known that he made a considerable investment in the firm at or near this time, and for some years afterward he was one of the principal financial backers of the enterprise. The *State Banner*, in its issue of March 8, 1851, contained the following advertisement:

FLINT ENAMEL
WARE

The undersigned, manufacturers of FENTON's PATENT FLINT ENAMEL WARE have heretofore sold their ware under a contract and have not felt at liberty to sell at their pottery. Having been discharged from this contract, they now give notice that they are ready to fill all orders on the shortest notice.

They have on hand a considerable quantity of second quality Ware, as good for use as the first, but not suitable for market, which they will retail at the Pottery at a low price.

LYMAN & FENTON

Bennington, March 5, 1851.

Many collectors have wondered why specimens of Bennington wares found in and near Bennington are so often defective, showing marked imperfections in the making — warped bases, sagged and misshapen forms, poor surfaces which show cracks, specks, and bubbles due to over-firing, and so on. The above advertisement offers a sufficient explanation. The wares which were rejected by the inspectors employed for the purpose, as being below the standard and unsuitable for the market, were sold as 'seconds' at the pottery at very low prices. Employees were also permitted to take these 'seconds' away, more or less freely. The natural result was that people in the neighborhood who wanted pitchers or other articles were in the habit of going to the pottery and buying the marred pieces. A pitcher which had an unglazed and rough spot, due to accidental contact with the side of the seggar when the gloss kiln was fired, could be bought for five or ten cents, and would serve practical purposes as well as a perfect one at several times the price. I know of several small collections in and near Bennington, with not a single perfect specimen among them. The collector who buys his specimens in the neighborhood of Bennington, therefore, should be on guard against 'seconds.' One is far more likely to find good specimens in and around Boston.

Although such an enormous quantity of the ware produced bore the trade-mark of *Lyman, Fenton & Co.*, that firm did not exist very long. We do not know exactly when Lyman left the firm, but it is certain that by the end of 1852 he was out of it, and Oliver A. Gager was to a large extent managing the finances of the enterprise. As we note his departure from the scene of this history, a brief outline of Lyman's career seems appropriate:

ALANSON POTTER LYMAN

Alanson Potter Lyman was a native of Woodford, Vermont, the town adjoining Bennington. He was born December 4, 1806, and was, therefore, about ten months younger than Christopher Webber Fenton. His education was virtually all obtained in the common school and the village Academy in the lower village at Bennington. As a young man, he taught in the Academy for a short time. He read law and was admitted to the bar and to practice in the County Courts in 1832, and three years later was admitted to practice in the Supreme Court. In 1837 he went to Gardiner, Maine, where he engaged in the pottery business, manufacturing stoneware. He had no practical knowledge of the business, however, and maintained a purely financial relation to it. He returned to Bennington late in 1841 and soon made the acquaintance of Fenton. How the two drifted into business association we have already seen. They had much in common: they were both men of uncommon energy; they were both strong Whigs; they were both full of ambition, and they were visionaries who believed that each latest enterprise must surely make them rich; finally, both were too fond of the convivial glass and paid heavily for their weakness in that respect.

From the many industrial and commercial enterprises with which he was associated during his life, it would be natural to infer that Lyman was less a lawyer than an *entrepreneur*. Such an inference would, however, be wholly wrong. He was one of the most brilliant lawyers in southern Vermont, and ranked high in his profession. An excellent speaker, he was unusually successful as a pleader, and many stories are still told of his triumphs in jury cases. For some time he was in partnership with Hiland Hall, who later became Governor of Vermont. At one time he was State's Attorney for Bennington County; at another, United States Registrar under the Federal Bankruptcy Law. In 1850 he was a candidate for Congress and was defeated by a small margin of votes. He died in 1883, in his seventy-seventh year.

OLIVER A. GAGER

Oliver A. Gager, who was a dominant figure in the enterprise from 1852 onward, was a native of Massachusetts, and, in early life, carried on business in Fall River. Removing to New York City, he became the head of one of the best-known firms in the china trade, O. A. Gager & Co., whose establishment was on Barclay Street. In the early seventies he succeeded to the business of the well-known Charles Field Haviland, which placed him at the summit of the trade in this country. Mr. Gager was a man of considerable wealth, with large interests in western gold and silver mines. He was treasurer of the Hudson River Tunnel Company. For many years a resident of Brooklyn, he was an active member of Plymouth Church and associated with many philanthropic undertakings. He had a profound faith in the Bennington enterprise and spent a great deal of his time in the Vermont village. Few now remain who can remember him personally, but the memory bequeathed by an older generation still lingers in the tradition of a man of sterling character, courtly yet benign manner, and unfailing cheerfulness. He died in 1889 at the age of sixty-four.

Between the time when Lyman's association with the firm as one of its principals ceased — toward the latter part of 1852 — and the reorganization of the business and the adoption, in 1853, of the name United States Pottery Company, there appears to have been an interval during which Gager took matters into his personal control and the name O. A. Gager & Co. was used. In the official *Catalogue* of the New York Exhibition of 1853, I find that, when the entries were made, some months in advance of the opening of the Exhibition, that of Bennington ware was made by 'O. A. Gager & Co., *manu.* Bennington, Vermont.' There are but seven entries in the American section, porcelain and other ceramics, the first one being of Bennington ware. It reads as follows: '1. Fenton's patent flint enamelled ware. — O. A. Gager & Co., *manu.* Bennington, Vermont.' As local accounts of the firm were charged to and paid by O. A. Gager & Co. at this time, there seems to be no room for reasonable doubt upon this point. By the time the New York Exhibition was opened, however, the name United States Pottery Company had been adopted. This is clearly shown by the following facts: The Bennington exhibit bore signs with that name printed upon them; the reports of the Exhibition, without a single exception that I have been able to find, refer to the exhibit of the United States Pottery Company; some of the pieces of porcelain exhibited were so marked.

BENNINGTON WARE AT THE NEW YORK EXHIBIT

It would seem, from the manner in which the entry was made, that the original intention was to exhibit only the Flint Enamelled Ware of the company. It may well be that both Gager and Fenton hesitated to exhibit their Parian and other porcelains, knowing well as they did the high standards of some of the British and French firms, with which they would seem to be challenging comparison. Gager knew even better than Fenton what the comparison meant. He knew the masterpieces in Parian produced by Copeland, Minton, and other English firms, compared with which the best of the Bennington Parian was crude and poor. But whatever the reasons, the firm entered only Flint Enamelled Ware, and no porcelains of any kind. The fact that the exhibit displayed other wares was passed over in most of the newspaper accounts, which, being based upon the official *Catalogue*, described the entire exhibit of the firm as Flint Enamelled Ware. More careful commentators upon the exhibits have been puzzled by the entry in the official *Catalogue* in connection with the exhibit itself. Silliman and Goodrich, for example, writing about the Parian exhibited by the firm, say, 'We do not know why it should be styled "patent flint enamelled ware," as from the specimens of feldspar, white quartz, and clay, shown as the raw materials of its manufacture, it is obviously a hard porcelain.' *

* Silliman and Goodrich, *op. cit.*, p. 188.

The center of the firm's exhibit, its *magnum opus*, was the large monumental piece referred to in a previous chapter, which for many years past has stood upon the porch in front of the house on Pleasant Street, Bennington, in which Fenton lived for so long. It was modeled by Daniel Greatbach, one of the foremost modelers in America at the time, who had come to Bennington in 1852. The design itself is said to have been the work of Fenton, assisted by Decius W. Clark. It is, of course, an interesting piece of work, but it has no artistic merit whatever. The design lacks originality, distinctiveness, and, above all, unity. The lack of unity is emphasized by the arbitrary and sharp division of the dissimilar parts. The Parian bust of Fenton* is good in itself, being well modeled and executed with considerable skill. It is so placed, however, as to convey the impression of a man's head in a sort of cage. As a matter of fact, it does not belong in its present position. It was not intended to be in any way associated with the large monument. Neither was the Parian statuette on top, representing a mother handing a Bible to her child. This statuette, which is so much better in its execution than in its modeling, has, like the bust of Fenton, been added to the large creation without any warrant. Properly to judge the 'monument,' as it is called, both these figures should be eliminated. It should also be remembered that the piece was originally designed for use as a *stove*. Half a dozen others were made, one at least having been smashed to bits in the Fenton cellar. When we view it as a stove, our judgment is likely to be more lenient. The addition of the Parian figures, giving it a pretentiousness not originally intended, has brought a great deal of misplaced criticism upon a work which was already bad enough.

* There is some doubt whether this bust was made at the Bennington pottery. The late Dr. S. R. Wilcox told me that he understood it was made elsewhere and presented to Fenton.

New Conditions, New Difficulties

In many respects, 1853–1854 was the best period of the Bennington enterprise. The favorable impression made by the exhibit at the Crystal Palace, the strength derived from Greatbach's work on the technical side, and, more than all, the financial strength given to the company by Gager and such associates of his as came into it, combined to make the future appear rosily bright. In the summer of 1853 the works were considerably enlarged to cope with the growing volume of business. It really appeared as if financial difficulties had all been safely surmounted and that the concern had been placed at last upon a sound and enduring basis. But by the beginning of 1855 the firm was again in trouble.

The policy of direct dealing with country stores, while it had brought a large volume of trade, was attended with many drawbacks. Payments were often tardy, and the cost of collection was unexpectedly high. The expense of delivery by wagons was great, and, with every step in the direction of making finer wares, this cost increased. It was quite different from the stoneware trade. Packing had to be more carefully done; and this involved additional expenditure in the making of the tierces in which the goods were packed; it called for more packers, and, likewise, it sensibly decreased the quantity of ware which a team could carry. That, of course, meant employing more teams. Thus the factory 'overhead' was steadily increasing. Finally, fuel, one of the large items in operating cost, was constantly growing dearer.

New capital had to be obtained somehow, and to that end another reorganization took place. The United States Pottery Company was incorporated in June, 1855, stock being sold at twenty-five dollars per share. The capital stock of the new company was placed at $200,000, the incorporators being J. H. Archer, of Wrentham, Massachusetts,

O. A. Gager, of Boston and New York, S. H. Johnson, of New York, Christopher Webber Fenton, and H. Willard.

The amount of capital actually raised by the new company, though considerable, was altogether inadequate to its needs, as the event proved. O. A. Gager increased his holdings; a Dr. Hollis invested a large amount, said to have been virtually his entire savings; W. H. Farrar, who later established the Southern Porcelain Company at Kaolin, South Carolina, put some twenty-five thousand dollars into the concern during 1856–1857. Yet, all the time, the situation was growing worse, while, paradoxically enough, the prospects appeared brighter and better. While orders came in steadily increasing volume, overhead expenses grew out of proportion to the total of the business. Production costs increased and it was impossible to raise prices sufficiently to cover such costs without losing the business.

Always the firm was 'turning the corner at last,' according to Fenton. As one reads many of the paragraphs in the various newspapers of the State, doubtless inspired by Fenton, who had something of a *flair* for publicity, one is impressed by the fact that then, as always, he saw golden success just ahead. When the production of Rockingham and Flint Enamelled cuspidors reached twenty-five hundred a week, the fact was heralded as a sure sign of success and prosperity. And when the firm introduced mortars and pestles made of thick, heavy semi-porcelain, which they called Wedgwood Mortar Ware, and found a ready market for them, the newspaper publicity attained an almost lyrical quality.

At this time, 1855, in an effort to reduce operating costs, the kilns of the company were altered so that coal might be used for fuel in place of wood. It was hoped that this and other economies would save the situation. How important the fuel question appeared can be gathered from a statement issued by the company and published in the local press:

FUEL. — The present high rates at which wood merchants in this vicinity hold their wood, and the constantly increasing demands in price made upon the purses of consumers, has induced many this winter to adopt coal in its stead. The 'United States Pottery Company,' carrying on business in this place, are making the necessary arrangements, in the re-construction of kilns, &c., for immediately commencing the burning of coal. One thousand cords of wood have been consumed annually at this establishment. Others will, if the high price of wood is continued, also adopt coal, as it is deemed fully as cheap and a good deal more convenient and comfortable. Fifteen years ago, wood sold here, and we had the pleasure of burning some, *for one dollar fifty and two dollars per cord* — the latter *body wood*. Now it is selling for *three and a half and four and a half dollars!* which goes to show conclusively that wood dealers either made a *poor living then* or they are growing *rich and fat now*. We like to see men do *well*, but it does seem to us that our wood merchants, in trying to heap up the 'dust' too high, are only 'biting off their own noses.' But they, of course, know their own business best, as every one ought to; and they will not complain if consumers also study their own interests too, as they most certainly are and will continue to do.*

FAILURE

Things were going badly. It was more and more difficult to meet the big weekly payroll in full. Workmen were frequently paid in cash only part of the wages due to them, the balance being taken by them in trade at local stores and charged to the account of the company, this trade being offset against sums due to the latter by the stores for wares. As I have examined some of the ledgers of these old stores, I have been impressed by the evidence thus afforded of the precarious condition of the company from 1856 onward. In the early months of 1858 it was quite evident that the company could not go on for long, unless from some unexpected source new capital should come, coupled

* *Vermont State Banner*, December 21, 1855.

with sound management. At this time about one hundred and fifty persons were employed — a considerably smaller number than had been employed twelve months before. The firm had more orders than it could fill, more than at any time in its history; but it could not collect its bills promptly, and many of the workmen went unpaid, or only partially paid, during the entire winter of 1857–1858.

Then came the inevitable day of doom. The manner in which it was met by the company was highly creditable to Fenton, to the company, and to all concerned, and it deserves to be recorded here. As money was received from collections, the workmen were called into the office in little groups and told the situation. They were informed that they were preferred creditors, and, as fast as money was received, they were paid what was due to them. In this way the claims of the workmen were met before the doors of the plant were closed. On Saturday, May 15, 1858, the last bell was in the nature of a requiem. The United States Pottery Company was unable to continue. The *Bennington Banner* published the following account of the closing down of the works:

CLOSED DOORS. — Officer Dewey took charge of the United States Pottery in this village at an early hour on Monday morning. The Company finding themselves unable to make collections sufficient to meet their present demands, gave their workmen notice of the fact that they might secure what the company were indebted to them. By this act of the Company the workmen have secured pay for their winter's work. — This magnanimous act of the U.S. Pottery Company is worthy of imitation by all large and small manufacturing companies. The daily laborer should receive pay for his labor. Although we regret that the doors of this mammoth establishment must be closed for a few weeks, and perhaps months, we feel that it will be for the benefit of both the Company and our village in the end, for when it shall again start in business, it will be upon a sure and sound foundation. — The days of experiments have passed in this establishment. The reputation of their ware is established, and we hear from all sections that the quality of their ware is now better than ever before. We also learn from the Company that they have been unable to keep up with the orders which have been made upon them for the last few months. We hope soon to hear the bell at these works calling their workmen back to labor.*

Thus ended one of the most interesting and fruitful chapters in the history of the pottery industry in America. In accordance with the half-hearted prophecy of the article quoted from the *Bennington Banner*, various attempts were made subsequently to reconstruct the business. With these, and with Fenton's later career, we shall deal in a separate chapter. It is sufficient to say here that the United States Pottery had finished. Its restoration was impossible. For a little more than a decade, in the face of almost endless difficulties and discouragements, Christopher Webber Fenton had struggled to raise the standards of the industry. That he fell short of his ideals, that even his ideals were sometimes crude, that his personal weakness contributed in some measure to his failure — may all be urged with literal truthfulness. But when all that has been said, the truth, nevertheless, remains that the Bennington experiment contributed largely to the advancement of the pottery industry in this country, and that Christopher Webber Fenton is entitled to be held in honorable esteem as one of the great pioneers to whose efforts the present high state of the industry in America is, in no small measure, due.

* *Bennington Banner*, May 21, 1858.

VAIN ATTEMPTS AT REVIVAL

A S soon as the United States Pottery was shut down, in May, 1858, the subject of its revival began to be discussed. At the same time, however, so many of the most skilled workers began an exodus from the town as to make it apparent that any genuine revival of the business was impossible. It might be feasible, indeed, to reopen the works and to manufacture pottery — at a profit even, but without Fenton and Clark, Greatbach, and others, the enterprise would be different. It would not be a revival, but something new.

The story of the attempts that were made to resuscitate the business may best be told by quotations from the local press from 1858 to 1860. In August, 1858, after having been idle for three months, the works were reopened by the firm of A. A. Gilbert & Co. Of this new firm O. A. Gager was an important member. He was still confident that the business could be made profitable. Calvin Park, Fenton's old partner, was another important member and, for a time at least, manager. The *Bennington Banner* of August 20, 1858, chronicled the reopening in the following paragraph:

RE-OPENED. — The United States Pottery was re-opened on Tuesday morning. It is now in the hands of A. A. Gilbert & Co., and we are informed is to be a 'permanent institution' so far as running it is concerned. The sound of the bell on this mammoth establishment is a cheering sound to many families in this place, and it is our wish that it may not again cease to send forth its daily notes to the 150 employees.

The new firm carried the business along for little more than a year. They used the old moulds and pottery marks. As a general rule, no mark was used to differentiate the wares produced by A. A. Gilbert & Co. from those produced prior to 1858 by the United States Pottery Company. Many of the inferior Rockingham and porcelain pieces which every collector of Bennington pottery encounters, and which are known to have been produced here, were made by the Gilbert firm. I have traced dozens of these inferior pieces — many of them bearing one or other of the marks of the United States Pottery Company — to this period. On the other hand, some exceptionally fine ware was made by the new company. This is true of some of the Rockingham, but more especially of the directly glazed hard porcelain that was produced at this time.

In the spring of 1859, Decius W. Clark was granted a patent for an improved enamel glaze for application to crockery and pottery wares and other materials. Even before the patent was obtained, this new glaze was used by A. A. Gilbert & Co. under the personal supervision of the inventor. Coarse bodies covered with this glaze presented an appearance which gave no indication of coarseness. My friend and fellow collector, Mr. George S. McKearin, has a pair of highly glazed creamy white poodle dogs of the familiar type, but slightly modified, which belong to this period and are interesting examples of this enamel glaze. The body differs radically from that of the Parian dogs. The use of this new glaze was regarded by the firm as its chief asset.* O. A. Gager was exceedingly optimistic concerning it.

To this period also belongs a type of ware which has occasioned much trouble and perplexity to not a few collectors. From time to time pitchers are found which are quite unlike any of the well-known Bennington types, but with Bennington 'pedigrees' which are appar-

---

* A long account of the newly patented invention was published by the *Bennington Banner*, June 10, 1859.

ently unchallengeable. The ware resembles granite in body and glaze. The background is pitted in the same manner as the hard porcelains, and there appear various designs in relief. These pitchers are gray in color, but of shades ranging from a rich silver gray to what may best be described as a grayish white. I have investigated the history of several of these pitchers and in each case have been satisfied that they were made at Bennington during the period 1858–1860.

THE VENTURE AT WEST TROY

By the latter part of September, 1859, the firm of A. A. Gilbert & Co. was engaged upon the task of winding up its affairs. It had found itself confronted by exactly the same problems as those which its predecessor found insoluble. There was no lack of demand for its wares, but the cost of production and transportation, instead of being lowered, had increased. A group of the most skilled workers employed by the concern formed themselves into a joint stock company to go into the manufacture of pottery at West Troy, New York. In its issue of September 30, 1859, the *Bennington Banner* published this announcement:

NEW JOINT STOCK COMPANY. — It having become apparent to every one, and particularly to the workmen in the U.S. Pottery of this village, that operations in that establishment would soon cease for the present at least, eight of the best workmen came together and formed a joint stock company, sent an agent to Troy, and made arrangements with the proprietors of the old stone-ware pottery for their works, and are now engaged in rigging it up for the manufacture of the same kind of ware as has been turned off at the United States. The names of those connected with the enterprise are as follows: Enoch Moore, S. Theiss, G. B. Sibley, T. Frey, Peter Stienbach, Wm. Leake, John Leigh, Jacob Mertz. They have our best wishes and we hope they will meet with good success.*

Some of these men put into this little venture the savings of a life-

* I have corrected the spelling of some of the names. — Author.

time. The company started with high hopes. It was believed that West Troy would prove to be a favorable location in two important particulars, namely, nearness to a large market for wares and great economy in the transportation of raw materials, especially the New Jersey and Long Island clays. O. A. Gager had promised to take all the ware the new concern could not market locally. The enterprise lasted only a few months, however, and most of the men returned to Bennington, having lost all their capital. William Leake went into bankruptcy, and so, I believe, did some of the others.

FURTHER EFFORT AT BENNINGTON

In the meantime, from the end of September, 1859, to the beginning of 1860, some of the members of the Gilbert firm tried to carry on part of the works under the trade-name of the New England Pottery Company.* Later on, in the summer of 1860, some of the old employees of the United States Pottery, including the solvent members of the West Troy concern, organized themselves into a company to restart the works at Bennington. Encouraged and inspired by D. W. Clark, and by Gager, who undertook to sell their ware for them upon most favorable terms, this group started with a pitifully inadequate capital. There seems to have been some confusion as to the name of the new company, for contemporary references to it make use of several different titles. The two following extracts from the *Bennington Banner* chronicle the formation of the new company and the renewal of operations:

We are glad to see that some of the recent employees in the United States Pottery, at this place, have joined hands in the worthy enterprise of again running that public institution. They will try the experiment for a short

* *Bennington Banner*, December 23, 1859.

time, and if successful, they intend to make a permanent thing of it. We hope it will go along, and the 'boys' reap an adequate reward for their undertaking.*

THE UNITED STATES POTTERY. — We are glad to see this establishment occupied and worked, or a portion of it at least, altho it may not be on so large a scale as formerly. It is now being run by a number of the old workmen who have formed themselves into a company, and intend enlarging their operations as soon as it may seem advisable. We wish them all the success they deserve, as we have no doubt do our entire community, and trust that from the beginning now made a result may spring that shall not only enrich those intimately concerned, but prove a prominent business lever to our village, making it a *permanent* and not a *temporary* institution.

The first kiln was drawn last week Thursday, and the ware is said to equal, if not surpass, that manufactured there heretofore. They propose taking up the coming Spring, if prospered, the making of white ware also. Mr. O. A. Gager, a partner in the firm of A. Gilbert and Co., who recently carried on the works, guarantees them to find a ready market for all the ware they can turn out.†

This venture lasted only a few weeks, when the works were once more shut down. Most of the men could not wait for money to come in. Credit was hard to obtain and they and their families must live. It was discouraging to have to take ware and go from store to store trying to exchange it for goods. Some of the men moved away — to Burlington, Vermont, Fort Edward, New York, Trenton, New Jersey, and other places.

T. A. HUTCHINS & Co.

Once more there was a reorganization, under the leadership of Thomas A. Hutchins, a presser, and the firm of T. A. Hutchins & Co. reopened the works. They started with high hopes, as will appear from the report in the *Bennington Banner*. In conformity with what

* July 27, 1860.
† August 31, 1860.

appears to have been a custom having almost the force of law, they began by presenting a pitcher to the local newspaper office:

THAT PITCHER: We have received from Messrs. T. A. Hutchins & Co., the new Pottery Company in this place, a splendid pitcher, a sample of what they are turning out of their establishment. It is, we think, in advance of ware made by the 'United States Pottery Company,' notwithstanding it is made from Bennington clay, which they condemned. The new company has discovered a new process of mixing which renders it fully up to (if not in advance of) the New Jersey clay. The last lot of ware burned by them is of *very superior* quality. The ware sells readily. Indeed they have more orders than they can fill. We are glad to be able to record this evidence of their success, and our citizens we know will be most happy to hear of it.*

Of the various successors to the United States Pottery Company the firm of T. A. Hutchins & Co. was the only one to use any other identification mark than those of the old company. Although I know of only one piece — a cuspidor — stamped with the name of this firm, the fact that such a stamp was used may be taken as an indication of the fact that the firm adopted a distinctive mark of its own. This firm managed to keep going in a small way for a few months, and then the works were once more closed down.

H. F. DEWEY

They remained closed until 1863, when they were partially reopened by H. F. Dewey, who started grinding feldspar upon a small scale, for sale to other potteries elsewhere. No ware was made at this time, and Pitkin is in error in ascribing the 'Phrenological Head' inkstand to this period, just as he is wrong in describing it as 'Parian.' † In its issue of May 7, 1863, the *Bennington Banner* published the following news item:

* October 10, 1860.
† See Pitkin, *op. cit.*, p. 54. (No. 22.)

THE POTTERY: H. F. Dewey, Esq., has fitted up a part of the United States Pottery buildings, the water power, etc., and has commenced the grinding of feldspar. At the present high rates of crockery ware, and the ready sale it meets, we cannot see why a company could not make it pay to start up the works at once.

Nothing came of the suggestion contained in this paragraph, however, and in 1870 the buildings were torn down and the Graded School erected upon the site.

CLOSING YEARS OF C. W. FENTON

We may well close this chapter with a brief sketch of the career of Christopher Webber Fenton from the time of the failure of the United States Pottery Company, in May, 1858, to his untimely death. Almost immediately after the closing of the works at Bennington, in May, 1858, Fenton and D. W. Clark went to Kaolin, South Carolina, taking with them Daniel Greatbach and other leading artisans. Both Fenton and Clark had a sentimental interest in the pottery which had been established at Kaolin, for the enterprise was in a sense the offspring of the United States Pottery at Bennington. About six miles from Augusta, Georgia, and an equal distance from Aiken, South Carolina, there were large deposits of kaolin. Farmers and others in the surrounding districts used the clay for whitewashing fences and buildings, but no other use had ever been made of it, so far as is known. Various English pottery firms had been interested in these deposits, including the noted firms of Wedgwood, Clews, and Ridgway. In a small way, the clay had been experimentally tried out at Bennington, and it was as a result of these experiments that, in the summer of 1856, William H. Farrar, one of the principal stockholders of the United States Pottery, had gone to South Carolina and established a pottery near the clay banks. He likewise interested some of the leading citizens of Georgia and South Carolina, with the result that a stock company was formed, Farrar himself being a large stockholder. It is interesting to note that, among those who were actively interested in the company, was Alexander H. Stephens, who some years later became the Vice-President of the Southern Confederacy.

Farrar was not himself a practical potter; all that he knew about the industry was what he had picked up at Bennington as a result of his interest there. He was quite convinced that the management of a pottery would not be materially different from the management of any other industrial enterprise; that so long as he employed skilled workmen he could not fail to succeed. He controlled a plentiful supply of clay of good quality; a great market lay close at hand, so that transportation costs would not be high; a pottery was needed in that section of the country, and he was assured of the good will and active support of the most influential citizens. Farrar took with him to Kaolin the master carpenter who had built the United States Pottery buildings, and the bricklayer who had built the kilns, the main features of which were now reproduced. When the plant was ready he sent to Bennington for the nucleus of a working force.

When Fenton and Clark went to Kaolin after the closing of the Bennington works, they seriously contemplated the possibility of joining forces with Farrar and his associates in the southern enterprise. They were perfectly well aware that the experience of the concern so far had been discouraging. During the whole of the first year the greater part of the ware produced was so poor that it was not fit for the general market. Much of it was ruined in the firing, and there were other difficulties. Clark had been appealed to and had gone to Kaolin, late in 1857, to study the problems on the spot and to make recommendations. When he returned to Bennington he sent his son, Lyman W. Clark, to supervise the mixing of bodies and glazes.

The real difficulty seems to have arisen from the fact that, while a genius like Decius W. Clark could make a ware of good quality from the South Carolina clay exclusively, less competent men could not do it. The manager of the works was Josiah Jones, a native of Staffordshire, England, one of the best designers of his day. He had achieved distinction by his work at the pottery of his brother-in-law, Charles Cartlidge, at Greenpoint, New York. Although he was a designer by profession, Jones was also a practical potter, thoroughly competent. He stoutly contended that it was necessary to get some other clay to mix with the local clay, and most of the potters agreed with him. Farrar, however, was adamant in his refusal to permit this.

In the early part of 1858, when Fenton and Clark went there, the establishment was turning out some fairly good hard porcelain, as well as Common White and Common Yellow of excellent quality. The cost of production, however, was excessive. Much of the inferior blue and white ware with pitted background, which resembles the Bennington ware of this type, but is inferior to it, was made at Kaolin and sent north.

Fenton stayed at Kaolin only a few weeks. Clark remained there some time longer, supervising various experiments intended to find a solution for the technical problems which were perplexing the struggling company. Fenton moved on to Peoria, Illinois, where he at once began to interest a group of capitalists in the possibilities of the pottery industry in that section of the country, and to raise capital for the most ambitious undertaking of his life — in some respects the most ambitious in the history of the pottery industry in America. He was soon joined by Clark, who had sold to the southern concern a number of formulas for bodies and glazes which he had evolved and success-fully used in its plant, thus making it possible for the concern to continue.

The foundation of the ambitious enterprise of the two men at this time was a new enamel which Clark had invented and patented, and to which reference has already been made. This will be described at some length in a subsequent chapter. For the moment we are concerned with its relation to the Peoria enterprise. They projected an immense 'departmental pottery' at Peoria which would employ more than one thousand workers. An elaborate diagram was prepared, showing a series of buildings, arranged something like an enormous wheel, each building being devoted to a separate branch of the industry and all converging at a common center of administration and distribution. In one unit Rockingham Ware would be produced; in another White Ware; in a third Stoneware — and so on. Their greatest hopes were founded upon an entirely new branch of industry, the manufacture of enamelled bricks, blocks, and ornamental architectural pieces for building purposes. Clark's new patent enamel was the basis upon which this new branch of the industry was to be built. While manu-facturers of brick in other parts of the country were to be licensed to use the new patent enamel, upon a royalty payment, as will be ex-plained later, the Peoria concern was to have the exclusive use of the enamel for a large district, and it was confidently expected that this of itself would ensure financial success.

Fenton was extraordinarily successful in his appeal to the business men of Peoria and the surrounding country. In the summer of 1859 work was begun upon one wing of the projected mammoth plant, and, when Fenton returned to Bennington, in December of that year, on a visit, one wing of the building, one hundred and fifty feet by forty feet, three stories in height, had been completed and was ready for the installation of machinery. Fenton and Clark contracted with a Bennington firm, Grover and Harrington, to manufacture the machinery for the Peoria pottery. They also bought and leased many deposits of feldspar and contracted with more than twenty mills for the grinding of feldspar to be used in the manufacture of Clark's patent enamel. One of the mills thus engaged was situated in Bennington, a small plant, later used as a pottery, owned by Enos Adams.

Among the capitalists who joined Fenton & Clark in this great enterprise was G. W. Lascell, of Syracuse, New York, who seems to have been the principal factor in bringing about a close relation between the group of Peoria capitalists and a similar group belonging to New York and New England. Arrangements were made with the New England Pottery, of Bennington, successor to the A. A. Gilbert Company and the earlier United States Pottery Company, to supply designs and moulds for use in Peoria. Undoubtedly, a great many moulds were sent to Peoria from Bennington, which explains why so many pieces of Rockingham identical with well-known Bennington models, but either believed or known to have been made at Peoria, are encountered by the collector.

Upon the occasion of Fenton's return to Bennington at this time the local paper published an editorial in which, while it was broadly intimated that Fenton was responsible for the failure of the local pottery — that he had dealt it a 'parricidal blow' — he was greatly eulogized:

The return of our old friend, C. W. Fenton, the pioneer potter of the United States, to the field of his former exploits, has dispelled the fear that he had transferred his *entire* interests to the home of his adoption in the great West, leaving to others less favored by the touch of genius and energy, the task of conducting the enterprises that sprung at his will into a living reality among us, giving to his name and to our town an enviable notoriety throughout the Union. One of the evidences of this is seen in the fact of his having confided the charge of manufacturing the machinery for the great Pottery at Peoria, Ill., to Messrs. GROVER & HARRINGTON, which is not only an assurance that he has not forgotten his old friends, but that he has exercised the best business sagacity on the score of economy, as the practical experience of these gentlemen acquired in the manufacturing of machinery for the several potteries Mr. Fenton has constructed during the past fifteen years, is to those interested a sure guarantee of the utmost perfection in its construction and operation.

We also learn that Mr. Fenton, in connection with Mr. Clark, has brought the New England Pottery, in this village, into requisition in the manufacture of designs, moulds, &c., for the use of the Peoria (Ill.) Pottery, which, together with the preparation of glazes for the already celebrated *enameled building material*, will require the full capacity of the factory both day and night for the Winter at least. This is really *some* compensation to the enterprises of our Village for the parricidal blow one of these gentlemen dealt the United States Pottery, which has paralyzed it for the present at least.

We have never doubted the ability of C. W. Fenton, in a fair field, to accomplish all that he might undertake; but we confess that, with all our confidence in his energy and executive abilities, we are fearful that in his efforts to supply the great valley of the Mississippi with Pottery wares, he will so far forget the attention due to the Pottery business in Bennington as to fail in the full realization of his early aspirations of making this the Staffordshire of the Union. Peoria, Illinois, is indebted for his preference of locality only from its possessing very superior facilities for the manufacture and distribution of Pottery wares; but from whatever motive his preference of any other locality than this may have been, and however much we may regret the loss of one who has done so much for Bennington, we can but admire his praiseworthy efforts to rid this country of her abject dependence on Great Britain for an article so indispensable to the comfort and convenience of the people at large. We congratulate MR. FENTON upon the generous and hearty response of the people of the West to his wishes in carrying forward so worthy an enterprise, as evidencing their high appreciation of the man and his mission.

Hasty preparations are being made by CLARK, JOHNSON & Co., in their arrangements, preparatory to their early departure for Peoria, which we understand will be in a few days.*

The next issue of the same paper contained an endorsement of this

* *Bennington Banner*, December 23, 1859.

tribute, signed by the Governor of the State, that great Vermonter, Hiland Hall, and by other distinguished and influential citizens. It was an endorsement of the newspaper's high praise by men whose names stood for all that was best in the community. There were, in addition to Governor Hiland Hall, ex-Governor John S. Robinson, Pierpont Isham, a former judge of the Supreme Court of Vermont and a distinguished lawyer, Samuel H. Blackmer, Clerk of the Court of Chancery and one of the most honored men in the community. With these were associated the leaders of the bar, the principal clergymen and a number of the business men and manufacturers of the town, thirty-four signers in all. The text of the endorsement, and the editorial prefatory note which accompanied it read:

MESSRS. FENTON & CLARK

We find by the following that we are not alone in the expression of our admiration and appreciation of MESSRS. FENTON AND CLARK, and are much gratified to be able to record an endorsement from so high a source; and of a character so complimentary and deserved; and so characteristic of the good and generous qualities of the subscribers.

EDITOR OF THE BANNER:
DEAR SIR:
Your notice in the last issue of the *Bennington Banner*, of the return of C. W. Fenton from his late protracted visit in the West, and the contemplated removal of himself and his associate, Mr. D. W. Clark, from this community, in which they have resided for so many years; whose enterprises they have contributed to so materially in building up, and who, by their genius and energy, have reflected so much credit on the manufacturing character of our State; together with the high commendations they have received from the 'Press' of our State, admonishes us that some expression of appreciation is also due them from this community. We, therefore, beg leave to assure you that we cheerfully endorse all that you and your contemporaries have said in their behalf — with the hope that this expression of appreciation of their services, and regret for their loss to our town and State, will bespeak for them the confidence and esteem of the citizens of

Peoria, and the West; where and among whom, we understand they are about to remove.

We remain, yours, Very Truly,

[Signatures.]

We have taken the liberty to prefix the titles to the names of the above individuals, that the public may be better prepared to judge of the character of the testimony which they bear toward the gentlemen whose names head this article.*

The response which Fenton and Clark made to these flattering encomiums is of especial interest because it summarizes so well their own estimate of their achievements at Bennington, and, more important still, their view of the Middle West as a field for their efforts.

CORRESPONDENCE

EDITOR BANNER:
DEAR SIR:
Through your Journal we beg leave to assure those gentlemen who have so generously and so publicly given the expression of their approval of our efforts to succeed in the difficult though interesting art we have labored so long to develop, and the influence our labors have had in forwarding the enterprises of their village, that if anything could add to the regrets we naturally feel on leaving a place which for thirty years has been our home and the field of our labors and which is endeared to us by a thousand pleasing recollections, it is the evidence they have given that they leave behind us the regrets and good wishes of those valuable friends, who have by their countenance and encouragement contributed so materially to whatever of success may have awarded our efforts; we, therefore, assure them that though we are not so presumptuous as to lay claim to all the credit and skill they have been pleased so generously to award us, we are as grateful for the tribute bestowed upon us as though it were more fully deserved. Therefore, in tendering our thanks for an endorsement, at once so complimentary to ourselves, and so well calculated to secure for us the confidence and esteem of the strangers among whom we are about to locate, we beg leave to assure them that the public evidence they have given us of their appreciation and

* *Bennington Banner*, December 30, 1859.

good wishes, will stimulate us to deserve their esteem and the confidence they have bespoken in our behalf.

To yourself and to those of your contemporaries who have spoken so favorably of our enterprises, and so flatteringly of our skill in the develop-ment of the plastic art in this country, we also beg leave to tender our thanks; but in so doing, we owe it to ourselves as well as to those skillful foreign manufacturers, who have attained so high a degree of eminence in an art on which they have reflected so much credit, to declare that with all our aspirations for public favor, we are not so vain as to suppose that in the mastery of the intricacies of an art requiring in its development the utmost proficiency in the science of chemistry, practical geology, mineralogy, the art of design and the chemistry of Pottery, without access to the secure laboratories of foreign manufactories, where lay hid the accumulated ac-quirements of ages in the art — with material untried and differing widely from that used elsewhere — forced thus to grope our way in the dark, relying on ourselves alone, aided only by such skill in its mechanical department as we could reach from abroad, we have been able to attain that degree of proficiency in the manufacture as to entitle us to the skill you and your contemporaries have been pleased so generously to award us — nor are we so unjust as to claim that precedents* in the art of fine Pottery that our better judgment tells us has not yet been transferred to this country. We are, however, proud to believe, from practical observation, that no country contains better material for the fabrication of Pottery Ware, than the United States, and we hazard nothing in saying that the art has been so far developed on this side of the Atlantic, as to warrant the hope that the day is not far distant when this country, by virtue of the knowledge of the art already acquired — the proverbial skill and energy of our people — the convenience, quality and abundance of the raw material — the extent of the market to be cultivated, and the tempting remunerative character of the trade, will be able to secure all the advantages to be derived from this great industrial art in our own country at least.

In transferring the prosecution of our business from Vermont to the great Valley of the Mississippi, we are influenced only by the superior advantages that that locality presents over the Atlantic States, in the abundance and quality of Pottery material — its unrivalled facilities for cheap freights — the extent and rapid growth of its markets, and the superior advantages it possesses for a more successful competition with foreign manufactures — a consideration not to be overlooked in this early stage of the enterprise in this country. With these advantages in our favor, and the practical foreign skill

* *Sic!* 'precedence' is meant.

that a more liberal international sentiment has opened to our reach, we doubt not we shall meet the full reward our efforts may deserve.

Yours truly

C. W. Fenton

D. W. Clark

Bennington, *Jan.* 2, 1860.*

It would take us too far afield to follow in detail the fortunes of either the Kaolin or the Peoria enterprises. Of the former, with which Fenton was only slightly connected, it is sufficient to say that in 1859 or 1860 it was reorganized as the Southern Porcelain Company, and that it continued until the works were burned down, in 1864. It was the only porcelain factory in the South during the Civil War.

The Peoria enterprise was also short-lived. There is a tradition to the effect that the first kiln of ware was drawn late in November, 1859, immediately prior to Fenton's visit to Bennington, already described. According to this tradition, Fenton brought with him to Bennington a lot of samples of the Peoria ware — principally pitchers and mugs — which were decorated in Bennington by Théophile Frey and presented to various persons. This tradition at first seemed to me to be supported by contemporary evidence, for in its issue of February 17, 1860, the *Bennington Banner* expressed the thanks of the editor's 'better half' to the 'gentlemen comprising the American Pottery Company' for 'the elegantly decorated pitcher presented to her by them last week.' The paper goes on to say that 'if it is to be taken as a fair sample of what they are to turn out of their Peoria Pottery, their ware, it seems to us must take the preference over all others. The glazing is most excellent Clark's best.' The credit for the gilding is credited to 'friend Frey, who goes to Peoria to do the gilding for the Company.'

* *Bennington Banner*, January 6, 1860.

I am now convinced that the tradition is the outgrowth of a mis-understanding — possibly of this very paragraph from the *Bennington Banner*. It is certain that when Fenton returned to Bennington in December, 1859, operations had not commenced at the Peoria plant; the machinery was not even made. It was late in the spring of 1860 before even the first wing of the Peoria Pottery was in operation. The pitcher presented to the 'better half' of the local editor, therefore, could not have been made at Peoria. It was undoubtedly made at Bennington, possibly of the Illinois clay, and was a souvenir of the pottery there.

It would appear that, at this time, there were two distinct organizations, the American Pottery Company and the Peoria Pottery Company. Fenton is always described as 'President of the American Pottery Company' in all statements relating to the patent enamel business. On the other hand, the office stationery of the Peoria Pottery is headed *Peoria Pottery Company*, and that mark is known to have been used upon Rockingham and other wares. In the spring of 1861 a new department — stoneware — was added to the pottery in pursuance of the elaborate plans announced in 1859. This is made quite certain by a letter which Decius W. Clark wrote on April 24, 1861, to James Gregg, a potter formerly employed at the United States Pottery, but then residing in Fort Edward, New York. The letter reads:

> Office of the Peoria Pottery Co.
> Peoria, Ill., *April* 24, 1861
>
> James Gregg:
> The new stone-ware Pottery is now being built. War is being inaugurated in the most splendid and qualifying style; so hold yourself ready, for either or both, as the case may require, assured that both in the end will be a complete success. But of all things for our country first — first, last and till the death, for our old, glorious Star Spangled Banner. — Sooner than permit Traitors' stock in our midst, and traitors' triumphs, let us use the Stars and Stripes

for our winding sheet in death. The war excitement with us is most intense; C. Manchester, F. B. Fenton,* and Thos. Johnson, and two other boys you do not know, have joined the Zouaves from our works, and the rest of us have joined the Home Guards, and so it goes. This State represents a military company, so aroused are the people with just the right feeling, a feeling of patriotism that will, with the united North, squelch out rebellion and hurl every secessionist into the deep, dark grave of the traitor.

Three times three for the old Union, for liberty and the prosperity of our free institutions.

D. W. CLARK

The Peoria Pottery Company failed early in 1863, according to the most reliable information that I have been able to obtain; and the American Pottery Company appears to have fizzled out about the same time. Thus ended the most ambitious enterprise in the history of the pottery industry in the United States.

In the meantime, Christopher Webber Fenton had lost his first wife and married another. His first wife, Louisa (Norton) Fenton, did not go with her husband to Peoria, but continued to live on at Bennington. She died there, December 3, 1860, aged forty-nine years. Fenton married in Peoria, Illinois, on July 3, 1861, a Mrs. J. E. Smith, of that city. By her he had at least one child, a daughter, Louisa. On the occasion of a visit to Bennington by Fenton and his second wife and their infant daughter, his oldest daughter by his first wife, who had become the wife of Calvin Park, adopted her little half-sister, who grew to womanhood under her care. This daughter of Fenton by his second wife became the wife of Henry D. Fillmore, of Bennington. Christopher Webber Fenton died from accidental causes at Joliet, Illinois, June 7, 1865, aged fifty-nine years.

* C. W. Fenton's oldest son.

III

VARIETIES AND TYPES OF WARE MADE

NUMEROUS enthusiastic collectors in all parts of the United States, and not a few in other lands, have for years competed against one another for good specimens of the pottery and porcelain made at Bennington by Christopher Webber Fenton and his associates under various firm names. Collecting Bennington ware has been a hobby as seriously pursued as any other form of collecting. Great museums have attributed as much importance to Bennington ware as to historical china, Staffordshire figures, or any other forms of ceramic art. They have installed large collections, have issued catalogues, and have arranged for lectures descriptive of them. In books and numerous magazine articles the products of Bennington potteries have been described, praised, and illustrated. It is not strange, therefore, that the competition of collectors has resulted in absurdly high prices, exceptionally good specimens — particularly of the finer animal pieces — having brought several hundred dollars each.

In view of the foregoing facts, it is strange and almost inexplicable that the collector who desires a reliable guide is unable to find, among all the books, catalogues, and magazine articles devoted either wholly or in part to the subject, a comprehensive list of the varieties and types of ware produced at the Bennington potteries. Of all the people who have collected Bennington, and of all the hundreds of dealers who have bought and sold it, it is safe to say that not more than half a dozen understand how many and what kinds of ware are known to have been produced by Norton & Fenton, C. W. Fenton,

Lyman & Fenton, and the United States Pottery Company — to name only the principal companies that operated the Bennington plant. In such circumstances, how can there be intelligent collecting, buying, or selling?

It is often said, and quite seriously believed by many collectors and others, that the monumental piece made for the New York Exhibition at the Crystal Palace, 1853–54, by the United States Pottery Company — which formed the center of its exhibit — was designed in part to show, in a single piece of gigantic proportions, in its component parts every variety and type of ware produced by the company. According to this interesting theory, the firm manufactured four types, as follows: (1) Scroddled or Lava Ware, of which the bottom section of the base of the monument is made; (2) Flint Enamel Ware, of which the second section of the base and the corniced top are made; (3) Rockingham Ware, of which the Corinthian columns enclosing the bust are made; (4) Parian, of which the bust of Fenton and the surmounting figure of a mother and her child are made.

It is a pity to spoil such an interesting theory; but it must be done. The truth is that the firm made several varieties and types of ware in addition to those exemplified in the monumental piece in question, and that even the foregoing classification is arbitrary and misleading.

PITKIN'S CLASSIFICATION

Pitkin, in his book, refers to and describes the following varieties and types: Rockingham (flint enamelled); Rockingham (not flint enamelled); Parian ware, white and colored; Granite ware; Scroddled or Lava ware; Tiles, inlaid and enamelled; Marbled ware. Under these heads he classified the well-known collection bearing his name in the Morgan Memorial at Hartford, and also the lists in his book.*

* With the exception of the Tiles, of which he never found a specimen.

It is a great pity that so many collectors have had to rely upon a classification so incomplete and faulty.

Pitkin makes a separate category of Marbled as distinguished from Lava or Scroddled Ware; yet in his description of the latter he clearly identifies it with the former.* This is confusing. Marbled Ware is quite distinct from Lava or Scroddled Ware, of course; and the distinction between the two is very clear, as we shall see later on. But Marbled Ware was not made at Bennington. Again, after having enumerated the varieties and types of wares included in his classification and already quoted above, Pitkin adds this statement: 'Porcelain, both hard and soft paste, was made at this pottery, but in small amounts with only partial success.' †

It is clear enough that he meant this statement to be taken literally. In the lists he offers for the guidance of the collector he does designate a single item as 'porcelain,' though many others are undoubtedly porcelain. In the *Catalogue of the Pitkin Collection of Bennington Pottery*, prepared by Frederick J. Williamson and included in the book, only two items are classified as porcelain. Of course, the Parian Ware, which Pitkin says was made in large quantities, is a true porcelain, and it is clear that the statement that Parian was made in large quantities is not to be reconciled with the other statement that porcelain was made 'in small amounts with only partial success.' The plain and easily ascertainable truth is that an immense amount of hard porcelain was made at the Fenton Potteries; that greater technical and artistic success was achieved in this branch of manufacture than in any other; that some soft paste porcelain was made; that, finally, the amount of Parian, properly so-called, that was made was relatively small.

* Pitkin, *op. cit.*, pp. 38–39.   † *Op. cit.*, p. 39.

It is fairly indicative of the confusion that exists concerning Parian Ware that at least seventy-five per cent of the pieces, which Pitkin designates as Parian, both in his book and in his collection, are not Parian at all. By his own showing, and using his own definitions as standards, these pieces should be classified as ordinary hard porcelain. Presently we shall have to discuss in some detail the distinctive features of Parian and its relation to other types of porcelain. For the present, therefore, it will suffice to quote Pitkin's own definition. On page 35 he correctly defines Parian in the following terms:

Parian was *an unglazed porcelain supposed to imitate Parian marble.* It was moulded with elaborate floral designs in relief. Besides pitchers and vases a few statuettes were produced for mantel ornament, such as the Praying Child in the Pitkin Collection. . . . When not too thick Parian is translucent. Many of the ornamental forms have much delicacy of modelling and a velvety surface probably obtained by coating the interior of the seggars in which they were fired with glaze which vaporized with the heat, gave the ware a glossy finish. *Only those pieces intended to hold liquids were actually glazed and then it was on the inside.*

On page 20 he defines Parian in the following words, 'This is a hard porcelain, and took its name from the resemblance to Parian marble.' On page 38 he says, 'The Parian Ware they made in large quantities and great variety of articles, useful and ornamental.' Then on page 39 comes the statement, already quoted, that 'Porcelain . . . was made . . . in small amounts with only partial success.' Could confusion be worse confounded than this, or greater perplexity offered the collector? Let us summarize the essence of these statements:

(1) Parian is a hard porcelain.
(2) This hard porcelain was made at Bennington in large quantities with success.
(3) Porcelain was made at Bennington only in small amount with little success.

Finally, although we are told that Parian is 'an unglazed porcelain,' and that it was never glazed, except that 'those pieces intended to hold liquids' were glazed, but only 'on the inside,' the first item in the *Catalogue* is a white pitcher, described as '*Glazed outside and inside*,' and listed as 'White Parian.' The same mistake is committed several times throughout the *Catalogue*.

THE ACTUAL PRODUCT, 1845–1858

It is exceedingly doubtful that any American pottery of the period 1845–1858, manufactured a greater variety of wares than was produced in the Bennington potteries directed by Christopher Webber Fenton. It is certain that few produced anything approaching an equal variety. The following discussion does not complete the list, but it is at least illuminating:

I. Common White

The output of table ware, pitchers, toilet sets, and similar articles of domestic utility, in the white earthen ware known to the trade as Common White, was always large, and at times enormous. Common White differed in no particular of quality, design, or appearance, which the most expert can discover, from similar ware produced in numerous American potteries during the same period, as well as before and after it. Never marked in any manner, it is quite impossible to identify it. Almost all of this Common White was thrown and turned upon the wheel: only a small proportion was pressed into moulds. In and around Bennington, as in virtually every other part of the United States, a great deal of this Common White is to be found. It is possible, and even probable, that much of that found in and around Bennington was made at the United States Pottery, but the collector has no means of knowing this, except in rare cases, where the history of the piece, or pieces, is unimpeachable. I know of only three pieces of this ware the authenticity of which is, in my judgment, beyond dispute or question.

These pieces constitute part of a child's toy tea-set, consisting of tea-pot, cream-pitcher, and covered sugar-bowl. They were made at the United States Pottery. A Mrs. Cartwright, who was employed in the Pottery assisting in the manufacture of Common White, had them made there for her small daughter, Nettie Cartwright. W. G. Leake, whose father was employed in the pottery, and who, as a boy, worked there, himself, after school hours and on Saturdays, clearly remembers Mrs. Cartwright as working on the Common White. He also remembers the little daughter for whom the toys were made.

The Leake family and the Cartwright family were near neighbors on Pottery Street. In the first year of the Civil War, Nettie Cartwright, having outgrown such toys, gave the tea-set to a little girl named Knapp, whose family also lived on Pottery Street and whom W. G. Leake also knew. Little Miss Knapp in the course of time became Mrs. Frank Hill, of Bennington, and the toys were used by her children and grandchildren. It was from Mrs. Hill that I bought them, and, by a curious coincidence, W. G. Leake was present at the time, and so met Mrs. Hill whom he had not seen in fifty years. He not only remembered the parties named in this account, but also recalled having seen just such children's sets made at the United States Pottery. Although the tea-pot in its long history was often filled with tea or coffee and set upon the kitchen stove, it is much less discolored than the sugar-bowl. For a long time I could not account for this fact, but now I know that the old-fashioned brown sugar frequently had this effect upon all sorts of white china.

II. Common Yellow

This is also the trade name of a ware that was made at Bennington in great quantity. There was a large demand for milk pans, mixing-bowls, mugs, baking-dishes, pitchers, custard cups, and similar domestic utensils in this cheap, clean-looking, substantial, and almost fireproof ware. Like the Common White this Common Yellow was never marked, and it did not differ in any way from similar ware produced in numerous other potteries then in operation throughout the United States. Specimens cannot, I believe, be positively identified by any human being.

I know of only one sample of this ware made at the United States Pottery concerning which there can be no least shadow of doubt. When William G. Leake was a boy of ten,* under the supervision of his father, William Leake, who was working at the pottery, he made a small mug of Common Yellow for his sister, who has kept it all through the years, a precious and, to her, priceless possession. I have other specimens of Common Yellow that were indubitably made at Bennington, and I know of still others in the hands of other collectors, but it is not certain whether they were made at the United States Pottery or in the Norton Pottery, or whether they were made during the period of Fenton's control or later. Of the little mug, and of it alone, I can say with absolute certainty, 'This is a specimen of the Common Yellow earthenware made at the United States Pottery.'

III. Stone China

This also is a familiar trade name, somewhat differently used by most manufacturers to-day than it was at Bennington sixty-odd years ago. For this reason, it seems necessary, or at least desirable,

---

* This was not long before the United States Pottery closed down.

to make clear the precise nature of the ware to which Fenton himself applied the term 'Stone China.' It is different from the Common White, already described, principally in that it is finer in texture, can be used in much thinner forms than the latter, and may be said to occupy a place midway between Common White and porcelain. Because of its fine texture and dense, hard body, it is often called 'semi-porcelain.' Like the wares previously named, the Stone China was never marked, so far as I have been able to discover. Its identification must always be uncertain, therefore, except where a specimen is accompanied by a history of unimpeachable authenticity. Without claiming too much expert knowledge in a field where there is so much uncertainty and so little positive authority, I content myself with the observation that the Bennington product, so far as I have been able to study authenticated specimens, seems to equal in fundamental quality the best English and American products of the period, and to be superior to most contemporary ware of similar substance.

By 'fundamental quality' here I mean fineness of texture, purity of color, perfection of shape, lightness of weight, freedom from specks and defects due to impurities in the clay or to over-firing, and, lastly, approximation to porcelain in all except the characteristic translucence of the latter. Some of the Bennington Stone China tea and dinner services, decorated with gold bands,* and the basket-work fruit-stands, most of which were similarly decorated, were of a high order of excellence. They are often erroneously classified as Granite Ware, a result, no doubt, of the fact that in present-day usage 'Granite' and 'Stone China' are used interchangeably, as different names for the same thing. Fenton, however, in all his announcements, and in

---

* There were some gold-banded white table services made in a finer grade — true porcelain in fact.

every article about his work which he inspired or wrote, kept the two apart, as distinct wares.

IV. Granite Ware

This name was given to a ware the body of which may be said to represent a middle quality between the Common White and the Stone China. It has not the porcelain-like appearance of the latter. Harder and more vitreous than the body of Common White, it is both coarser and less vitreous than that of Stone China. Its glaze is not so closely akin to the body in its composition as is the glaze of Stone China, but is more like that of the Common White. It was extensively employed in the manufacture of toilet sets, cuspidors, water-pitchers, and the like. It was also used quite largely for the manufacture of pieces intended for presentation to individuals, and to be embellished with the names of recipients or with appropriate inscriptions, in gold or colors, the nature of the glaze used making it particularly adaptable to such decoration and embellishment. In this ware, water-pitchers, cow-creamers, and trinket-boxes bearing the names of their original owners, or presentation inscriptions done in gold, are most sought after by collectors. Sometimes the design used includes vine leaves and bunches of grapes in a rich blue outlined with gold, in addition to the customary gold decoration.

This ware is never marked. Collectors have almost wholly relied upon the shape of pieces and the style of their ornamentation in identifying specimens of this ware — especially in the case of pitchers. These last are nearly always of the rather squatty, bulging pattern known as the 'Saint Nicholas Pitcher' — a name derived from the fact that this form of pitcher was specially designed for the Saint Nicholas Hotel, a once famous New York establishment which stood at the corner of Broadway and Spring Street, and, for some years after its opening in 1854, was one of the great show places of the city. During the Civil War the Saint Nicholas was the favorite stopping-place for army officers. The water-pitchers used in the guest rooms bore the name of the hotel in gold and were especially designed for the place.

The design was reproduced by a number of potteries, and came to be known as the 'Saint Nicholas' pitcher. The pitchers for the hotel itself were made, principally, at the works of Houghwout & Co., at Greenpoint, Long Island, and, from the fact that pitchers of this 'Saint Nicholas' pattern are frequently found bearing well-known old Brooklyn and New York names, which are not found in the neighborhood of Bennington, it would seem a fair inference that such pitchers should be attributed to the Greenpoint firm, and not to Bennington. In other words, in the case of Granite Ware presumably produced at Bennington, positive identification is virtually impossible, except on the basis of the known history of each piece. If one has a pitcher, a trinket-box, a cow-creamer, or any other piece of Granite Ware, which bears a name that is common in the Bennington neighborhood, and especially if one knows something of the history of the item, then one is entitled to call it Bennington with some assurance. On the other hand, a pitcher which is, in all other respects, identical with those made at Bennington, but bearing some name common to Brooklyn or New York, had better be tentatively attributed to the Greenpoint factory. The smallest of the pitchers illustrated here was given by Fenton's daughter 'Fanny' to a friend.

In connection with this 'Saint Nicholas' pitcher, it may be worth calling attention to a statement made by Barber to the effect that the Granite Ware pitchers of this model made at Bennington were sent to New York to be decorated.* This statement is wholly without founda-

* Barber, *op. cit.*, p. 442.

tion in fact. During the whole period of the Fenton Pottery — including Lyman, Fenton & Co. and the United States Pottery Company — there was at Bennington one of the best china decorators in the country, Théophile Frey who had worked for twelve years at the Royal Sèvres Porcelain Works in France. Why, then, should pitchers be sent to New York to be decorated? As a matter of fact, no such thing was done.

The most elaborate, and altogether most beautiful, example of this type of ware ever made at the United States Pottery, so far as is known, is the jewel-casket illustrated by Plate XXIX. It was made at the pottery, and decorated by Théophile Frey, and given to a young lady upon the occasion of her betrothal. It is now cherished by the daughter of the original owner. Although I have come across only one other piece of the kind, it seems to be a moral certainty that a good many others were made. Search among the waste-heaps of the pottery has disclosed numerous fragments of such boxes, in the 'biscuit' state. It is quite likely that the use of the little figurine on the cover was unusual — an inspiration of the particular occasion. Altogether it is one of the loveliest things ever made at the Bennington potteries.

I cannot conclude this description of the Granite Ware without some account of the colored banded pitchers, basins, and mugs that were made at the pottery. Although these are known to have been produced in large numbers, they are absolutely unidentifiable now, even by the most expert. No marked specimen has ever been found, to my knowledge. In shape and coloring these pieces are precisely like those that have been turned out by numerous English and German potters, and are, in fact, still being made. From William G. Leake, who worked in the Bennington pottery as a boy, and made the 'snips' or pouring lips for these pitchers, I secured the only authentic example that I know of.

Starting from the top the decoration of this consists of a narrow black band or stripe, rather less than an eighth of an inch wide. A still narrower white stripe separates this from a wide gray band or stripe, little more than one and one half inches in width. Then come alternate white and black stripes, and then a broad band of blue, about two and three quarters inches in depth. Then come narrow rings, white, black, white, followed by a band of gray, about one and one half inches, followed in turn by narrow white and black stripes. Mr. Leake is authority for the statement that this ware was called 'Banded Granite.' Satisfied as I am that no human being could possibly identify the Bennington product with certainty, or distinguish it from similar earthenware made in other places, I have given this description of it for no other reason than to make the list reasonably complete.

V. Common 'Slip' Covered Red Ware

It will probably startle and shock not a few students of our ceramic history, and even more collectors, to be told that, at the Fenton potteries in Bennington, where so much ware of a high standard was made, pitchers and vases of crude red earthenware covered with 'slip' were also manufactured. I confess that the discovery was something of a shock to me. Searching along the banks of the stream near the site of the old pottery, where much of the débris used to be dumped, I was astonished to find, along with fragments of other wares — broken pieces of Rockingham, Parian, and so on — several bits which were undeniably of red earthen body covered with brown 'slip,' the surface of the latter being finer, however, than is usually found in the similarly made old pots and pans of an earlier day. Of course, finding the pieces in that locality did not prove that the ware had been made there, though finding them in association with the other fragments, in quantity, tended to create a presumption to that effect.

Later, I came across in Bennington, a pitcher which the owner was positive had been made at the United States Pottery, an uncle having brought it from the works at the time he was employed there. This pitcher was of the same shape and design as one of the best, and also best known, of the white porcelain pitchers made at the United States Pottery — the Pond Lily design. There could be no mistake about it: beyond all question, it was red earthenware covered with a 'slip' of a deep brown color, almost like chocolate. The question was, whether this specimen was just a 'freak piece,' perhaps the work of some boy, or a sample of a regulation type of ware. That the latter is the case now seems to be assured. Other pieces of the same type turn up from time to time. I have a beer-pitcher in this ware of the Pond Lily design which was used for years in the barroom of the Stark House, a local hostelry.

My friend, Mr. George S. McKearin, of Hoosick Falls, New York, has in his collection three pieces of this ware. One is a pitcher of the Pond Lily design referred to. Where it has been chipped, especially on the edges of the raised design, and where it has been broken and repaired, it is quite easy to see the red earthenware body, which is both crude and coarse. Another pitcher, of identical quality and appearance, bears the well-known Paul and Virginia design in relief. This piece is stamped with the familiar 'ribbon' stamp of the United States Pottery Company. Finally, in many respects most interesting of the three, occurs a Paul and Virginia vase, partly in the 'biscuit' state. The inside has been covered with brown 'slip'; the outside is uncovered. A piece broken out of the bottom rim shows plainly that the body is red earthenware, of a very coarse and crude quality. This has been washed over with a thin wash of yellowish clay, but whether as a preparation for the 'slip' — which seems quite unlikely — or as an experiment for some other purpose — perhaps long after the piece left the pottery — there is no means of knowing.

This 'slip' ware, is well remembered by some of the older residents. Nothing further need be said about it here. It is irredeemably ugly, and has nothing on earth to recommend it. Had it been produced some sixty years earlier, when the industry was in its infancy here in New England, we might regard it differently. It would then be possible to discern it as a praiseworthy step in the direction of a conscious quest for beauty, and away from the crude standards of the time. As it is, one can only look upon it as an ugly example of atavism. It must however, be added to the list of the varieties and types of ware produced at the Bennington pottery under Christopher Webber Fenton.

VI. Flint Ware

This little known Bennington product must not be confounded with the Rockingham and the brilliantly colored Flint Enamelled wares that bear the well-known impressed mark — *Fenton's Enamel Patented 1849*, which it does not resemble in the least. Flint Ware was used principally, if not exclusively, in the manufacture of insulators for telegraph wires, in which the United States Pottery Company specialized. It was composed of a vitreous body containing a large percentage of calcined flint, and was of great hardness. It was regarded as a remarkable non-conductor of electricity, and from it several types of insulators were made. Occasionally specimens are found — crude, ugly, heavy objects, but rather interesting in their construction, nevertheless. Historical interest is the only claim that the Flint Ware has to our attention, and the product is mentioned here solely in order that the record may be as complete as possible.

VII. Rockingham

One sign of the dawn of the millennium will be the general recognition by amateur collectors and by dealers in antiques of the fact that Rockingham, as applied to pottery in this country, is the name of a *type of ware*, commonly made by potters in many parts of the country, including the Bennington potteries of both Fenton and his associates and of the various Nortons. *It is not the name of the product of a particular pottery or maker.* This common and familiar ware with a yellow body and mottled or splotched brown glaze, sometimes of several tones, which give it a resemblance to tortoise shell, would seem to present no great problem to collector or dealer; but it does, nevertheless.

On the one hand, there are the persons who think that every piece of ware of this general type must be Bennington, and who, in consequence, ask ridiculously high prices for nondescript rubbish. Once it becomes known that one is 'collecting Bennington,' people write from all sorts of places offering for sale what they regard as choice specimens. Often, of course, it is possible for the experienced collector to tell from their descriptions what these 'choice specimens' are, and to make intelligent decisions. Quite as often, however, the descriptive powers of the writers are so limited that no such decision is possible. There is consequent waste of time and energy all around. Unfortunately, the worst sinners in this respect are found among antique dealers of a certain type — folk who have no real knowledge of antiques, beyond the merest smattering, in which misinformation and information are jumbled together, and who are either unable or unwilling to learn. Fortunately, this type is being replaced by a much higher and better type.

On the other hand, there are the persons who submit specimens or descriptions and photographs and ask, 'Is this Bennington, or is it Rockingham?' or who complain, 'I bought this for Bennington, and now I am told that it is Rockingham.' These and similar inquiries and statements are quite common. When one answers, as one some-times must, that the specimen submitted is both Bennington and Rockingham, that it is Bennington Rockingham, the result is usually to make the person so advised grasp thereafter at every bit of Rock-ingham and label it 'Bennington.' It would, therefore, seem to be worth while to attempt here to define and describe Rockingham with greater care and detail than is customary.

In the first place, then, it should be borne in mind that the type of ware commonly known in this country as 'Rockingham' is not at all what is meant by 'Rockingham' as that term is used in English books and treatises upon ceramics. In the British Museum there is a wonder-ful exhibit of Rockingham, as that term is used in England. It consists in large part of some of the most elaborately modelled and exquisitely decorated figures ever produced in England by the potter's art. Fine specimens of this Rockingham are among these rare and costly treasures which few collectors except the very rich can ever hope to possess.

This ware is a soft paste porcelain which derives its name from the fact that it was made at Swinton, in the West Riding of Yorkshire, England, in the latter half of the eighteenth century, at a pottery which was established under the direction and patronage of the then Marquis of Rockingham.

In 1807 this pottery passed to the famous firm of the two Bramelds who operated it until 1842, when the works were closed. The Marquis of Rockingham employed the services of the foremost artists of the time to design and decorate the wares made, which bore the Rockingham crest, a griffin, as their distinguishing mark. After the works passed to the Bramelds the griffin mark was still retained, with the addition of the words *Rockingham Works, Brameld*, underneath it.

It may be wondered what this elaborate ware can have in common with the cheap brown glazed pottery that bears the same name in this country. The answer is as follows: In the nature of the case, the wares made at Swinton under the patronage of the Marquis of Rockingham were costly and commanded a limited market. In periods of depression the demand for them immediately fell off. On the occasion of such a depression, rather than have the works shut down and the employees discharged, the good Marquis made arrangements for the manufacture of a cheaper line of goods — in particular, cheap tea-pots for common everyday use. These tea-pots were made of a common yellowish clay body, covered with a brown glaze. In allusion to the name of the Marquis, the workmen among themselves called these tea-pots 'Rock's pots,' 'Rockies,' 'Rocky's pots,' and so on. As a matter of fact, the manufacture of this cheap ware, begun in the circumstances here outlined, developed into a substantial business that lasted at Swinton for many years, during all of which time the foregoing nicknames remained in use.

When, in the middle of the nineteenth century, English potters who had settled in this country began to make ware similar to 'Rocky's pots,' cheap ware of a common yellow body covered with brown glaze, it was quite natural for the nickname they gave it to be brought into general use — but in its refined form, Rockingham. Almost every general pottery in the eastern part of the United States, in operation from 1835 to 1885, or later, made Rockingham Ware, as the term is understood in this country. Of course, differences in the clay used in the bodies and differences in the formulas of the glazes used by the various potteries are reflected in the wares produced. Nevertheless, any pottery of a common yellow body covered with the *typical brown glaze* is properly called Rockingham — in our American sense.

I trust that the reader will not overlook the significance of the words 'typical brown glaze,' used above, for it is the distinguishing characteristic of Rockingham that *the color is mixed in the glaze*. Ordinary glazes are not colored; the glaze is transparent and colorless and such color as may be needed is applied to the body before glazing. In Rockingham the color is *always* mixed in the glaze. The brown is derived from manganese, but sometimes it is mixed with a small amount of umber, to give additional richness of tone.

Now, it does not matter, profoundly, whether the body of the ware is dipped in the Rockingham glaze, or whether the coating is applied with a sponge, a brush, or a stick, the ware so glazed is Rockingham. Different potteries applied the glaze differently, and, even in the same pottery, pieces of different character frequently had the glaze differently applied. The method most in use from 1847 to 1865 was 'spattering' with the paddle. The workman whose job it was to glaze the ware stood beside a tub containing the ready-mixed glaze. Holding in his left hand the piece to be decorated, and a long flat piece of wood called a 'paddle' in his right, he would dip the paddle into the mixture, strike it lightly against the side of the tub, to remove the surplus glaze, and then, holding the article just below the top of the tub and over the liquid, he would keep rapping the paddle against the edge of the tub, so as to spatter the varnish-like liquid upon the piece, which he turned the while.

He pleased his own fancy as he worked. If he thought that it would look better to produce a streaky effect by applying the glaze more heavily in some places than in others and letting it run down, he did that; if he fancied that his ware would look better to be spotted more or less regularly, he carried out that idea. If he sought to obtain a light tone, he used less color, or, what amounted to the same thing, a thinner coating of glaze. Then there were accidental results, the effects of haste, carelessness, poorly mixed glaze, and so on. This will explain why, almost literally, no two pieces of Rockingham are exactly alike.

It should be quite easy for any one to understand that the final appearance of a piece of Rockingham may be greatly influenced by other factors than the whim or skill of the workman applying the glaze. In the first place, a dark, coarse, muddy body and a body that is light, clear, free from impurities and relatively fine, treated with the same glaze, and in exactly the same way, will look quite different when finished. In the second place, if different processes of firing are resorted to, then, even if the quality of the body is the same, the final appearance of the pieces will differ. In a good many potteries the 'one-fire' process was used. This means that the green ware was first air-dried so as to be capable of being handled, and the glaze was applied to it in that state, before firing. When glazed it was placed in the kiln and baked or fired, glaze and body thus being fired at one and the same time.

In other potteries the 'two-fire' process was used. This means that the green ware was first fired, before any glaze was applied. When so treated, it became what is known as 'biscuit.' In that state it was given — by immersion — a coat of 'gloss' or under-glaze. This was a quick-drying preparation which covered the entire biscuit body with a glossy film. This gloss did not require firing or exposure to heat, for it dried in the air very quickly. Next, upon this was imposed the brown glaze, after which the piece so treated received its second firing. Anybody who can understand that a priming coat will greatly improve the appearance of the paint that is laid over it should be able to understand this simple technical exposition of glazing.

With this in mind, let the collector or the student compare one of the Rockingham pitchers marked *Norton & Fenton*, referred to in an earlier chapter, with one of the finer examples of Rockingham made at the best period of the United States Pottery. If he will look at the bottom of the former, he will at once see that there is no evidence of the extra coat of gloss, the under-glaze, or priming coat. He will notice, also, that the glaze is uniform, not irregular and 'mottled' in effect. The glaze was applied by dipping. On turning to the later specimen, and examining it in the same way, he will observe that the evidence of the under-glaze is unmistakable. He will also see that the glaze is not uniform in tone as in the other case, but presents variations which plainly indicate another mode of application.

Naturally, the ware produced by the two-fire effect is more brilliant than the other. There is a greater 'depth' to the color, to use a phrase of art criticism. Even if the two pieces had been glazed at the same time and from the same tub of glaze, the relative superiority of the twice-fired specimen would be apparent. When the United States Pottery had failed and closed, sundry attempts were made to start it up again, and an effort was made to hold the market by producing Rockingham more cheaply. With that object in view the 'one-fire' process was resorted to. Examples of Rockingham so made are common, and they are all inferior to that which had been produced in the best days of the United States Pottery.

It must not be understood, however, that the *quality* of the glaze used had no effect upon the ware. That would be nonsense. Every pottery making Rockingham had its own formula, or, rather, every glaze-mixer had his own formula, which he carefully guarded. A good deal of mystery was made about the composition of these glazes, much of which was pure bunkum. It is easy to understand that the glaze-maker would surround his formula with all the mystery and secrecy possible, for that was part of his working capital. But if a glaze-maker left his position it was usually possible to obtain in his place another whose product was quite similar. It might be a little better or a little inferior, but in the main the change was not a serious matter. There was very little difference in the constituents of the numerous Rockingham glazes used; and such differences as there were took the form of varying proportions of the same constituents. A little more calcined flint or a little less, as the case might be, would give a harder or a softer glaze — and so on.

The Fenton Potteries at Bennington made an immense variety of things in Rockingham Ware: Toby mugs, 'Coachmen' and 'Monk' bottles, pitchers of many sizes, patterns, and designs, inkstands, cracker-jars, mugs, door-knobs, name-plates for doors, soap-dishes, bed-pans, cuspidors, 'Tulip' vases, and numerous other articles. The famous hound-handle pitchers, most of the cow-creamers, jelly-moulds, and baking-dishes were almost always made in Rockingham. Mottled poodle dogs, and a great many of the tubular candlesticks were made of Rockingham.

Even when marked with the familiar stamp of *Fenton's Enamel*, pieces might be, and often were, simple Rockingham; and, in point of fact, the stamp had no legitimate place upon them, for they were not protected or covered by the patent to which that stamp referred. The demonstration of this must be left to the section on Flint Enamel. It is a notable fact, however, that the mark referred to is the only one that was used upon Bennington Rockingham Ware during the years that the United States Pottery was in operation. For the most part such ware was unmarked; otherwise it was marked in a misleading manner, which, in these days, would be regarded as illegal and might probably subject the responsible parties to prosecution for misbranding their wares and making unlawful use of a registered patent mark.

Pitkin * calls attention to an octagonal water-cooler in Rockingham, marked *Fenton's Works, Bennington, Vermont*. As already noted, I have one like it in my collection. I have to confess that I do not know how to regard these pieces. It is quite possible that they were really made at the United States Pottery and were marked with the earlier Fenton mark. This might be due to purpose, the whim of some workman, for example, or to some accidental cause. Many of the old moulds and stamps of the earlier period were preserved in the new pottery. Indeed, when the United States Pottery buildings were torn down, in 1874, moulds with the stamp of *Fenton's Works* were found. It is not difficult to believe that these may have been used at various late dates, especially when a workman took a fancy to make a particular piece for himself or for friends. On the other hand, it is quite possible that such pieces were really made at the earlier period when Fenton was in business upon his own account. In that case, one has only to compare a specimen with the Rockingham produced by Norton & Fenton to realize the great advance that was made by Fenton in the manufacture of this ware.

* Pitkin, *op. cit.*, p. 24.

For several reasons it is unfortunate that the name Rockingham ever came to be applied to this ware, which at its best development is identical with the 'Mottled' or 'Tortoiseshell' Ware of the English potters. The latter term is admirably descriptive of it, and it is quite a common thing for people who know absolutely nothing about the subject to write that they have pieces of old pottery 'that look like tortoiseshell.' This fact alone proves the fitness of the name. Rockingham must always be both a misnomer and a cause of confusion. Tortoiseshell Ware was made by some of the most famous of the English potters — Josiah Wedgwood, Thomas Whieldon and Josiah Spode, among them — and some of it was of a standard of excellence never attained at Bennington. At the same time, it is worth remembering that the so-called Rockingham of Bennington is neither more nor less than an American copy of English Tortoiseshell Ware.

The amateur collector who has followed the discussion thus far will naturally wish to know how the unmarked Rockingham Ware of Bennington may be identified and distinguished from other makes of Rockingham. It was long ago remarked that the Tortoiseshell Ware of the various English makers was rarely marked, making authoritative attribution almost impossible. While some of the Rockingham made at Bennington, and some of that made at other American potteries, was marked, much of that made at Bennington — perhaps the greater part — was unmarked. The same is true of most of the American potteries of the period. The answer, therefore, to the question of the amateur collector is that there is no absolute and unfailing standard, or test, by means of which such identification can be made. In a general way, one who is sufficiently familiar with the Bennington ware can distinguish it from most — although not all — other Rockingham, by its *quality*. High-grade Rockingham made elsewhere is likewise generally identifiable by those familiar with it.

The greater part of the unmarked Rockingham pitchers, mugs, and similar articles, which are picked up in various parts of the country, are inferior in quality to the best grade of the Bennington product, both in body and glaze. I have already indicated wherein the superiority of the Bennington product lies. All that is necessary to add, by way of warning to the amateur collector, is that this applies only to the better class of Rockingham Ware made at Bennington. A great deal of inferior Rockingham was made at Bennington in the form of pie-plates, baking-dishes, and the like, which no man can distinguish from a mass of similar ware made in scores of other places. Except in so far as one aiming at a comprehensive collection completely illustrative of every phase of the Bennington potteries must desire to secure a specimen or two, this latter ware should be regarded as worthless rubbish, with nothing to recommend it.

The collector may not, however, rely upon the quality test alone, for examples of Rockingham made at other American potteries are sometimes picked up which are in no wise inferior to the Bennington product, and which are so similar to the latter in the appearance of both body and glaze that they cannot be definitely distinguished from it.

I have in mind, as an example, some of the early work of Bennett & Brother, of Pittsburgh, and later of Baltimore, made in 1846. Not only is it not inferior to the best grade of Bennington Rockingham, but it is so like it as to be capable of deceiving a fairly expert judge. In addition to the quality test, therefore, the collector must rely, to no small extent, upon his knowledge of authenticated Bennington designs and patterns. It is here that he must be keen and must pay sharp attention to details.

In the case of the well-known hound-handle pitcher, for example, the Bennington model differs sufficiently from others of the same general type to make its identification fairly easy, notwithstanding that it was never marked, so far as we know. From time to time, I have heard rumors of examples of this pitcher bearing the Bennington mark, but in no single instance has investigation sustained the rumor. I have received letters from several people positively assuring me that they possessed one or more of these pitchers bearing a Bennington trade-mark. In some cases they have described the mark with such detail that I have felt certain that, at last, I had discovered what almost every collector has sought. In every such case I have secured the piece 'on approval' — and have invariably found that the mark was not that of any Bennington firm, but of other manufacturers. In all such instances, moreover, the hound has differed quite materially from the rather grotesque and un-doglike animal whose body makes the handle of the Bennington pitcher.

A more difficult matter is the positive identification of Bennington cow-creamers. So far as is known, these were never marked; certainly no marked example is known to exist. The manufacture of cow-creamers was in no sense an exclusive Bennington specialty. Such pieces were made at a number of American potteries from 1845 to 1885, and later. Large quantities were also made in England. Some of those made in Rockingham Ware at various American potteries — Jersey City, South Amboy, Baltimore, and Trenton, among others — are so like the Bennington model that the differences are easily overlooked. All these cow-creamers are virtually of the same size, differences in this particular being as marked between absolutely authenticated Bennington examples as between those made at Bennington and those made elsewhere. These differences are due, principally, I think, to inequalities in shrinkage, caused by variations in the quality of the clay used in the bodies, in the degree of wetness when moulded, in the firing, and so forth.

To sum up the whole matter as it relates to the cow-creamers, the collector must carefully study an authenticated model, learn its special and distinctive features, and firmly reject whatever is offered him which does not possess these distinctive features. *Caveat emptor* is the motto to be borne in mind. It does not make the slightest difference that the cow-creamer offered is known to have come from Bennington, even from 'an old Bennington family.' Offhand I could name nearly a dozen much-prized cow-creamers reposing upon the shelves of friends and neighbors of mine, and proudly regarded by them, which are 'Bennington cows' only by adoption. Once, to my knowledge, a good many years ago, a consignment of Rockingham cow-creamers was imported from England and sold in and around Bennington. And there is every reason to believe that long before that, soon after the close of the United States Pottery in 1858, the market for cow-creamers which had been developed in New England was supplied from without.

The foregoing résumé of the chief characteristics of Rockingham Ware in general, and of Bennington Rockingham in particular, should prove helpful to the student and to the collector who feels the need of a guiding hand through a way that is beset with difficulties and snares. Little more can helpfully be added. At the risk of indulging in wearisome repetition, I close this lengthy section with the admonition to the collector to make resolute choice between two courses: either to confine himself to the collection of marked pieces — in which case he will be obliged to forego much of interest and value — or to study carefully the details of well-authenticated specimens of each model, together with the technical points herein outlined, and to reject whatever does not conform to the standard which this study will erect in his own mind. Of course, he will make mistakes even then — but such mistakes are no small part of the pleasure of collecting.

VIII. Flint Enamel Ware

The patent which Christopher Webber Fenton obtained in November, 1849, protecting a certain process of applying color to pottery in connection with glaze, has already been discussed in an earlier chapter, as well as in the preceding section of the present chapter, in connection with our discussion of Rockingham Ware. It is not necessary to go over the same matter in detail, the briefest recapitulation of the essential facts being quite sufficient. If the reader will take the trouble to read the 'Specification' upon the basis of which the patent was issued,* no argument will be necessary to prove that the patent had nothing whatever to do either with the composition of the body itself or with that of the glaze used. The method was exclusively one of applying color in connection with the glaze. It is clearly set forth in the specification that the process can be used upon any kind of body, and it is quite plain, though not so explicitly stated, that it can be used in connection with any kind of glaze.

As early as 1846, Bennett & Brother, already referred to, had, with great distinction and success, used colors under a glaze containing a large percentage of flint. Because of the colors used, and the general resemblance of the result of enameling, this glaze was called 'Flint Enamel.' The colors were applied to the under-glaze with a brush, sponge, or rag, the workman placing the colors in precisely the manner and form he wished them to assume in the finished piece. When the color was dry, the piece was glazed and fired.

* See Appendix II, p. 250.

Fenton's patent covered an entirely different process: The article to be colored — or 'enamelled' — was taken, in the *biscuit* state, and first given a coat of transparent glaze. It was now ready for the application of colors. These, instead of being in liquid or paste form, were in powder, and, 'with a small box perforated with holes,' were 'thrown or sprinkled on through the holes over the surface of the article in quantity to produce deeper or lighter shades,' as desired, 'leaving a part of the surface for the body of the article to show through in spots.' When this was done, the piece was glazed and fired in the usual way. Since the colors employed were all of a metallic nature, the intense heat of firing fused them and caused them to flow and mingle with the under-part of the glaze, and, to a less extent — varying with the nature of the color and the degree of heat — to penetrate and mingle with the glaze itself. Anybody who will examine closely a typical piece of this colored Bennington ware, in which there are greens, yellows, blues, and browns of various tones, will see immediately that the colors have run down and spread; and he will be able to tell by the direction in which the colors have run exactly how the piece stood in the kiln during the firing.

As was pointed out in the section on Rockingham, it is obvious that it is a misuse of the protective mark of the Flint Enamel patent to apply it to articles not so colored. In particular, it is a misuse of the mark to apply it to articles glazed with Rockingham glaze, in which the coloring is part of the glaze itself. Pitkin, notwithstanding that he clearly and accurately explains the nature of Fenton's patent, utterly failed to apply that knowledge to his classification of the various types of Bennington ware. The Pottery's slipshod and loose method of using the *1849* mark — which was in keeping with careless and slipshod ways manifested in other directions — puzzled him as it has puzzled many others. Finding the patent flint enamel mark upon certain pieces of Rockingham, and unable to escape the obvious fact that some Rockingham is much superior in its glaze to other pieces bearing the same name, due, in part at least, to the use of more calcined flint in the glaze, Pitkin divides Rockingham into two categories. He refers to 'Rockingham Ware (not flint enamelled)' and 'Rockingham (Flint Enamelled).' * Thereby he effectually destroys the value of his description of the Flint Enamel Ware. Elsewhere he distinguishes between Flint Enamel Ware and Rockingham, and, although the distinction is not quite accurately stated, it is reasonably clear. He says: 'The "Flint Enamelled" ware . . . was similar to Rockingham, but harder and more brilliant in appearance, and was made in three colors, black, mottled with yellow, olive and yellow, with red, blue and green mixed.' †

We shall never get away from the confusion which has enshrouded all the discussions concerning Bennington pottery unless we rigorously distinguish between 'flint glaze' and 'Flint Enamel,' and confine the use of the latter term to the ware in which various metallic colors are used independently, and are not mixed in the glaze itself, as in the case of the manganese used in Rockingham glaze as a component part of the glaze itself. In ceramic history the term 'enamel' has almost always been associated with the use of colors for decorative effect, and that association should be maintained throughout. It is obvious that some such term as 'Flint Rockingham Glaze' can be used with advantage to describe that superior type of Rockingham to which reference has been made, but to call it 'Rockingham, Flint Enamelled,' or 'Flint Enamel Rockingham,' is equivalent to destroying the possibility of intelligent classification.

* Pitkin, *op. cit.*, pp. 43–44. The peculiar use of capitals is Pitkin's.
† *Idem*, pp. 39–40. The arithmetic in the passage quoted needs revision!

Although Fenton's patent covered only the particular method of applying colors which we have described, the older method of applying color by means of a rag or sponge was undoubtedly resorted to in some cases. This would still produce 'flint enamel,' of course, but it would not be Fenton's patented process. There was nothing in his patent which gave him an exclusive right to that trade term. Indeed, that term does not occur in the patent, the words used being 'Fenton's Enamel' — quite another matter. I have in my collection pieces in which it is evident that the colors under the glaze were carefully 'spotted in,' presumably with a piece of rag. Where the colors were laid on in definite shapes and patterns, they must have been applied in paste form. There is no possibility that powdered oxides were sprinkled in any such fashion, for the colors show none of the irregular running and spreading under the intense heat such as occurs with those applied according to the patented process.

We hear a great deal about the 'lost art' of the Bennington glaze. What people mean when they talk of this is not the *glaze* but the combination of the glaze and colors. Even so, this 'loss' is no more than an old wives' tale. There is nothing in connection with any phase of the manufacture of any type of Bennington pottery which may properly be viewed as a lost art. Every phase of every process is quite well known, local gossip to the contrary notwithstanding. Of course, students of ceramic history will recognize that the 'lost art' myth is constantly cropping out in all parts of the world. When William De Morgan made his tiles and vases decorated with colored lustres like those used by the Persians and the Syrians in the Middle Ages, there was a profound sensation in some circles because he was supposed to have 'found' the secret of an ancient art that had been 'lost.' He used to tell with great gusto how horrified his workmen were when he freely made public the methods by which those rich lustres were obtained. If ever the art had been 'lost,' he used to say, it had been too often rediscovered for any particular glory to be due to himself.

We know that the richness of the browns in the Rockingham made in Bennington under Fenton's management was derived from the oxides of manganese found in Bennington and Stamford in connection with the local hematite ores; and we know the effect of a mixture of the oxides of manganese and iron when fused together. We know that a mixture of oxide of manganese and cobalt, in proper proportions, will give a rich black; that different proportions of the same ingredients will give a blue so dark as to appear almost black. We know that oxide of uranium will give yellow; that oxide of cobalt will give blue; oxide of copper, green. There is no mystery about these circumstances — either chemical or mechanical — and if any manufacturer wanted to revive the manufacture of this ware he would not find it a task of extraordinary difficulty to evolve formulas which would substantially reproduce the most characteristic qualities of the Bennington product.

So much of the Flint Enamel Ware is marked that its identification is easy and calls for no special advice. It frequently happens that the mark is barely discernible, or is decipherable only in part, by reason of the fact that the stamp impressed into the clay has been partly or wholly filled in with glaze and thus largely obliterated. In not a few cases, indeed, such obliteration is complete. Then, too, many pieces were altogether unmarked.

Unless we accept the explanation of a rather slipshod way of working, it is virtually impossible to find any theory which will conform to known facts, and, at the same time, will explain the use and non-use of the pottery mark. Book flasks are unmarked in ninety-nine cases out of every hundred; but occasionally one is found bearing the small oval stamp of the United States Pottery Company. The stamp is generally on an edge of the book, but occasionally it appears on the side. Marks disfigure the book flasks in every case, and that would seem to be a good reason for the general practice of omitting them. There is no apparent reason, however, why one pitcher of a particular pattern and design should be marked and another, identical with it in all other respects, be unmarked. That the lions without bases should be unmarked is easily understood, for they offer no particularly good place for a mark, though one could have been placed on the bottom of the large ball, of course. On the other hand, there is no obvious reason why the lions on bases should be sometimes marked and sometimes unmarked.

The absence of a mark from any characteristic piece of the Flint Enamel Ware, however, need not trouble the intelligent collector. The ware itself is almost unmistakable, and there is no lack of marked pieces which the cautious collector can use as standards to guide his decision. I do not know of any other American pottery so easily and surely identifiable. It is quite unlike the Rockingham in this respect. What is important to the student is the clear understanding of the distinction between Rockingham Ware and Flint Enamel Ware, and the development of a judgment independent of the patent mark of 1849.

IX. *Scroddled Ware*

This is the ware which is sometimes also called 'Lava' and sometimes (erroneously) 'Marbled.' Almost invariably the name which Fenton gave to it is misspelled 'Scrodled' — and mispronounced accordingly. It is so misspelled by both Barber and Pitkin, and by nearly every other writer on the subject. I cannot recall a single article dealing with Bennington pottery in which the word is correctly spelled. The *Standard Dictionary* defines the verb 'scroddle' as follows: 'To variegate, as pottery ware, in different colors by the use of various colored clays.' This simple definition is itself almost a sufficient description of this ware. In its general appearance it somewhat resembles old-fashioned 'marbled cake,' irregular waving streaks of brown in two tones, light and dark, running through a cream-colored body. The intention was to imitate the general appearance of a certain type of lava — hence one of the names by which it was often called.

This ware is, in every particular, identical with the Agate Ware of the eighteenth-century Staffordshire potters and of their successors in the early part of the nineteenth century. Dr. Thomas Wedgwood, son of Thomas Wedgwood, of the Overhouse Works, at Burslem, Staffordshire, made it in great perfection. It was made also by Whieldon, who seems to have specialized in knife hafts for the cutlery trade of Sheffield, and by the famous John Dwight at Fulham.

It is important to note that, whereas the name 'Marbled Ware' has been extensively used in this country as a synonym for 'Scroddled Ware' or 'Lava Ware,' it is properly applied by English writers to quite a different type of ware. The amateur should make particular note of this important distinction: 'Agate Ware' is a perfectly proper and accurate synonym for 'Scroddled Ware.' On the other hand, 'Marbled Ware,' which is used by Pitkin and others, is neither proper nor accurate, and strictly belongs to ware of another type altogether. 'Lava,' 'Scroddled,' and 'Agate' are different names for a ware in which the lava-like effect is produced by the process of superimposing layers of clays of different colors, with the result that the coloration goes through the entire substance of the material. On the other hand,

'Marbled' and 'Veined' are different names for a ware in which the 'marbling' or 'veining' is *done upon the surface only*, sometimes by the use of slip and sometimes by the use of metallic oxides or other coloring agents. It is not difficult to understand this distinction. To put the matter another way: 'Marbled Ware' is 'marbled' on the surface much as old-fashioned 'graining' was done on woodwork, while 'Scroddled Ware' is produced by lamination.

Scroddled Ware was made at Bennington in precisely the same manner as it was made in Staffordshire in the eighteenth century — by 'wedging' different-colored clays. A lump of clay, prepared much as for ordinary white body, was first thoroughly kneaded; upon this was pressed, or 'wedged,' a similar lump into which coloring matter derived from oxides of iron, manganese, and cobalt had been thoroughly mixed; upon this, again, was placed still another lump, colored in the same manner, and of the same materials, but lighter or darker in shade, as required. The entire mass was then pounded and hammered, so that, when it was flattened out, a cross-section of it presented the appearance of stratified rock. Pounded back into a single cake, the mixed clay was sliced by drawing a strong wire through it. These slices were 'thrown' upon the wheel and worked or moulded into the desired forms. Treated to a clear glaze composed mainly of flint and feldspar, it was subjected to great heat for a much longer time than most other ware. From this description of the method of its manufacture, it will be understood that the marbled effect which appears upon the surface runs completely through the body, so that, if a piece is fractured or chipped, it is found to present the same characteristics throughout. It is exceedingly hard, and has often been called 'the strongest ware made at the United States Pottery.' The collector will do well, however, to remember that specimens of this ware are liable to prove brittle and to break with ease — its 'strength' notwithstanding.

It was probably the least popular of all the wares made at the United States Pottery, and good specimens of it are relatively rare and uncommon. It was used chiefly in toilet sets and cuspidors, but occasionally more ornamental articles were manufactured from it, notably the 'Tulip' vases and cow-creamers. These were, perhaps, individual pieces made by workmen for themselves, and not produced commercially. The principal pieces — wash bowls and pitchers, soap-dishes, toothbrush boxes, and cuspidors — were generally marked with a small elliptical stamp, impressed into the ware, bearing the words *United States Pottery Co., Bennington, Vt.* Vases, cow-creamers, door-knobs, and other articles were unmarked.

Even at the cost of some repetition, the collector may be warned that this ware was quite commonly made in England in the first half of the nineteenth century, and it is therefore necessary to be on guard against confusing the English product with that of the Bennington pottery. English Lava Ware is often found in antique shops in an ornamental form, especially in combination with Parian figures. It is a safe rule to reject every piece in which this combination is found. I know of no such use of the Scroddled Ware at Bennington. It is true that, in the collection of Bennington pottery exhibited at the Pan-American Exposition, there occurred a piece in which a Parian figure was combined with a Lava or Scroddled background, but, since close inspection of this specimen revealed the mark of an English maker, no more need be said about it.

It is perhaps of greater practical importance to the collector to be warned against a widely prevalent belief that Scroddled Ware was made at no other American pottery than Bennington; that it was distinctively a product of the United States Pottery; and that any cuspidor, soap-dish, pitcher, bowl, vase, or other article in this ware which may be picked up can be definitely attributed to Bennington, whether marked or not. As a matter of fact, Scroddled Ware was produced at a number of American potteries during the third quarter of the nineteenth century. Although the ware never attained any popularity, there are still a good many pieces scattered about, most of which were not made at Bennington. When Enoch Wood, who had worked at Bennington for some time, went to Perth Amboy, New Jersey, and conducted the Hall Pottery there, he went into the manufacture of Scroddled Ware quite extensively. Door-knobs, pitchers, bowls, vases, and many other articles, he produced in this ware. Perhaps ninety per cent of the pieces of Scroddled Ware that I examine appear to have come from this pottery. When Wood found that the New York dealers did not take kindly to the type, but preferred Rockingham, he went into the manufacture of the latter, William G. Leake taking charge of that department of the works.

To the nine classes of ware enumerated and described in this chapter must be added the various types and grades of porcelain made at the Fenton Potteries, including the Parian Ware. The enumeration and description of these require a separate chapter.

IV

PARIAN AND OTHER PORCELAINS

THE reader who has paid me the compliment of reading the foregoing pages with reasonable care will understand, without further discussion or explanation, the task I have set for myself in this chapter. It is neither more nor less than the establishment of a definite and intelligible classification for those Bennington wares which have heretofore been lumped together under the designation of Parian, regardless of the fact that they are manifestly of different types, and conform to no single standard.

My major contentions are these: (1) that Parian is the name of a distinct type of hard porcelain, differing quite definitely and importantly from all other hard porcelain; (2) that a great deal of the ware produced at Bennington which has heretofore been called Parian is, in fact, hard porcelain of another type, and not Parian; (3) that the dissimilar wares heretofore designated Parian should be differentiated according to their distinctive characteristics and scientifically reclassified as (a) hard-paste porcelain, (b) soft-paste porcelain, (c) Parian porcelain.

This is not intellectual formalism. Still less is it a contention over 'mere names.' It is, in the first place, the first serious attempt to describe accurately the most important products of the Bennington potteries, and, in the second place, to simplify the whole business of identification as regards these Bennington wares.

The purpose of this discussion, and of the entire volume, being to guide and assist the average collector, I am compelled to bear in mind that a collector's interest in Bennington pottery and porcelain does not necessarily imply technical knowledge of the composition of the various wares, the manner of making them, or their exact relation to one another and to other wares. If one were writing for experts, much could be taken for granted that must here be explained. I shall try to avoid being too technical, or using unfamiliar terms. Without setting up as an expert authority, but simply as an amateur collector and student writing for fellow amateurs and students, I shall try to present the gist of the whole matter as concisely and simply as I can.

The Composition of Porcelain

First of all, then, what is porcelain? This is a question of fact, not of opinion. The Chinese were the first to make porcelain, and its composition was long a jealously guarded secret. All that was generally known was that porcelain was a product of the potter's art compounded wholly or in part of clays, earths, or stones, or a combination of these; that it was exceedingly hard, strong, and durable, and that it was translucent, or semi-transparent. From the latter quality it was evident that porcelain possessed something of the essential character of glass; that in the substance of which it was composed there must be some part that was fusible. Of course, if all the materials had been fusible — and fused — the result would have been glass; had none been fusible — or fused — there would have been no translucence, but an opaque body, earthenware. Porcelain is, therefore, a distinct product, partaking of the qualities of both earthenware, or pottery, and of glass. It is related to both, and may be roughly defined as a product midway between them.

The great French scientist Réaumur discovered the secret of the Chinese. He took some clay, which the Chinese called *kaolin* and a substance called *petun-tse*, and made some interesting experiments.

He placed a small cake of each substance in a separate container and subjected them to intense heat. He found that the *petun-tse* fused completely — that is, it melted, and in that state became practically molten glass. The *kaolin*, on the other hand, instead of melting, became hard; it thoroughly petrified, and proved to be wholly non-fusible. The one was glass; the other pottery of the type we call stoneware. Next, Réaumur prepared a cake composed of equal parts of both substances and subjected it to the same intense heat. He found that the non-fusible *kaolin* became thoroughly permeated with the fusible — and fused — *petun-tse*. In other words, there was produced an amalgam composed of a non-fusible mass of clay completely saturated with molten glass. Owing to the absorption of the glass by the clay, the mass baked hard. In this state it was found to be identical with Chinese porcelain. It was semi-vitrified and semi-transparent. The secret of porcelain had been revealed.

Concerning these two substances, *kaolin* and *petun-tse*, two important facts should be noted here. The first is that neither of them is peculiar to China, both being found in great abundance in many countries. The second is that, notwithstanding the great difference in their properties, already explained, the two are closely related. *Kaolin* is a fine clay, a silicate of alumina, having its origin in the decomposition of the mineral feldspar, of which decomposition it is the residuum. Feldspar is one of the important constituents of granite, and *kaolin* is commonly found in valleys that are surrounded by granite. *Petun-tse* is also derived from the fine silicious matter of granite. It is feldspar in a state of partial decomposition. The difference between the two may be summed up thus: *kaolin* is a clay, highly plastic; *petun-tse* is friable and, of course, non-plastic. The plastic substance is non-fusible; the non-plastic substance is fusible, owing to the amount of potash or soda that it contains.

Numerous experiments have proved that there could be no substitute for *kaolin* in the manufacture of porcelain. On the other hand, substitutes for *petun-tse* can be easily found. Where the partially decomposed feldspar does not exist in quantity or condition for use, feldspar in quartz form, crushed into a fine powder, is equally good. Finely powdered flint also answers the same purpose, and so will a mixture of powdered feldspar and flint. All of these materials exist in great abundance in many parts of the United States, but especially in the New England States. Nowhere in the world, perhaps, is there better *kaolin* than in Vermont, where the material is found in great abundance and of exceptional purity.

Now that we know the principal properties of porcelain and the constitutents of which it is compounded, we are in a fair way to distinguish it from earthenware, and from all other forms of pottery. It is hard, light, strong, and translucent. So much for its body. We must now turn our attention to another distinctive feature, namely, the nature of its glaze. In the case of every other kind of ware, when glaze is applied to a biscuit body the composition of the glaze is different from that of the body and contains some elements not contained in the latter. In the case of porcelain, however (with the exception of soft-paste porcelain, to be considered later), the glaze is of the same substance as the body — powdered feldspar. Being of the same substance, of the same composition and hardness, it becomes one with the body. The coat of glaze may be light or heavy, but, in either case, it becomes absolutely a part of the body. It cannot chip off or crack, for the simple reason that there are no inequalities of expansion and contraction in body and glaze due to differences in the materials of which they are composed.

In all other glazed wares the glaze and the body being of different composition, of varying degrees of hardness, density, porosity, and so on, separation of the glaze from the body by peeling, chipping, or cracking is possible. The glaze can be scraped or filed off and the body revealed. In such wares the glaze is a coat of one composition imposed upon a body of another composition. This is not the case with porcelain. If a porcelain body in the biscuit were covered with 'slip' composed of other materials, or with a lead glaze, for example, the finished product would not be porcelain, but something else, and would have to be otherwise classified.

In general, hard-paste porcelain is glazed by direct application of the glaze to the body. The biscuit piece is dipped into a vessel containing the glaze materials, and is then placed in the kiln for a second firing. This melts the glaze materials, and a thin varnish-like coating of glass is spread over the whole body. Sometimes, however, hard-paste porcelain is finished with a gloss, called a 'smear glaze.' This is not applied directly to the ware as a coating, but is obtained indirectly by evaporation. The inside of the seggar — the container in which the ware is held while in the kiln — is coated with glaze before being placed in the kiln. The greatest care is taken to see that the ware does not touch the seggar at any point. When the seggar becomes sufficiently hot, this glaze melts and, the seggar being closed, a vapor is created which surrounds the ware and 'smears' it. This gives to the surface a gloss or polish, rather than a glaze. It will be apparent to the reader that this does not affect the validity of what has been said about coating the biscuit with glaze directly applied.

Such, then, is hard-paste porcelain. Ninety-five per cent of the porcelain produced at Bennington was of this variety, as is by far the largest part of all porcelain produced in America. It is therefore the type in which we are most interested. Soft-paste porcelain was made at Bennington, though not in large quantity. It has also been made at other American potteries from time to time. Such porcelain is characteristically English, however, and the greatest part of the soft porcelain made in the world, as well as the best, is produced in England. The English have been notably successful in the manufacture of this type of porcelain.

The process of manufacturing this soft-paste porcelain differs from that employed in the manufacture of the hard variety. As a substitute for *petun-tse* — instead of the powdered feldspar quartz and flint used in this country for hard porcelain — a mixture containing a large percentage of ground and calcined bone is used, the other elements being ground flint, soda, borax, and oxide of tin. These materials are fusible at a much lower temperature than are those employed in making hard porcelain. The *kaolin* is also mixed with other clays not generally used in this country. The fusible elements are first compounded and then mixed with the clays. The result is a porcelain body. It is translucent, like other porcelain. The body is softer, however, and less vitreous than the body of hard porcelain. It is less completely non-porous, and the texture of the body is less compact, being somewhat flaky. This soft-paste porcelain is usually glazed with a glaze containing lead, the components being borax, soda, and lead, though the latter is sometimes omitted and additional borax used. In this respect — its glazing — soft-paste porcelain differs radically from hard-paste porcelain. As the body and the glaze used are different in composition, and vary in their expansion and contraction, crackling, peeling, and chipping of the glaze are common. The glaze can be scratched through with the sharp point of a knife.

It is necessary to warn the amateur at this point that the foregoing descriptions are of what may be called 'standard' examples of the two types of porcelain, and that a great deal of the porcelain made in this country and in Europe does not conform absolutely to either standard, but varies widely, the variations ranging all the way from the one standard to the other. *Hardness* and *softness* are relative terms, of course, like 'lightness' and 'heaviness,' and like many other terms which will suggest themselves to the mind of the reader. Some manufacturers of hard porcelain use no calcined bone dust, some use a little, others use much, with the result that some makes of 'hard' porcelain are less hard than others. Sometimes, indeed, it is a matter of opinion, and not of fact, whether a piece of porcelain should be described as having a hard-paste body or a body of soft paste. One who is fairly expert will find no difficulty in distinguishing between hard-paste and soft-paste porcelains, when the specimens conform to the 'standards' above described. But there is probably no person expert enough to be able to distinguish with certainty, and to classify with absolute accuracy, the varying degrees of hardness exemplified in the numerous variations of porcelain bodies.

PARIAN WARE

We now come to Parian Ware. The first requisite to an intelligent judgment of this ware and its properties, its relation to and differences from other wares, is an accurate and authentic answer to the question, 'What is Parian?' To answer that question is our first task.

(1) The name itself furnishes the first hint as to what the answer to our question must be. It is the name given to a new ware — produced for the first time in England, in 1842, by Copeland, of Stoke-on-Trent — because of its close resemblance in appearance to Parian marble. The ware was, in fact, expressly designed to imitate Parian marble, both in appearance and in texture, and it was used principally

for the reproduction of sculpture, well-known classic marble statues and bas-reliefs constituting the subjects. For this reason, it was also called 'Statuary Ware' — an important fact that should be borne well in mind. It would seem to follow from these considerations, concerning which there is not the slightest dispute or question, that objects which do not by their appearance or their texture suggest Parian marble, but are radically unlike it, may not properly be called Parian, and that the designation when applied to such objects is a misnomer.

(2) The material in which this imitation of Parian marble was achieved was a hard porcelain, and it was invariably so described. Parian or Statuary Ware is, therefore, a hard porcelain which, in texture and appearance, closely resembles Parian marble. A porcelain which does not have this resemblance is not Parian; neither is any compound other than porcelain Parian, even though it may resemble Parian marble. Compounds of marble dust and plastic clays are used to reproduce statuary, and some of them closely resemble Parian marble in texture and appearance; but they are not Parian Ware, since they are non-translucent and non-vitreous.

The foregoing paragraphs comprehensively summarize the distinguishing characteristics of Parian Ware, by which it may be definitely identified. There has never been any doubt in the mind of any responsible authority concerning these points. A few quotations will serve the twofold purpose of illustrating this and of giving the collector added assurance:

The *Standard Dictionary* defines Parian Ware as follows: 'Parian-porcelain, a fine variety of hard porcelain used for statuettes and bas-reliefs: so called from its resemblance to Parian marble.'

The *Encyclopædia Britannica* speaks of 'a special porcelain known as Parian,' and says of it, 'This in its finest expression was a "biscuit" porcelain used for the production of statuettes and groups rivalling the finest 18th century "biscuit" figures of Sèvres and Derby.' *

Horace Greeley, in his little known work, *Art and Industry at the Crystal Palace, New York,*† makes quite clear the nature of Parian Ware. He speaks of the 'introduction of statuary porcelain, or Parian figures,' and calls it 'a branch of porcelain manufacture,' and 'this imitation of marble,' ‡ and sums up with the following:

We have lingered over the collections of Parian Ware with great pleasure, as the introduction of this material is destined to effect for statuary what electrotyping accomplishes in the harder metals; it facilitates the reproduction of the works of the finest artists in a material less costly than marble, with their multiplication to any number of copies, and the elevation of the public taste in articles of fancy.§

It is plainly evident that Greeley held Parian to be a distinct type of porcelain, having, as its special and distinctive quality, a close resemblance to marble, and the imitation of statuary as its principal use.

In their elaborate and exhaustive volume, devoted to an illustrated descriptive and analytical account of the exhibits at the New York Exhibition of 1853–54, Silliman and Goodrich devote much attention to the exhibits of Parian Ware, both English and American.¶ It is safe to say that more competent authorities have rarely discussed the subject. Their book is the most valuable work of its kind ever published in this country. These authors say that statuary porcelain, or Parian, is a true hard porcelain. Of the Bennington Parian exhibited

* *Encyclopædia Britannica* (11th Edition), art. 'Ceramics.'
† Pitkin, *op. cit.*, p. 40, refers to this exhaustive book as 'an article in the *New York Tribune.*'
‡ Greeley, *op. cit.*, p. 118.
§ Greeley, *op. cit.*, p. 119.
¶ *The World of Science, Art and Industry Illustrated by Examples in the New York Exhibition, 1853–54.* Edited by Professor B. Silliman, Jr., and C. R. Goodrich, Esq. New York: G. P. Putnam and Company. 1894.

at the Crystal Palace, specifically, they say, 'It is obviously a hard porcelain, of which the raw materials are superior to the skill which has been bestowed on them.' * Parian in general — which they repeatedly term a hard porcelain — they describe as 'this exquisite material, the happy substitute for marble.'†

Finally, both Barber and Pitkin, notwithstanding the confusion which is common to both, declare Parian to be a hard porcelain, named on account of its resemblance to Parian marble. Says Barber:

Parian derives its name from its resemblance to a beautiful, ivory-tinted marble found in the island of Paros. It is a fine grade of porcelain, the ingredients being thoroughly ground together. It is usually moulded by the 'casting' process, in the same manner as most thin china, and possesses the translucency and vitreous nature of porcelain, but is seldom glazed.‡

Pitkin, as we have noted in an earlier chapter, defines Parian as 'an unglazed porcelain supposed to imitate Parian marble.' He says that 'When not too thick, Parian is translucent,' and that 'Only those pieces intended to hold liquids were actually glazed and then it was on the inside.' § And, again, Parian 'is a hard porcelain, and took its name from the resemblance to Parian marble.'¶

It would be easy, but entirely superfluous, to make many additions to the foregoing quotations, all emphasizing the same points. It is sufficient for our purpose to take note of the fact that no authoritative writer, in England or America, has ever expressed any other view than that Parian is (a) a hard porcelain, and (b) that its distinctive and distinguishing characteristic is that it resembles Parian marble in appearance and texture.

* Silliman and Goodrich, *op. cit.*, p. 188.
† Silliman and Goodrich, *op. cit.*, p. 78.
‡ Barber, *op. cit.*, p. 20.
§ Pitkin, *op. cit.*, p. 35.
¶ *Idem*, p. 20.

It is obviously absurd, therefore, to apply the name 'Parian' to wares which are as little like Parian — or any other — marble as chalk is like cheese. It cannot be too often reiterated that the porcelain which is quite unlike marble in appearance must be placed in some other category than Parian. Let the collector examine his specimens of Bennington porcelain with this standard in mind: he will at once find himself engaged in reclassifying them, and, in the end, a small percentage of his pieces — if he has an extensive collection — will be classified as Parian and the remainder into the following categories: (1) hard porcelain with direct glaze; (2) hard porcelain with indirect, or 'smear' glaze; (3) soft-paste porcelain.

Long before this stage of our discussion was reached, the interested reader, whether amateur collector or dealer, must have wished to ask, 'What of the Parian — or supposed Parian — pieces with colored backgrounds?' Certainly, by no stretch of the imagination can the brilliant blue backgrounds of some of the vases and pitchers which have been called 'Parian' be regarded as possessing any close resemblance to Parian marble; yet we know that the name has often been applied to pitchers and vases with backgrounds of blue, brown, and sage green, of English as well as of American make.

If the reader who is puzzled by this question will take the trouble to go back to first principles, to elemental definitions, the answer will become self-evident. Let him go back, then, and start with the original conception of Parian as a material especially designed for the reproduction of sculpture, and to the alternative name Statuary Ware. Then let him think of the definition of the *Standard Dictionary* which correctly defines Parian as 'a fine variety of hard porcelain used for statuettes and bas-reliefs.' The same test must be applied to the reliefs as to statuettes, namely, do they resemble marble closely enough to be regarded as good imitations of it, both in texture and in surface appearance? The colored background is to be disregarded entirely, so far as this primary classification is concerned. It is obvious that the background was not intended to represent marble. It is just a background against which the bas-relief figures are displayed. It may be blue or green or some other color; it may be glazed or unglazed.

If the figures are glazed and do not resemble marble, then they are not Parian figures, but something else. If both background and figures are directly glazed, the proper classification is hard porcelain, directly glazed and colored — assuming that the material is hard porcelain. If the colored background is directly glazed, but the figures unglazed and resembling marble, then its classification is hard porcelain directly glazed and colored, with Parian figures. If the entire piece, background and figures, is indirectly glazed, it should be so classified. Finally, if both background and body are unglazed, since only the white relief will bear any resemblance to Parian marble, its proper classification is hard porcelain, colored, unglazed, with Parian figures.

It may be necessary to warn the reader that, just as in the classification of porcelain into 'hard-paste' and 'soft-paste,' many variations will be encountered, and not a few indeterminate examples, so with this classification. I have several pitchers and vases in my collection which I am never quite certain how to classify. They are so close to what I may term the Parian 'norm' that it seems almost a meticulous conceit to exclude them from that category, and yet I am aware that they do not absolutely meet the test. On the other hand, they do not any better fit into any other of the categories. In this border zone, so to speak, the question is always one of opinion rather than of fact. Is this or that piece enough like Parian marble in its general appearance and its texture to be called Parian? One qualified expert answers

that, in his opinion, it is; another equally well-qualified expert answers
that, in his opinion, it is not. We must not seek the absolute.

Unfortunately, the differences between the several types of porcelain
which we have indicated and described cannot be photographically
represented. The amateur collector must, therefore, depend more
upon the text for guidance than upon the illustrations. Reliance upon
illustrations as guides to identification has led numerous collectors
and dealers into a bog of difficulties. It is important to remember
this, because design and pattern are rarely found to be exclusively associated with any one type of porcelain. In any extensive collection of
Bennington ware will be found various specimens of the same pattern,
size, and design which yet represent every type of hard-paste porcelain
that was made, and all the indefinite intermediate variations. This
applies to statuettes, vases, and other ornaments as well as to pitchers.
In my own collection, for example, the familiar white Palm Tree design
syrup-pitcher occurs in three quite distinct types. The pitchers are
identical in size, pattern, and design, but differ radically in quality and
finish.

The upper half of Plate XIII illustrates four pitchers which have
been represented as Parian by numerous writers, including Barber and
Pitkin, though in fact none of them resembles Parian. The largest is
the Rose design, one of the rarest of the several designs made by
Fenton when he was in business alone. It bears the raised medallion
mark with *Fenton's Works, Bennington, Vermont*, impressed. It is
not at all like marble, and to classify it as Parian, as, without an
exception, every writer has done heretofore, is wrong and destroys the
whole classification of which it is part. It is a typical example of
indirectly glazed or 'smear'-glazed hard-paste porcelain, and should
be so classified.

Next on the right is one of the Daisy designs. It bears the same mark as the other. Of this design there are variants, it should be noted. This is also a typical example of hard-paste porcelain with indirect or 'smear' glaze. I have never seen this design, in any of its variants, in what I should call true Parian. It is, however, quite frequently found in an unfinished, biscuit state, generally unmarked. When china painting was in vogue, in the middle of the last century and later, as one of the 'accomplishments' to which nearly every lady aspired, a great many pitchers of this variety were sold in the biscuit state for decoration. Second from the left is the Niagara Falls pitcher. It has the raised medallion mark of the United States Pottery Company. The entire surface is 'smear' glazed, and it is quite unlike Parian marble. Indeed, it is not Parian, but a fine example of indirectly glazed, hard-paste porcelain. This same pattern is frequently found in the directly glazed porcelain.

The other is a Palm Tree syrup-pitcher, pewter-covered, and bearing the large ornamental medallion mark of the United States Pottery Company. It is not nearly so white as the other pitchers, probably because of the presence in the clay of oxide of iron in unusual quantity. It is less hard than either of the other three, a result, probably, of the use of bone dust. It is a hard-paste porcelain, nevertheless. Its surface has a peculiar appearance and it feels like wax to the touch. It is utterly unlike Parian in texture and surface appearance. It is a 'smear'-glazed hard-paste porcelain with some unusual features which are probably of accidental origin. Syrup-pitchers of this size and pattern are found with the deep glaze attained only by direct glazing and in various degrees of 'smear' glazing, but rarely — if ever at all — in true Parian.

Plate XIII also shows four colored porcelain pitchers, each of which has been designated Parian by Barber, Pitkin, and other writers copying from them. Neither one has a single characteristic feature of Parian. Each is as unlike Parian as the colors are unlike marble. The tall pitcher is of the design commonly called Paul and Virginia. On the bottom it bears the well-known ribbon mark. The background is a bright blue, pitted like the skin of an orange. The raised design is white. The whole exterior is brilliantly glazed, and the piece may be classified only as a notable example of colored, directly glazed porcelain. The same general description applies to the smaller pitcher with the Oak Leaves and Acorns design. This also bears the ribbon mark. The blue and white pitcher with the Pond Lily design, which also bears the raised ribbon mark on the bottom, is a good example of 'smear' glaze. The small syrup-pitcher with the Palm Trees design, is not quite so easy to classify. The background is pitted in the usual manner, but the color is a light brown. It is an exceedingly rare piece. It was apparently intended to have this represent true Parian upon a colored background. Probably due to accidental causes, one side of it is 'smear' glazed, the other remains unglazed. This pitcher, like the others on this plate, has the ribbon mark.

Plate XXIV contains reproductions of a number of pieces of Parian, concerning the classification of which there can be neither doubt nor dispute. The large white pitcher with the Pond Lily design bears the ribbon mark with the initials of the United States Pottery Company. It is a splendid imitation of Parian marble, both in its texture and in its surface appearance; and no one having in mind the differences which I have attempted to describe in these pages, as the basis of a correct classification, would hesitate to classify it as Parian. It is a hard-paste porcelain, unglazed, made to imitate Parian marble.

Pitchers of this design are frequently found in the various types and variations of hard-paste porcelain.

No other design was ever made at Bennington which so well lent itself to the Parian medium. The broad flat surfaces and low relief of the design are such as might well be wrought in marble, a consideration which is not true of the Daisy design, for example.

Of the vases it is sufficient to say that, while their resemblance to marble in texture and the appearance of the surface itself leave no doubt as to their proper classification, they represent a base and improper use of the material. The one on the right of the plate is inexpressibly ugly and has not a single good feature. The design is as crude and ugly as even the mid-Victorian era could produce. The one at the left of the plate could not be wrought in marble, except as a *tour de force*, and then only at the cost of destroying every characteristic appearance of the material. It is not lacking in a certain gracefulness, but the high relief of the leaves and the tendrils of the grapevines, and the resulting fragility, which is so painfully obvious, are not in consonance with the actual material, or the substance which it is supposed to imitate. Delicate and graceful as are these elements of the design, they are not in harmony with the material and serve to illustrate how readily a really fine material could be debased.

The same criticism must be made of the ornamental pitcher in the center. This is so fine in its workmanship, and the imitation of Parian marble so perfect, that I have sometimes doubted whether, after all, it was actually made at Bennington — whether, indeed, it may not be one of the English pieces brought here and used as models. Yet its 'pedigree' seems unassailable. Pitchers of exactly the same pattern and design were made by S. Alcock & Co., the noted potters of Burslem, Staffordshire, and also, I believe, by T. R. Boote, of that city, but the same thing may be said of many of the Bennington pitchers. There is no denying the gracefulness and beauty displayed in this piece, or the exquisite workmanship. Yet the pitcher is heavily overburdened with ornament which detracts from its beauty and charm by distorting its outline. Above all, the ornamentation is in violent opposition to the nature of the material used and to the purpose for which the pitcher was intended.

The fine granular surface of Parian, like that of the marble it is designed to imitate, is easily soiled and difficult to clean. This is true even of the flat surfaces; of course, it is still more pronounced in the case of broken surfaces. When we come to high relief with extreme undercutting of vine leaves, the drawback is greatly intensified. It is almost impossible to clean such inaccessible places. Moreover, the sharp edges and points of the leaves catch in any cloth that is used for washing or drying them, and they are so delicate and fragile and break so easily as to warrant the statement that it is practically impossible to wipe them. A vase or pitcher so fashioned that it must be handled with painful and laborious care violates every sound principle of art. Whatever skill of design or execution it displays is worse than wasted. This pitcher is wholly unsuited to use as a pitcher, or to use of any kind; it is fitted only to be kept under a glass shade, like the old-fashioned wax flowers.

In justice to the Bennington potters, it should be said that they simply followed precedent in this sort of debasement of a really fine and beautiful porcelain. Parian had no sooner been introduced in England than its misuse began. Such pitchers as the one we have been discussing, and others which were even worse, were made by Copeland, Minton, Boote, Alcock, Rose, and others. Some of the pitchers and vases made in Parian by the English firms named, and others, are unspeakably hideous. Yet the same firms made statuettes and bas-reliefs of exquisite beauty. Writing of the English Parian exhibited at the New York Exhibition, in 1853, Silliman and Goodrich discussed this subject with great sincerity and a keen perception. I quote two typical paragraphs:

We are sorry to see this exquisite material, the happy substitute for marble in statuettes and works purely ornamental, misapplied and degraded by being moulded into jugs, cups, candlesticks, and all sorts of commonplace articles, of which there are so many to be seen in the exhibition.*

A small Parian bracket, which follows, in the Raffaelesque style, is a work in which beauty and propriety equally appear. We heartily wish that this fine material [Parian] had been altogether confined to purely ornamental objects like this, instead of being misapplied to ordinary table furniture, as has been done in the Tea Service, which, except for this fault, would be unexceptionable. The fine granular surface of Parian has a positive attraction for dirt, and we like not to be compelled to remember the inevitable impurities of Parian tea cups, butter dishes, and beer-jugs, in connection with the divine creations of art, fitly enshrined in the same material.†

At its best, the Parian Ware produced at Bennington was decidedly inferior to the best of the English Parian. No one who is familiar with the finest of Copeland's reproductions of classic sculpture will ever claim that anything done at Bennington approached them. At its worst, of course, the Bennington Parian was extremely crude in workmanship and dreadfully inartistic, possessing all the worst characteristics of the mid-Victorian degradation of taste, to which even Wedgwood and Copeland sometimes succumbed. The best work was done in statuary, the natural fitness of material and purpose being in itself an important element of successful achievement. The excellence of the bust of Fenton has already been noted. Excellent, also, are many of

* Silliman and Goodrich, *op. cit.*, p. 78.   † *Idem*, p. 94.

the little statuettes and figures, some of which are illustrated on Plate XIX. The Little Red Riding Hood, the Tight Shoe, the Child at Prayer, and the trinket box in the form of a book surmounted by a recumbent lamb, are beautiful examples of Bennington Parian, which are not only as fine as anything ever produced in this country, but worthy to be ranked with the best English work of the same class.*

THE MAKING OF PARIAN WARE: CASTING

It may be well to bring this discussion to a close with a brief account of the methods employed in the manufacture of Parian. At the outset it must be understood that this ware was never made by the 'throwing' process — that is, upon the potter's wheel. It was invariably moulded, either by the 'pressing' or the 'casting' process.

In casting, the materials are ground together and mixed with water to the consistency of liquid paint. This creamy liquid is called 'slip.' It is poured into hollow moulds made of plaster, the porousness of which insures the absorption of the water contained in the slip. As the water is thus absorbed and evaporated, the solid matter settles down and additional slip has to be poured in. When the mould is opened and the piece taken out, the next step is the addition of handles, ornaments, and so on.

The next process is firing. As it is of the highest importance to keep the article from being soiled by smoke or dust while in the kiln, this firing is done in large containers called 'seggars.' When the firing has been completed, the material is 'biscuit.' If a direct glaze is to be applied, that is the next process. If only a 'smear' glaze is required, the inside of the next seggar, in which the article is placed in the special

* The collector is reminded that most of these pieces, if not all of them, are found in the other types of hard-paste porcelain as well as in Parian. In such forms they generally lose much of their charm.

kiln used for glaze firing, is glazed. If Parian is wanted, this 'smear' glazing is reduced to almost nothing — to the merest suggestion, for the true Parian standard is a surface that has no visible glaze, yet to the touch suggests an imperceptible, dull polish, as though the granular, marble-like surface had been rubbed down.

Handles of pitchers, and the vine leaves and bunches of grapes, and similar ornaments, were not cast with the body, in the same mould, but separately, and were applied to the body by hand, before firing, while both body and the part or parts to be added were 'green.' In the case of statuettes and animal pieces, the base, torso, head, and principal members were all moulded and cast separately and then assembled before firing. This work required a high degree of skill, as may be readily imagined. The pitting of the surface of a background so that it would resemble the indented surface of a thimble, was accomplished in the mould, which had raised points on its surface, each point making an indentation.

THE MAKING OF PARIAN WARE: PRESSING

The 'pressing' process, which was largely confined to pitchers, vases, and similar articles, differed from the 'casting' process in that the slip was reduced to a state resembling dough. It was passed through fine cloth, allowed to settle and the water drawn off. This dough-like paste was then pressed by hand against the sides of the mould. The subsequent stages of the manufacture were identical with those already described.

Where a colored background was desired, the casting process was used. At Bennington, the color was not applied to the moulded body, either in the green state or in the biscuit, as many have supposed, and as was done in many places: the desired color was mixed with a certain quantity of slip which was then applied on the mould itself, to those parts which it was desired to color. This colored slip was carefully applied with a camel's-hair brush, after which the slip for the body was poured into the mould. The two materials would immediately unite by adhesion, yet without intermingling. Firing, of course, completed the union. A great deal of the blue porcelain with white Parian designs in relief which is found in the antique shops up and down the country, and frequently mistaken for Bennington, shows plainly enough that the blue was applied to the body, and is not a part of it. Much of it looks as if water-color paint, or kalsomine, had been applied to the biscuit and then fired. The colored porcelain of Bennington never has that appearance. Since the color was thoroughly mixed with the outer coating of slip — which is always of considerable thickness — the colored part gives much the appearance of penetrating the entire body of the ware except for the white inside glaze. This is one of the best tests to apply to the mass of blue-and-white porcelain on the market, offered — honestly in many instances — as Bennington Parian.

Let the amateur beware, however, for even this test is not absolute or infallible. The only safe course is to insist upon obtaining marked pieces of those patterns and designs which are known to have been marked — sometimes at least, if not always; and for the rest — in the case of patterns and designs which were not marked — to take expert advice or to require a detailed 'pedigree' which can be thoroughly investigated and checked up. Not ten per cent of the pitchers and vases in Parian, or in blue porcelain with white ornamentation, decorated with vine leaves and bunches of grapes, are Bennington, a widespread belief to the contrary notwithstanding. It is safe to say that virtually every pottery in this country and in England that made Parian and other porcelains at any time between 1842 and 1892 used this decoration more or less extensively.

SUPPLEMENTARY NOTE TO CHAPTER IV

The 'Wedgwood Mortar' Ware

This is perhaps the most fitting place to make record of another of the many interesting experiments made by Fenton, and of the high hopes which were entertained concerning it. The following extract is from an article published in the *Bennington Banner*, March 28, 1856, which was either written by Fenton or inspired by him:

We cannot enumerate in detail the multitude of different wares manufactured here, all of which are of exquisite delicacy and beauty, nor can we forego the mention of one more article of great value, and never before manufactured in this country. We refer to the Druggist or Wedgwood Mortar, some specimens of which were shown us at the factory. The body of these mortars is of a semi-vitrified compound, in which one portion remains infusible at the greatest heat to which they are exposed; while the other portion vitrifies at that heat, and enveloping the infusible part, produces a smooth, fine, compact body that will resist the action of all acids, and defy for endless ages the destroying hand of Time. We are glad to learn that these mortars are pronounced by the large importers of New York and Boston fully equal to those manufactured in England (France makes none) and have left their orders for large quantities of them, and we venture the prediction that in five years no more mortars will be used in America than are manufactured in America.

This speaks volumes for our friends, Fenton and Clark, who have accomplished in ten years what it took England ages to perform.

I had heard, years ago, that, at one time, the manufacture of mortars and pestles was carried on at the United States Pottery on a large scale, and that almost certain financial success had been generally predicted from this branch of manufacture. It was not until I read the article containing the foregoing paragraphs, however, that I determined to find one of these 'Wedgwood Mortars,' if possible. If there was one left in any attic or 'buttery' in New England, it must be found. Before long, my search was rewarded with success. A mortar and pestle, both perfect, with an indisputable 'pedigree' were found at a farmhouse near Bennington. Even if there had been no such pedigree, however, I believe that I should have been quite content, once I had heard the wonderful tones that resounded when the mortar was struck, bell fashion. It seemed impossible to believe that such strength and clarity of sound could emanate from any product of the potter's art. Comparison with many other mortars of the same general appearance left no doubt that here was something quite superior in quality. Obviously, it was a hard porcelain, too thick to be translucent (the ware is half an inch thick), but of a quality that, presumably, might be translucent in a thinner body. It seemed to be practically indestructible, and the hardest blows with the pestle did not injure it in the slightest degree.

Every collector who reads this will understand why I prized these homely articles more than some of the handsomest specimens in my collection. Of course, such pride had to be humbled; it invited the proverbial fall. One day, while displaying my collection to a good friend and neighbor, I beat a light tattoo upon the mortar with the pestle, using my left hand while arranging something on the shelves with my right hand. Without warning, and without my being aware of it even, until my friend called my attention to the fact, the mortar which was supposed to defy for endless ages the destroying hand of Time, lay in two pieces upon the rug. Repaired and wholly well-seeming, but silent, it now rests upon the shelf. What happened to my cherished prize was, in all probability, what had happened to many another of the vessels which the makers believed to be practically indestructible. Perhaps that was the reason why the glowing hopes expressed in the article quoted were never realized.

V

SOME OF THE BENNINGTON CRAFTSMEN

Decius W. Clark

IN any list of the craftsmen who were associated with the Fenton Potteries at Bennington the place of honor unquestionably belongs to Decius W. Clark. He was not only by far the ablest of the men who worked at Bennington; he was one of the most remarkable men ever connected with the pottery industry in this country. As already pointed out in an earlier chapter, a great deal of the credit usually bestowed upon Christopher Webber Fenton in reality belongs to Clark. From 1847, when the firm of Norton & Fenton was dissolved and Fenton went into business on his own account, until the winding-up of the United States Pottery Company, Clark was responsible for every formula used, both for bodies and for glazes. This fact was attested to by Christopher Webber Fenton on more than one occasion. In Bennington it was well known. This of itself would entitle Clark to a high place among American potters. That he was the real inventor of the Flint Enamel process patented by Fenton may be regarded as a moral certainty, even though direct proof is lacking.

He was a native of Vermont, having been born, in 1815, at Burlington, where his father was stationed in the service of the United States Government. The elder Clark was transferred to the Watervliet Arsenal and removed his family to West Troy, New York, while Decius was still a small boy. There was a stoneware pottery at West Troy, and here young Decius served an apprenticeship of seven years. As a young man, even before the completion of his apprenticeship, he acquired some reputation among his fellows for his skill as a potter and for the assiduity with which he studied the problems of his art. It is said that he was always reading and experimenting, and his knowledge of the chemistry of his craft gave him a place of recognized leadership among the potters of Troy and its vicinity. His advice was always sought when there were difficult problems to be solved, even the men from whom he had learned the rudiments of his trade deigning to consult him and to seek his advice and aid.

He was barely twenty years of age when he married, his wife, who was Miss Harriet Grace, belonging to one of the oldest and most highly respected families of Troy. He was twenty-five years of age when he came to Bennington with his wife and children. Young as he was, he had acquired such reputation as one of the best stoneware potters in the country and as a student of all pertaining to the pottery industry, that Julius Norton had sought him out and induced him to accept employment in the Norton Pottery.

Working there at the time were such men as Frank Norton, Frederick Hancock, and John Webb, acknowledged master-craftsmen, whose skill and achievements have become traditions. The fact that Decius W. Clark immediately assumed a position of leadership in such a group proves that he was a craftsman of far more than ordinary ability, and a man of character besides. But he possessed little or no artistic sense, and it is said by those who remember him well that he frequently lamented the fact that he could hardly draw a simple sketch to help elucidate his ideas.

His mind was peculiarly well fitted for investigation and research. He studied the properties of clays and experimented in the compounding of bodies and glazes. Intensely patriotic, he resented the dependence of this country upon Great Britain for china ware, and stoutly held that from our native clays could be made ware of every variety, equal to, if not surpassing, the British product. To use only the native clays, feldspar, flint, and ores was his inflexible determination. Helpless in the matter of designing and modelling, in every other branch of the industry he excelled.

His association with Fenton during many years has already been sufficiently described. From the time Fenton went into business on his own account, after separating from Julius Norton, to the date of his death, in 1865, Clark was always at his right hand. It was Clark who supervised the first experiments in porcelain-making by Norton & Fenton, compounding the bodies for the pieces modelled by John Harrison, working out the problems of firing, glazing, and so on. All through the vicissitudes of Fenton, Hall & Co., Lyman, Fenton & Co., the United States Pottery Company, and, later, A. A. Gilbert & Co., his was the brain that was always at work mastering the technical problems and evolving new and improved processes.

Between Clark and Fenton there existed a strong bond of attachment that was quite extraordinary, and that appears all the more remarkable when we consider how difficult it was for Fenton to form and hold intimate friendships with other men. Following the failure of the United States Pottery Company, strong efforts were made to persuade Clark to dissociate himself from Fenton, and to assume direction of a reorganization. Rightly or wrongly, it was felt locally that Fenton was the prime cause of the failure of the concern; that, as the local newspaper put it, he had dealt the enterprise a 'parricidal blow.' But the friendship of the two men, and their close association, could not be broken.

In the brief sketch of the attempts that were made to revive the United States Pottery, reference has been made to a patent which

Clark obtained in 1859 for a new process of enamelling. This invention was something of much larger significance than a mere enamel glaze for various kinds of crockery. As one reads the accounts of the invention in the newspapers of the period, and of the arrangements that were being made to use it in manufacturing, one is almost staggered by the magnitude of the conception and the boldness of the imagination displayed. Briefly stated, the invention applied not only to crockery, but also — and more especially — to building materials. Ordinary common red brick, terra-cotta, or stone could be given a coating of this enamel, which would make the surface perfectly smooth, hard, absolutely impervious to moisture, and incapable of being chipped or peeled off. It was unaffected by acids or by the most extreme changes of temperature. The enamel could be perfectly white, or it could be tinted any color by the use of metallic oxides.

The *New York Day Book* published in November, 1859, an exhaustive description of the new invention. A few extracts from this article will show how it was regarded by a responsible authority of the time:

The development . . . which we are about to describe, is the result of the persevering efforts of Messrs. D. W. Clark and C. W. Fenton of Bennington, Vt., in their determination to bring out an article of crockery made from American materials fully equal to the best productions of France and England, and which would neither craze nor check by use or exposure to atmospherical action; in the course of their recent experiments they fortunately hit upon a combination of metallic and mineral substances, which, in its effects, has more than met their most sanguine expectations not only in producing a perfect enamel for crockery ware, but is found to be equally fusible upon the most common red brick as well as almost every variety of stone, giving to either of these substances a perfectly smooth polished surface of the purest white, and which can be changed (by the use of metallic oxides) to any conceivable color desired, representing the color of anything in nature or art; and the same can be variegated to represent all kinds of marble, free-stone or granite. It is difficult to conceive of anything more beautiful or better adapted to the wants, tastes, and capacities of all.*

What this paper foresaw as a result of the invention amounted to nothing less than a revolution in the building trade. That the same view was entertained by the inventor himself, and by Fenton, his partner, there can hardly be any question. This appears not only from the publicity which they inspired, but equally from their plans. They proposed to use the new enamel not merely in manufacturing crockery for domestic purposes, but also in the manufacture of brick. Not only that, they arranged to license others to use the invention, themselves supervising the erection of the kilns. To all the firms licensed to use the patent, upon a royalty basis, Fenton and Clark were to furnish the enamel, prepared ready for use. They actually leased and bought up a large number of quartz and feldspar deposits and arranged contracts with no less than twenty-four mills to grind these materials. Some of the largest and most important brick manufacturers in the country secured licenses for the exclusive manufacture, in their respective districts, of building and ornamental architectural material. Such firms as J. Park & Co., the largest manufacturers of brick in New York, and Fisk & Ring, of Boston, one of the largest firms in New England, became licensees under Fenton and Clark for the use of the invention. Something of the vision of the inventor and of the hard-headed business men who manifested their confidence in its success may be gathered from the following additional paragraph from the *New York Day Book:*

Men of moderate means whose highest ambition may have been to possess an ordinary brick tenement, can, with but a trifling additional expense, live as it were, in a porcelain palace, in comparison with which, (for elegance) polished marble bears but a slight comparison. In an *economi-*

* Reprinted in the *Bennington Banner*, December 23, 1859.

cal point of view, it surpasses the most ordinary building material, from the fact that a slab or block of any size or shape, plain surface or carved, that can be moulded of common brick clay, can be enamelled in the most beautiful manner, with only the additional expense of immersing the article in the liquid enamel, and subjecting it to a low degree of heat for about six hours' duration to fuse, leaving a perfectly smooth and polished surface. Thus it will be seen that enamelled slabs of any desired color, such as gray, sky blue or straw color, &c. &c., must take the place of plastering and plain or gilded paper, and be as durable as the building itself, and always be clean, bright and beautiful. The mantels, table, bureau and stand tops, as well as complete toilet sets, can be made to correspond exactly with the color of the rooms or drapery. The outside of the building may be made equally elegant by taking common brick from any brickyard and enamelling them in the same manner, and which may be finished with a gloss or not at the will of the operator, while burning or managing the kilns.

The *Buffalo Republic* reprinted the article from the *Day Book*, together with a long editorial upon the subject. From the news columns of the same paper we learn that D. W. Clark and C. W. Fenton had arranged to visit Buffalo for the purpose of introducing the new invention, and that their visit was eagerly discussed in business circles. The editorial to which reference has been made said, in part:

The importance of the subject treated upon to the United States is almost incalculable. If, as the gentlemen say, and we have no reason to doubt the statements put forth, that they can manufacture brick and all manner of architectural work and cover it with a porcelain finish at a slightly advanced cost, from ordinary clay brick, it will at once produce a wonderful revolution in all our building operations. . . . They have already made arrangements in Boston, Providence and New York with the most extensive brick makers at those several points for the manufacture of all manner of building material. Thus it would seem that in a very short time we shall be able to see houses finished inside and out with this beautiful composition. We have not learned whether any one in this city has as yet secured a license for manufacturing the work in this section, but presume that some of our large brick-making concerns will lose no time in securing the right. It seems to us that its introduction here would open a very large field for enterprise and labor. It will give us great pleasure to welcome any project to our city that will give a new impulse to the manufacturing interests of our people, and hope in a short time to be able to chronicle an event of so much importance to every landholder in this city.*

The State Assayer of Massachusetts, Professor Charles T. Jackson, who was regarded as being perhaps the foremost chemical authority in the country, made a report upon the finished products made according to this invention which would seem to justify the high expectations of the newspapers. In a letter to the inventor, he wrote, on October 20, 1859:

I have examined and tested your Patent Enameled or Porcelain Faced Bricks, and find that the enamel is a fine, hard, opaque porcelain which imparts great strength to the brick or body to which it is applied — rendering it indestructible from the action of the elements, as the enamel resists all atmospheric causes of decomposition and disintegration, and that it cannot be peeled off by pressure or by frost, or by any exposure to the weather in any climate. . . . They must form a perfect security against the admission of moisture, and unlike marble, will never stain or fade, and will endure for ages without the slightest change or deterioration.

This enamel or porcelain facing can be tinted of any color desired, and may be successfully applied to any kind of bricks and to blocks for buildings, or for Tiles for Tessellated or Mosaic Pavements, as also for Table Tops, Mantels, and for various other furnishing and architectural materials, to which it imparts a beauty and brilliancy unrivalled.†

A more stupendous scheme was probably never conceived by any manufacturers of building material anywhere in the world. That it was not wholly visionary, but had a basis of sound and enduring merit, is evident from the fact that the leading firms of brick-makers, in various parts of the country, became licensees under the patent and actually went into the manufacture of the enamelled bricks. Despite the auspicious beginning, which seemed to insure success upon a

* The *Buffalo Republic*, December 3, 1859.
† Quoted in the article published in the *New York Day Book*.

national scale, and the apparent merit of the enamel itself, the scheme failed after a little while. As to what were the reasons for the failure, there seems to be no available evidence; at least, none is known to the present writer. Perhaps some research directed to that end would discover them. Clark himself never lost faith in the merit of his invention, and some years after the failure of the Peoria enterprise he started to manufacture his Patent Enamelled Brick at Croton, New York, and carried on the business for a few years.

In 1862 his wife died. She was the mother of a large family, eight children surviving both parents. Soon after her death, Clark announced his conversion to Christianity, and from that time onward was a devout Christian and active church member. He was married again, in 1875, in Chicago, his second wife being a Mrs. Margaret Morehouse. In 1876 he settled in Croton, New York, where he established a brick enamelling works, which he successfully carried on for some years. He died at Croton, April 1, 1887, in his seventy-second year.

Much of this sketch of the career of this remarkable craftsman has been devoted to the ambitious, but long forgotten, undertaking based upon his Patent Enamel; but mention, at least, should be made of the fact that his inventive genius found many other expressions. For example, he invented an enamelled retort for use in the manufacture of gas, which was of tremendous economic importance and value. That he was the profoundest student of the chemistry and physics of the pottery industry in America during his day, and perhaps at any time, is not too much to claim for him. He was self-taught, yet his scientific attainments were of a high order. A great craftsman, admired for the excellence of his work by men who themselves were great craftsmen, he was always unassuming and modest, and the old potters who as boys and young men worked under him have preserved a rich remembrance of his genial and kindly personality.

Daniel Greatbach

It is probable that for every collector of Bennington and other pottery who knows anything of Decius W. Clark there are a hundred to whom the name of Daniel Greatbach is familiar and well known. This is due, of course, to the fact that Greatbach's name is associated with some of the designs and models most sought after by collectors everywhere. While Decius W. Clark was incomparably the greater man, and there can be no comparison of their respective contributions to the pottery industry at Bennington, Greatbach achieved the wider popular fame. Although he was not a great designer and modeller, in the sense that Flaxman and Hackwood — whose names are associated with the greatest achievements of Wedgwood — were great designers and modellers, or even in the lesser sense that Josiah Jones, of Cartlidge & Co., of Greenpoint, New York, was a great designer and modeller, he was a man of marked ability who attained a national reputation. While his work was not remarkable for originality or for artistic distinction, it possessed the elements of popularity. Its quaintness, its whimsicality, and sometimes even its crudeness, made direct and instant appeal to a public possessed of no highly developed artistic taste; simple and kindly folk who were attracted by things that were 'just too cute for words.'

Like so many other potters who left their impress upon the pottery industry in this country, Daniel Greatbach was of English birth and ancestry and belonged to a family of famous pottery workers. In the history of the Staffordshire potteries the name Greatbach holds an ancient and honorable place. In the *Staffordshire Pottery Directory*, published in 1802, at Hanley, we find the name of James Greatbach, a potter at Shelton, and the same publication lists John Greatbach, dealer in earthenware, at Burslem, and Oliver Greatbach, oven-builder at the same place. When, in 1754, Josiah Wedgwood entered into partnership with Thomas Whieldon, at Little Fenton, or Fenton Low, as it was more often called, among their early apprentices were four youths who were destined to achieve eminent position among English potters. These four apprentices were Josiah Spode, William Greatbach, Robert Garner, and Uriah Sutton. Associated with great masters, each of these youths became himself a great craftsman and left his name indelibly impressed upon the history of his industry.

When his apprenticeship to Whieldon and Wedgwood was finished, William Greatbach set up in business for himself, at Fenton. He made wares of superb quality, specimens of which are still extant and are highly cherished. He made the famous tea-pots upon which was printed in black the 'History of the Prodigal Son,' engraved by Thomas Radford, a famous engraver of the time. He also made the 'World in Planisphere' mugs, the design by Radford being reproduced by the transfer-printing process. But William Greatbach failed in business, owing, it is said, to the dishonesty of a business associate, though I do not know of any detailed authority for the statement. As soon as the failure became known, Josiah Wedgwood went to his former apprentice, whose skill he had long admired, and entered into a most remarkable agreement with him. This was to the effect that Wedgwood was to pay Greatbach five shillings a day for the rest of his life, and provide him with a good house and garden free of rent, regardless of whether he worked or not, provided that anything he designed or modelled should be the exclusive property of Wedgwood. Five shillings a day in addition to house and garden free of rent was a high wage for that period, and the agreement shows how highly Josiah Wedgwood esteemed the work of his old pupil and apprentice. The agreement was faithfully kept on both sides until Greatbach's death. It is unfortunate that identification of the Wedgwood productions which were designed and modelled by William Greatbach should be almost wholly a matter of guesswork and inference.

This William Greatbach was the grandfather of Daniel Greatbach. The latter came to this country about 1839, and went to work as a modeller at the works of the American Pottery Manufacturing Company, Jersey City, where, since 1825, excellent work had been done. The Jersey City Porcelain and Earthenware Company, established in 1825, was, in 1826, awarded the silver medal of the Franklin Institute for 'the best china from American materials.' In 1829, the works were purchased by D. and J. Henderson, who made 'flint stoneware' of a high quality. After various changes of ownership and management, when Greatbach arrived, the concern had become the American Pottery Manufacturing Company. He was then in the prime of life. He had been previously employed as a modeller by the famous English potters, the Ridgways.

At Jersey City, Greatbach made what I believe to have been the first of the many varieties of pitchers having a dog's body for handle which became so popular all over the United States, and which toward the middle of the nineteenth century were made by so many potteries. Of course, he was not the original creator of this general design. Pitchers with handles in the form of a dog's body had been made in England long before, most of the leading Staffordshire firms having adopted the general idea. The Wedgwoods had one, modelled, according to tradition at least, by William Greatbach soon after he had entered the service of Josiah Wedgwood. The Doultons made a hound-handled pitcher that was very popular. Another was made by the Ridgways, and so on. The latter firm also used the body of a fox for a handle. There is some reason, indeed, to believe that the proto-type of all pitchers of this general type displayed the body of a fox as a handle. The association of the grapes in the border design with the hunting scene on the sides lends plausibility, at least, to this theory.

The hound-handled pitcher which Greatbach designed and modelled at Jersey City differs in several important particulars from the one he made at Bennington some years later. It is, I think, far inferior to the latter. The general features of the two designs do not differ greatly, but the shape of the Bennington pitcher is the better, while its model-ling is greatly superior. The hound on the Bennington pitcher is more striking, mainly owing to the manner in which the head is arched and raised above the paws. As a matter of fact, however, in neither case is the dog anything better than a travesty. Neither bears any resem-blance to any breed of dog known to mankind. In the Jersey City model, the 'hound' is a mere impressionistic sketch; in the Benning-ton model, the modelling is more ambitious and detailed, but the result bears no semblance to a real dog. It is more like some sort of serpen-tine creature around the head, while the body with its sharp edge all along the under-side is an anatomical absurdity. If one were to gather together a representative collection of the many varieties of dog-handled pitchers made in this country — to say nothing of the Eng-lish — he would find several which are markedly superior to either of these Greatbach creations.

At Jersey City, Greatbach also designed and modelled a number of Toby jugs and mugs. He designed and modelled the Apostle pitcher made by the American Pottery Company, having raised fig-ures of the Apostles in panels, and being an adaptation of one made by the Ridgways, which Greatbach may or may not have executed at an earlier date, when employed by that firm. In many respects, the finest work he did for the Jersey City firm, and perhaps in his entire career in this country, was a tea-set in Cream Ware, with floral decorations in relief. While the several pieces were greatly over-ornamented, after the fashion of that day, they were excellent in shape, and the floral design was in itself pleasing and well executed.

Barber says that 'In 1852, Mr. Greatbach entered into partnership with James Carr and commenced the manufacture of pottery at South Amboy, New Jersey, but this connection only lasted about a year. Greatbach went to Peoria, Illinois, where Mr. George Wolfe ... found him in 1861.' * This account is erroneous in some respects, at least. It is as certain as anything can be that Greatbach was not in partnership with James Carr at South Amboy during the year 1852–53. During the whole of that period he was residing in Bennington, and it is possible that he was there somewhat earlier. He modelled many of the pieces which were exhibited by the United States Pottery Company at the New York Exhibition, in 1853, including the great monumental piece which formed the center of the firm's exhibit. He was working upon this in the latter part of 1852 and the first months of 1853. On the other hand, James Carr had another partner at the period mentioned. When Carr left the Jersey City firm, in 1852, he went to South Amboy and took the Swan Hill Pottery. As Barber correctly states, on another page,† his partner in that enterprise was Thomas Locker. That partnership lasted just a year, and until October, 1853, when Carr left South Amboy and opened a pottery in New York City, where his partner was one Morrison. The firm of Morrison and Carr became famous for its majolica. It is quite pos-

* Barber, *op. cit.*, pp. 438–39.   † Barber, *op. cit.*, p. 178

sible that Greatbach was at South Amboy for a few weeks, at most; it is probable that he made some models for Carr, which were used at South Amboy during the year of the association of Carr and Locker. Barber's account passes over eight or nine years of the most fruitful period of Greatbach's life and then says that 'Mr. George Wolf . . . found him, in 1861,' at Peoria. It would have been equally correct to have said that it was Greatbach who found Wolf.

The facts are that, from 1852 to the spring of 1858, Greatbach was residing at Bennington and was employed by the United States Pottery Company as chief designer and modeller. He went with Decius W. Clark and Christopher Webber Fenton to Kaolin, South Carolina, and worked there for a brief period. After that he went to Peoria and joined with his old friends and employers. That was late in 1859 or at the beginning of 1860. He was so employed when he was 'found' by Mr. George Wolf.

At Bennington, Greatbach modelled, in addition to the pieces already mentioned, a whole series of Toby mugs and bottles. (Plate XI.) The Franklin Toby, with a handle in the shape of a man's leg and foot, is an adaptation of a larger Franklin mug made at Jersey City. The one with the grapevine handle is, except for the handle, almost a copy of a Toby jug in pink lustre made in Staffordshire, England, and quite popular during the latter part of the first half of the nineteenth century. The 'Coachman' and 'Monk' bottles were principally used in saloon bars for whiskey. The 'Duke of Wellington' Toby is perhaps the least common of all. It is sometimes called the 'John Stark' Toby by country people in Vermont. For a long time I did not believe that this model was ever made at Bennington, but in the course of my investigations discovered what seems to be indisputable evidence of my mistake. Not the least convincing of the circumstances which forced me to change my opinion was the fact that a laborer digging near the Graded School, where waste from the old pottery had been used for filling in, dug up a piece of ware in the biscuit state, which was undoubtedly the lower half of one of these Duke of Wellington Toby mugs, the epaulettes and the high military collar plainly showing. Charles Kimball, who worked in the United States Pottery, said that these Wellington mugs were made there, but not in large numbers.

There is every reason to believe that Greatbach modelled the famous 'Bennington Lions,' though positive evidence to that effect is lacking. Dr. S. R. Wilcox, who worked at the United States Pottery in his youth, while only vaguely remembering Greatbach himself, remembered that old-time potters always spoke of the lions as having been modelled by Greatbach. William G. Leake, who retains a vivid memory of Greatbach, likewise 'always understood' that the latter modelled the lions. Charles Kimball, who as a lad was 'jigger-turner' for Greatbach, and remembered him quite well, said that he knew that Greatbach modelled the Toby mugs and bottles, and, while he did not see the master at work upon the lions, he recollected that shop gossip credited Greatbach with their design. Kimball also attributed the Cow-Creamer to Greatbach. In neither case can any originality of conception or design be credited to Greatbach. The Bennington cream-pitcher in the form of a cow is an exact reproduction of a familiar English model, which has little to commend it except a certain naïve quaintness.

The lions were made in two quite distinct types, each of which was made both with a base and without. In every case the lion has one of its forepaws resting upon a ball. One type of lion has a curly mane smoothly glazed like the rest of the body. This is generally supposed to represent a lioness. The other type has a rough mane in the so-called 'cold-slaw' effect, having the appearance of rough-cast plaster. It is precisely like the mane of the poodle dog carrying the basket of fruit. The lions on bases are generally — but not always — marked; those not mounted on bases are never marked.

These lions are sometimes finished in Rockingham, and sometimes in Flint Enamel with the usual metallic coloring of that glaze. (Plates I and XXXVIII.) If Greatbach modelled these animals, he copied from English models. The Whieldon lions are well known. Both the types described were quite extensively made in England, and I can quite well remember seeing them in many English homes when I was a boy. Many old potters who came originally from England have confirmed my recollection in this respect.

Some years ago a lion on a base, with the rough cast, or 'cold-slaw' mane, was identified by several of the best-known collectors of Bennington ware, as being 'Bennington beyond any question.' Yet that particular beast had been brought from Staffordshire, England, by its owners, and there was not the slightest shadow of doubt that it had been made there. Not only was it identical with the Bennington lion in appearance, but in its dimensions. The amateur collector, therefore, will do well to regard unmarked lions with some skepticism and to seek expert advice before purchasing any of them. This advice is proffered, not alone because of such incidents as the one related, but because, within a period of about eighteen months, I have been offered, on two separate occasions, 'Bennington' lions which, most certainly, were never made at Bennington.

Other animal pieces modelled by Greatbach while at Bennington include the large Recumbent Cow and the two deer, Stag and Doe, recumbent, each upon a separate base. All three pieces, which rank among the best that Greatbach ever modelled, are copied from English originals. The Bennington pieces differ from their prototypes, however, in the nature of the material of their bodies and also in the coloring. There is no likelihood of confusing English and American pieces of this description; nor should there be difficulty in identifying them. Even when the Bennington pieces are unmarked — which is rare in the case of these animals — they may be quite readily identified.

In all probability Greatbach did not model the famous Bennington Dog Carrying a Basket of Fruit. According to Charles Kimball, it was gossip of the shop, even while Greatbach was working there, that the original models for this pair of dogs, right and left, were made by John Harrison, and that they were intended to be made in white porcelain. When the fire of 1845 caused the abandonment of the Bennington experiments in porcelain-making, and the return of Harrison to England, the moulds were laid aside, no satisfactory pieces having been made from them up to that time. Later, during the time of Lyman, Fenton & Co., the Harrison moulds were brought out and Parian dogs successfully made from them. It was then decided to produce the dogs in Rockingham and the patent Flint Enamel. This required some modification of the design in order to secure good results in glazing; the top of the dogs' heads in front was flattened and the peak in the center of the head common to the Parian dogs done away with. Comparison of the pictures of the two types will illustrate this point quite clearly. In support of this bit of tradition, which is given for what it is worth, it may be pointed out that there are some features of the modelling of the basket of fruit carried by these Bennington dogs which are identical with certain features of the one definitely authenticated example of Harrison's modelling that we have. Occasionally, one finds a Parian dog to which a mustache has been added, giving it a grotesque appearance. Such additions were inspired by the whimsical humor of individual potters, who made such pieces for themselves or their friends, not for the trade. (Plate XXXI.)

It is noteworthy that Charles Kimball did not, and William G. Leake does not, agree with the description of Greatbach given by both Barber and Pitkin. Barber says that he was 'large and handsome in appearance,' * and Pitkin quotes Mr. Henry S. Gates, of Chicago, formerly of Bennington, as saying that 'Daniel Greatbach was inclined to be a recluse. . . . He was about sixty years old and weighed about two hundred and forty pounds.' † Kimball knew Greatbach well.

As his 'jigger-man' he worked with him and under his immediate direction for years. He knew all the moods of the older man, to whose beck and call he was subject. Many years afterward he could mimic the voice, gestures, and gait of the man, whom, by the way, he almost worshipped. As Kimball remembered him, Greatbach was small in stature, well below the average height, and weighed not more than a hundred and forty-five or fifty pounds. Too fond of 'lifting the glass,' as Kimball expressed it, Greatbach was anything but a recluse. He was what is termed 'a good mixer,' fond of chatting with people on the streets and elsewhere. A man of highly convivial habits, he was a regular attendant at a local bar-room where the potters gathered in the evenings, and there he used to sit night after night, delighting in telling stories and singing songs.

Leake remembers Greatbach as a man about five feet five inches in height, weighing about ten stone — one hundred and forty pounds. He was an exceptionally small-boned man, with notably small and graceful hands and feet. Always fastidious in his appearance, he was

* Barber, *op. cit.*, p. 439.   † Pitkin, *op. cit.*, p. 33.

as neat as the proverbial new pin. He invariably wore a tall silk hat on the street, even when going to and from his work. His appearance was more like that of a minister than a mechanic. Leake also says that Greatbach was a delightfully sociable man; that he was always 'one of the boys.' His regular attendance at the bar-room and his conviviality were well known. In all respects the accounts of Charles Kimball and William G. Leake tally, and, in turn, they agree with the local tradition that Greatbach had his own seat in the bar-room and was one of the leading spirits in organizing evening rides to a well-known drinking-place some miles away, from which most of the potters returned in hilarious mood.

I find these recollections of the man by those who knew him well, who saw him daily for years, and who, regarding him as an extraordinary man, would be likely to retain exceedingly distinct impressions of his appearance and personality, far more convincing than the picture quoted by Pitkin. Somehow, the idea of a recluse does not harmonize with Greatbach's work. At least, I find it impossible to believe that the creator of those Toby mugs and bottles, quaint and whimsical as they are, was a recluse, or indeed, anything other than a 'good fellow.'

After the failure of the Fenton and Clark enterprise at Peoria, Greatbach went to East Liverpool for a time, and while there he worked for a short time for William Bloor, I believe. Apparently he removed to Trenton, New Jersey, at the end of 1864 or the beginning of 1865, for his name appears for the first time in *Lant's Directory of Trenton for 1865-66*, in which he is described as a 'Designer,' residing on Kossuth Street. By that time he had fallen upon evil days. Always an improvident man, old age found him in dire poverty. Mr. Joseph Lawton, one of Trenton's oldest potters, gives the following information:

Upon returning from the Civil War, I was employed as mould maker at the pottery of William Young & Sons in this city. During that year, which I believe was 1866, Mr. William Young, deceased, employed Daniel P. Gretbech, an expert modeller. His work was the finest that I have ever seen. I made moulds from his creations. He had a daughter. I believe that she was married in this city. Gretbech was an old man at this time. His manner and make-up were very refined. In fact, he impressed me as a man who had seen better days — a man of polish and knowledge who apparently was up against it — Gretbech at last disappeared. To the best of my recollection he went to the poorhouse and was buried in the paupers' cemetery.*

Mr. Lawton's memory of the old modeller is that he was 'rather tall' and of 'medium build,' which varies from other descriptions already quoted. Another old potter, Mr. John P. Beech, remembers that, for a time, Greatbach worked in Trenton at the John Maddock Pottery. The vital records of Trenton do not, apparently, contain any record of his death. Mr. Harry J. Podmore, to whose researches I am indebted for practically all that I have been able to discover concerning Greatbach's closing years in Trenton, tells me that the present Poormaster has informed him that it is hardly likely that Greatbach's death would be placed upon any city or State record if he died in the poorhouse, as no records of pauperism were kept at that time. Presumably, then, Greatbach died in the Trenton Poorhouse and was buried in the old Paupers' Cemetery, of which not a trace has been left, the entire tract of land which it occupied having been built over long ago. Thus in complete obscurity ended the career of the best-known of all the men who worked at the United States Pottery.

Partly because some of the pieces most sought after by collectors of Bennington pottery are associated with his name, Greatbach has been greatly overrated and the merits of his work have been exagger-

* I have reproduced Mr. Lawton's spelling of Greatbach's name. I know of no authority for the middle initial 'P.' The surname was frequently spelt 'Gretbetch,' 'Gretback,' 'Gretbech,' etc.

ated. He has been acclaimed as a great genius — frequently by persons who should know better. He was no genius, though his talent was unquestionable. He lacked originality, but he was a competent modeller. Nothing that he designed may be said to possess great and distinctive artistic merit; and not a little that he produced was commonplace. Yet it must be admitted that, in general, his work was well executed. If he was not a great creative artist, he was at least a craftsman of more than ordinary skill, and he possessed the integrity and devotion to ideals which all the great master craftsmen have possessed. He left the mark of his personality upon the products of the Bennington pottery, whose merit is in no small measure due to his fine craftsmanship.

In judging the work of Greatbach, and his place in our ceramic history, we must always bear in mind what the Bennington potteries were, and what they were intended to be. They were manufactories for the production of the domestic wares used by a simple people, and of such homely ornaments as such a people could appreciate and afford. To compare these products with the rare and costly specimens produced for rich patrons by Wedgwood, the Worcester Porcelain Company, Duesbury, and other noted English makers, would be extremely foolish. These latter firms employed the greatest artists of their day to make designs, and for individual pieces they sometimes received prices which to-day seem almost incredible. Yet even high prices did not always cover the cost of production. Josiah Wedgwood paid Webber twenty-five hundred dollars for modelling a copy of the famous Barberini vase belonging to the Duchess of Portland. From this model fifty vases were made. They sold at fifty guineas each. In other words, for the entire output Wedgwood received just what he had paid for the modeller's work alone — counting as nothing the enormous expense of manufacture, including numerous experiments.

It is not with such enterprise that we must compare the work of the Bennington potters. Greatbach was not a Webber. The Bennington pottery directed and inspired by Christopher Webber Fenton and Decius W. Clark must be judged by quite different standards. We must see it as the courageous and sincere attempt of American craftsmen to raise the standards of an important industry; to make its products more attractive and pleasing to the eye without sacrifice of utility; to make it dependent upon American materials only; and, finally, to establish for American workmen standards of excellence hitherto rarely attempted. Daniel Greatbach was a leading figure in that experiment.

ENOCH WOOD

Enoch Wood, who worked at the United States Pottery for some years, was a mould-maker. He was descended from a long line of famous English potters. His great-grandfather was the brother of Ralph Wood, of Newcastle, Staffordshire, father of the famous designer and modeller, Enoch Wood, who is so often called 'The Father of English Pottery.' It was after this great English potter, whose beautiful border designs encircling American historical and scenic pictureware are so greatly prized by collectors, that the American Enoch Wood was named. One of the uncles of the latter was Thomas Wood, of the firm of Wood and Challinor, of Tunstall; another uncle was John Wood, long identified with the firm of Copeland, of Stoke-on-Trent, and one of the most brilliant china painters of his day; another uncle was Hugh Wood, a successful English engraver. Josiah Wedgwood was related to the Wood family.

Enoch Wood came to Bennington as a young man and worked at

the United States Pottery, as a mould-maker. He was regarded as one of the most skillful workers of his day in that branch of the industry. He left Bennington in 1853 or 1854, and went to South Norwalk, Connecticut, where he was employed by a potter named Wheeler, whose daughter he subsequently married. About 1857 or 1858, he purchased a half-interest in the business and with his brother-in-law for partner carried it on for some time. He served in the Northern Army during the Civil War and attained the rank of Captain. After the War, the pottery at South Norwalk having been destroyed by fire in the meantime, he became the superintendent of the Hall Pottery at Perth Amboy, New Jersey. Here he went in for the manufacture of Scroddled Ware upon a large scale, but, finding that style unpopular and unsaleable, he soon turned to the manufacture of Rockingham Ware, producing numerous pitchers and Toby mugs which are frequently mistaken for Bennington, even by careful and discriminating collectors. Captain Enoch Wood was held in high repute by the potters of his day. By all accounts, he was a conscientious and highly skilled artisan who strove to live up to the traditions of his family.

STEPHEN THEISS

Stephen Theiss was a designer and modeller who worked at the United States Pottery from 1850 to its suspension in 1858. He was a native of Mons, Belgium, and came to the United States in 1848, at the age of twenty-four years. Before Greatbach joined the staff of the United States Pottery, Theiss was its chief designer and modeller. Greatbach, however, when he came, was given the chief position and Theiss was placed under him. Unlike Greatbach, Theiss had mastered every department of his trade, and could mix bodies and glazes, make moulds, 'throw' or cast, or set kilns. It was said of him that he was one of the best 'all around men' employed at the United States Pottery. When the latter suspended operations, he was one of the group of workmen who formed the joint stock company that for a short time operated the pottery at West Troy. He lost practically all his savings in that enterprise. Later on, he was one of those who undertook to re-start the United States Pottery. From Bennington he went to South Amboy, New Jersey, and thence to Worcester, where he worked for Norton & Hancock. At a still later time he was employed as foreman in the pottery of J. Jefford, in Philadelphia.

THÉOPHILE FREY

Théophile Frey was a Frenchman, who entered the employment of the United States Pottery Company in 1849 and remained in Bennington until the close of 1859. Turning over the files of the local newspapers of the period, one soon discovers that Frey was one of the most popular men connected with the pottery, and the old potters so remember him. He was regarded as one of the most expert china decorators in the country, perhaps the most expert; and one is forced to the conclusion that the wares produced at Bennington did not afford him an opportunity to do his best work.

Before coming to Vermont, Frey had been employed for twelve years as a decorator at the Sèvres Porcelain Works in France. He is said to have had a collection of specimens of Sevres porcelain, decorated by himself, which was greatly admired, the beauty and richness of many of the pieces frequently forming the topic for conversations among the workmen at the pottery and among the townspeople in general. Frey was an ardent Freemason, a member of Mount Anthony Lodge, F. & A. M., and was much given to political discussion, his radical views sometimes astonishing the more conservative. When Fenton and Clark opened up their Peoria factory, at the end of 1859, it had been planned that Frey should accompany them, and the fact that he was to do so was duly announced in the local press. It appears, however, that he changed his mind at the last moment, and went to Trenton, New Jersey, instead. Although the tradition that he was a great artist survives to this day, I do not know of any example of his work which can be regarded as particularly notable. The decorated pitchers which have survived show competent workmanship but no more; they display neither originality of design, nor any trace of superlative talent.

MEN FROM STAFFORDSHIRE

Among the workmen who came from Staffordshire were William Hollins, William and Charles Leake, John Sedman, Leonard Wray, William Umpleby and William Maddock — all pressers; Enoch Barber, John Leigh, mould-makers; Joseph Tunicliff, James Baker and William Wray, turners; Enoch Lear and John Caldwell, Jr., throwers; James Caldwell, slip maker; John Caldwell, clay maker; Joseph Alsop, John Molds, William Anderson, Richard Moon, William Seabridge, William Owens and Thomas Platt, all kiln-pacers. This list is not complete; it is merely given as representative of the English workmen who were employed at Bennington, and to show in how large a measure the working force was recruited from the Staffordshire potteries.

Some of the men mentioned in this list were artisans whose work was of such quality that their fame endured long after them. Enoch Barber is an example. Until a few years ago, whenever old potters gathered together and indulged in reminiscent talk the skill of Enoch

Barber was almost certain to be spoken of. William Leake was another whose skill was long celebrated. I have a small collection of pieces modelled and made by him at Elizabeth, New Jersey, when he and his son, W. G. Leake, were in partnership with L. B. Bierbower, under the firm name of Bierbower & Co. These show that Leake must have been a potter of uncommon ability and skill. His photograph frames in flint enamel, wonderful in coloring, greatly excel anything in the same line that was made at Bennington. His vases, too, beautifully modelled and richly colored with cobalt blue, are most effective. A napkin ring in black and gold, with a floral design in colors, is as fine as anything of the kind ever produced at any American pottery.

NATIVE VERMONTERS

Among the native Vermonters employed at the United States Pottery, Decius W. Clark, of course, stood head and shoulders above all the rest. Enoch Moore, foreman; William Wells, Byron Sibley, William and Henry Moore, John Keough, Thomas A. Hutchins, Rufus Godfrey, Charles Kimball, Thomas Cullien, Daniel and Patrick McGuire, Augustus Danforth, Charles and Dwight Riddle, Silas R. Wilcox and Charles Sanford — these are a few of the names of Bennington men who were employed at the United States Pottery at one time or another.

The ideal of Christopher Webber Fenton and Decius W. Clark was the maintenance of a wholly American industry — native workmen, using native materials and supplying the American market. The employment of foreigners was, to them, an unavoidable evil to be continued only until the industry had established itself, and had trained enough competent native workmen to carry it on without foreign assistance. They would not use foreign clays;* they looked forward to the time when only American skill would be required.

* Pitkin says — apparently quoting Mrs. Emmons — that a large amount of the clay used at the United States Pottery was brought 'as ballast in ships from abroad.' (*Op. cit.*, p. 39.) I have made careful inquiry into this matter and have not been able to find a single fact to support the statement. Fenton and Clark continually emphasized the fact that they did not use foreign clays, but native clays exclusively. This statement was often published in the local press and never challenged; it was also repeatedly made in the press of New York and other cities. I am convinced, therefore, that the statement about the use of foreign clays is incorrect, so far as the United States Pottery is concerned. Old Vermonters often used the word 'abroad' to indicate other states in the Union!

VI
BENNINGTON MARKS
A. Norton & Fenton Marks

NORTON & FENTON
East Bennington, Vt.

T HE two marks, shown here in reduced size, occur on stone-ware and Rockingham from 1845 to 1847. Neither is to be considered prior to the other.

B. Fenton Marks
1. fenton's works

This raised medallion with impressed lettering was used by Fenton from the summer of 1847 until late in 1848. He used it when he was in business alone and during his brief partnership with Henry Hall in the firm of Fenton, Hall & Co. The mark is found upon many of the white porcelain pitchers, and is not at all rare. It is interesting to note that the mark itself, both in design and general appearance, is remarkably like the mark used by a well-known English firm of the period — Jones & Walley, of Cobridge — some of whose designs Fenton seems to have appropriated.

II. LYMAN FENTON & CO.

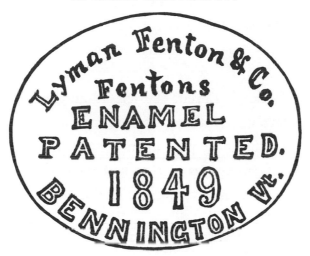

This is the familiar *1849* stamp that is found impressed on so many pieces of Rockingham and Flint Enamel. The misuse of this mark, and the resulting confusion, have been discussed in the preceding pages. It was first used late in 1849, and, notwithstanding the fact that the partnership of Lyman and Fenton was dissolved before the end of 1852, the use of the mark was continued, apparently, for some six years afterward — to the end of the business, in fact. It may well be, however, that its use from 1852 onward was occasional and limited, and that this fact accounts for the large number of pieces of Rockingham and Flint Enamel that are found unmarked.

III — U.S.P.

This mark came into use in 1852, at the time of Lyman's withdrawal. As noted in the text, the name 'United States Pottery' — and even 'United States Pottery Company' — was used some time before the incorporation of the United States Pottery Company. At the time when the business was carried on under the firm name of O. A. Gager & Co. the name 'United States Pottery' was applied to the works.

The 'ribbon mark' is raised, the letters and numerals being impressed. These latter are often quite obscure and even illegible. This mark is found for the most part upon porcelain pitchers and vases, including Parian. The figures at the right-hand side denote the pattern number; those on the left the size of the pitcher.

IV. UNITED STATES POTTERY CO.

This raised ornamental medallion appears to have been adopted in 1853, at the time of the incorporation of the United States Pottery Company. It is found upon porcelain pitchers, and, I believe, nowhere else. The lettering is, of course, impressed. This mark was in the mould, and could not be used upon any except 'cast' pieces.

V. UNITED STATES POTTERY CO.

This elliptical impressed stamp is found upon much of the Scroddled Ware. More rarely it is found upon pieces of Rockingham or Flint Enamel — including book-shaped bottles or flasks. Because it was in the form of a stamp, which could be impressed into any clay surface, while 'green,' its use was not limited to 'cast' pieces as was that of the raised marks.

VI. A. A. GILBERT & CO.

VII. NEW ENGLAND POTTERY CO., BENNINGTON

So far as I know, there is not a single specimen in any known collection containing either of the two foregoing marks. But because more or less circumstantial accounts of pieces bearing such marks have been current for some time, this notation is made with all due reserve.

VIII. T. A. HUTCHINS & CO.

This is the mark used for a brief time, after the failure of the United States Pottery Company, by the last of the successors of the concern. It has no significance and seems to have been used almost — if not quite — exclusively upon cuspidors.

APPENDICES

APPENDIX I

IDENTIFICATION HINTS

Cow-Creamers

THERE are many types of 'cow-creamers,' closely resembling those made at Bennington, and representing the product of many different potteries. The fact that none of those made at Bennington was ever marked, and the further fact that this fact applies to cows of almost every other make, renders identification exceedingly difficult.

The true Bennington cow is quite plump — rather bloated, in fact. Reject those with extremely prominent ribs. In the genuine Bennington cow the ribs are plainly indicated in the modelling, and are often emphasized by the coloring, but in passing the finger over the side of the cow the ribs, while perceptible, do not give the impression of marked corrugations. Reject the cows with blurred and poorly modelled eyes: in the genuine Bennington type the eyes are always well-modelled, clear and open. The nostrils should be well marked by crescent shaped indentations. The folds in the skin below the neck are clearly shown.

Disregard variations in color, mottling, and so forth, but beware of those cows which are in a single tone, either light or dark, without the mottled effect. Slight variations in size occur (mainly due to differences in the shrinkage of the clay according to its quality, degree of wetness, and so on) and should be disregarded.

Toby Mugs

There are several types of Rockingham Toby mugs which are sometimes mistaken for Bennington ware. As more than ninety per cent of the known Bennington Toby mugs are unmarked, it is well to be on guard. In all cases, the Bennington Toby mugs are almost flat at the bottom, whereas the most commonly encountered 'spurious' type has a concaved space underneath in which a good sized ball can be set. Notwithstanding that such pieces may be offered with a Bennington history — perhaps authentic and offered in good faith — they are certainly *not* Bennington pottery and should be rejected by the collector.

Dogs

In view of the fact that (except for the small paper-weights) none of the dogs made at Bennington was ever marked, it may be well to warn the collector against various types of dogs, in Rockingham glaze as a rule, but sometimes also in Parian and in 'Flint Enamel,' with touches of color. Such beasts are frequently offered as 'Bennington.' None of the dogs in a sitting posture, without bases, and none of those with bases (sometimes called 'Door Stops') was ever made at Bennington.

Hound-Handle Pitchers

Never marked. There are so many types of hound-handle pitchers in Rockingham glaze, some of which are frequently mistaken for the Bennington model, that the following points, which make sure identification possible, should be remembered:

The belly of the hound should have a pronounced ridge, instead of being flat or well rounded as in almost every other type. Note also the head of the hound: under the chin, and between it and the paws there is a space large enough to put the tip of the little finger through. The nose of the hound is really more like a duck's bill than a dog's nose. The collar of the hound is in the form of a chain, with the links clearly showing — not a band as in most other models. There is a border of grapevines, with fruit, around the top, a stag hunt on one side and a boar hunt on the other. The hound-handle pitcher with game on the sides, and the one with fish, are *not* Bennington.

Parian and Other Porcelain Figures

Various small ornamental figures in Parian and 'Smear' glazed porcelain, having letters and numbers impressed in the back (and in some cases on the bottom) have found their way into some of the best collections of Bennington pottery. It may be taken for granted, however, that these are not 'Bennington.' They are mostly foreign — English and German. Dr. S. R. Wilcox, who, as a young man, was employed in the United States Pottery making Parian ware, has assured me that 'No such letters or numbers were ever used at the pottery'; that when one of these 'foreign pieces' was copied, 'all distinguishing numbers and letters were eliminated in the mold.'

'Scroddled' or 'Lava' Ware

With only two exceptions, so far as I have been able to discover, the collector will do well to insist upon the small elliptical impressed mark (No. 6) on this ware. The exceptions are the so-called 'Tulip' vases with scalloped top, and the cow-creamers. These were undoubtedly made at the United States Pottery, but not for the general market. Apparently, they were made by workmen as 'individual' pieces. They were not marked. I have not been able to discover any evidence that they were made in other American potteries. The vases were, however, made in a number of English potteries. On the other hand, while there is no evidence that door-knobs, door-plates, or photograph frames were made at Bennington of this ware, there is abundant evidence that they were made, in considerable quantity, at Perth Amboy. Much — probably *most* — of the unmarked 'Scroddled' ware on the market was made at other potteries than Bennington. The exceedingly light colored 'Scroddled' ware, having little of the dark waving lines, should be especially regarded with suspicion and, if unmarked, rejected.

BLUE AND WHITE PORCELAIN

The unmarked vases and pitchers (especially vases) in this ware should be carefully investigated. Designs and patterns are not helpful here; indeed, reliance upon these will lead the amateur collector far astray. The same designs and patterns were used in scores of potteries, both American and English. The collector is referred to the description of this ware in the body of the book and warned to reject all pieces, no matter what claims may be made for them, in which the blue is thin and has the appearance of having been applied to the white after the drying or firing of the latter. A careful examination of a good marked specimen in comparison with one of these inferior pieces will show the great difference between the use of colored 'slip' applied to the mould and color applied to the body after drying or firing.

APPENDIX II

United States Patent Office

C. W. Fenton, of Bennington, Vermont

IMPROVEMENT IN GLAZING POTTERY WARE

Specification forming part of Letters Patent No. 6, 907, dated November 27, 1849.

To all whom it may concern:

Be it known that I, Christopher W. Fenton of Bennington, in the County of Bennington and State of Vermont, have invented a new and useful improvement in the application of colors and glazes to all articles made of potters' materials — such as crockery, earthen, and stone ware, signs and door-plates and knobs, picture-frames and architectural ornaments; and I hereby declare that the following is a full and true description thereof.

The article to be colored and glazed, being in the usual state for applying the glaze, is immersed in a transparent under-glaze, then with a small box perforated with holes the colors are thrown or sprinkled on through the holes over the surface of the article in quantity to produce deeper or lighter shades, as may be desired, leaving a part of the surface for the body of the article to show through in spots. By fusion in the kiln the colors flow and mingle with the under-glaze, and are carried about over the surface in various forms, and the article is thereby made to present a close imitation of the richest shells, variegated stones, or melting and running fluid, almost every variety of rich and beautiful appearance being produced by flowing and mingling of the colors with the under-glaze, and the appearance of the article being varied according to the complexion of the body of the article and the colors and quantity thrown upon it.

The colors may be applied to the article by other means than that of the perforated box, provided the same effect is produced. What I claim as my invention, and desire to secure by Letters Patent, is —

The coloring of the glaze of pottery-ware by the means substantially as herein set forth and described.

C. W. Fenton

Witnesses:

A. P. Lyman
L. Norton

APPENDIX III

FORMULÆ OF BODIES AND GLAZES USED AT THE UNITED STATES POTTERY

Students will be interested in the following formulæ of bodies and glazes used at the United States Pottery. They are from the cherished 'Secret Book' of one of the old glaze-makers, which I have been permitted to examine.

COMMON WHITE

'Common White' Body (a)
- 1350 lbs. Ball Clay
- 250 " China Clay
- 800 " Flint
- 425 " Feldspar

'Common White' Glaze (a)
- 75 lbs. White Lead
- 75 " Flint
- 128 " Feldspar
- 30 " Whiting
- 16 " China Clay
- 30 " Zinc

'Common White' Body (b)
- 1100 lbs. Blue or Ball Clay
- 100 " China Clay
- 800 " Flint
- 375 " Feldspar

'Common White' Glaze (b)
- 100 lbs. White Lead
- 60 " Feldspar
- 40 " Flint
- 5 " Whiting
- 4 " China Clay

GRANITE WARE

'Granite' Body (a)
- 1400 lbs. China Clay
- 200 " Ball Clay
- 1100 " Flint
- 500 " Feldspar

'Granite' Glaze (a)
- 15 lbs. Boracic Acid
- 20 " Whiting
- 70 " Feldspar
- 60 " Flint

The above calcined in glost kiln, ground and then mixed as follows:
- 80 lbs. of above
- 40 " White Lead
- 40 " Feldspar

'Granite' Body (b)

900 lbs. Golden China Clay
800 " Burgess China Clay
400 " Blue, or Ball Clay
1300 " Flint
500 " Feldspar

'Granite' Glaze (b)

140 lbs. Feldspar
130 " Flint
40 " Whiting
Calcine above in glost kiln, grind
and add
80 lbs. Feldspar
80 " White Lead

ROCKINGHAM GLAZE

Formula (a)

90 lbs. Red Lead
24 " Feldspar
26 " Flint
18 " Clay
7½ " Paris White
18 " Clay
36 " Manganese

Formula (b)

100 lbs. Red Lead (or Litherage)
20 " Flint
20 " Feldspar
20 " Clay
25 " Manganese

YELLOW GLAZE

Formula (a)

150 lbs. Red Lead
25 " Feldspar
35 " Flint
30 " Clay
10 " Paris White

Formula (b)

75 lbs. Red Lead
21 " Feldspar
17½ " Flint
6 " Clay

APPENDIX IV

NOTICE

ARTICLES OF ASSOCIATION OF THE UNITED STATES POTTERY COMPANY

TO ALL MEN TO WHOM THESE PRESENTS MAY COME, BE IT KNOWN

That we, Jason H. Archer, Henry Willard, Christopher W. Fenton, Samuel H. Johnson and Oliver A. Gager, have associated and do hereby associate ourselves together, under the provisions of an Act of the Legislature of the State of Vermont, approved December 5th 1853, entitled 'An act providing for the organization of private corporations.'

The purpose of this Association is to engage in the business of manufacturing Earthen and other Pottery Wares at Bennington, in the State of Vermont, and to engage in the sale and merchandise of such wares, under the corporate name of the 'United States Pottery Company.'

The amount of the capital stock of said corporation is Two Hundred Thousand Dollars, in shares of Twenty Five Dollars each, and said corporation is to continue for the time of thirty years from the date hereof.

Dated at Bennington, in the County of Bennington, and State of Vermont, this eleventh day of June A.D. 1853.

J. H. ARCHER
H. WILLARD
C. W. FENTON
S. H. JOHNSON
O. A. GAGER

APPENDIX V

EXTRACT FROM THE FIRST ANNUAL REPORT ON
THE GEOLOGY OF VERMONT, 1845 (*pps. 52–53*)

Bennington. — Half a mile north-east of the village is a deposit of excellent kaolin, which supplies the manufactory of Norton & Fenton in the village. This bed is overlaid by drift, but the state of the excavation did not admit of an examination of its structure. Mr. F. very obligingly shewed us the material, and the ware in various stages of process, and gave the desired information with illustrative specimens. With a public spirit more praiseworthy than common, Mr. F. freely communicates the valuable results of his experience.

For fire-bricks, the kaolin is made into paste with water, from which bricks are formed and burnt. These bricks, retaining the whiteness of the kaolin, and becoming very hard, are called 'clay bricks.' They are next broken up by a mill and sifted, so as to be of the coarseness of fine gravel. This is mixed with unburnt kaolin and arenaceous quartz, pressed in moulds of the required form and size and burnt in the same manner as before. These fire-bricks are very white and hard, and when fractured shew their composition of broken clay-brick and kaolin.

Other kinds of pottery are here manufactured, and a great variety of articles of stone-ware. The latter was made with a mixture of kaolin and arenaceous quartz. But since our visit, improvements have been made, both in the construction of the works and in the processes, and I therefore take the liberty of inserting the following letter from Mr. F.

BENNINGTON, *September* 15, 1845

DEAR SIR, — Your favor of the 5th instant came in due course, for which you will please accept my thanks. You have probably noticed by the papers the loss of our works by fire, which will be, I trust, a sufficient apology for me, for not furnishing you with some facts in relation to our business, as I had intended to do. The rebuilding of our works has occupied my whole attention since the fire, and has suspended all my experiments in the manufacture of porcelain, to an indefinite period. We are now erecting, under the firm of Norton & Fenton, the most extensive and best constructed pottery works in this country. The buildings are fire-proof, in form a hollow-square. 114 feet by 92. We intend to have a plan of our works taken when completed, of which we will furnish a copy if you should wish. Our works are constructed so as to use more of our own materials than formerly. We are building mills for refining the kaolin, and also for pulverizing and grinding the feldspar stone, which we showed you a sample of, a mixture of feldspar, silex, etc. My experiments have proved it to be a very valuable article for common stone-ware, especially for chemical and other important purposes. By uniting these materials in certain proportions, we produce a much better, handsomer, and stronger stone-ware than is made in this country. The other improvements which we have made, consist in the construction of our kilns, for which we are entitled to patent, but shall not ask it, having furnished models to the owners of nearly all the principal potteries in the Northern States, who have built, or are intending to build, upon our plan. We have also perfected a system of firing our kilns, different from any other. In short, we have reduced it to a perfect system, while others make it an uncertain guess-work. These improvements render our wares more durable and perfect, and give us the preference wherever we send our goods. The character of our fire-bricks is also well known. They are a composition of materials which we find here, consisting of arenaceous quartz and kaolin. Being very pure, they make a good fire-brick, which will stand longer in a strong heat than any other brick known. They are used for blast furnace hearths, and, in many places, where no other fire-bricks will endure. The amount of fire-bricks and pottery-ware which we manufacture yearly, will not vary much from $20,000. I intend to continue my experiments as soon as I have leisure, with materials found here, of which I will endeavor to keep you advised.

I remain your friend and ob't serv't,

C. W. FENTON

In East Dorset, Wallingford, Chittenden, and Brandon, kaolin is associated with the brown iron ore-beds, as before described. . . .

INDEX

of, dissolved, 16, 17; his apprenticeship in pottery business, 27; children of, 28; his family life, 28–30; a religious man, 30; a Freemason and charter member of Temple Lodge, 30; picture of, 31; an intense patriot, 31, 32; death, 32; Harwood's account of, 33–35; Harwood's account of his funeral, 35; his estate, 36.

Norton, John, son of Captain John Norton, becomes member of Norton firm, 16; at dissolution of firm, 17, 52; and Luman, Pottery owned and operated by, from 1823 to 1827, 19; withdraws from partnership in Pottery, 20; Director of Bennington Academy, 31; his connection with the Norton firm, 51, 52; establishes shop in lower village, 56.

Norton, Julius, son of Luman Norton, 20, 41; taken into firm, 20, 57; responsibility in firm shifted to, 42, 59; successful business man, 43; talks of going to Portland, Maine, 57; advertises under own name, 64; birth, 67; living in Captain John Norton's house, 67; schooling of, 67; an accomplished musician, 67; his first wife, 67; his second wife, 68; a good craftsman, 68; austere as a man, 68; his characteristics, 68; a money-maker, 68, 70; his partnership with C. W. Fenton, 68–70, 112; progressive, 76, 77; sends for John Harrison, 78; dissolves partnership with Fenton, 80–85, 112; confines himself to manufacture of stoneware, 88; takes Edward Norton into partnership, 88; death, 89, 90.

Norton, Laura, daughter of Luman Norton, 41, 60.

Norton, Louisa, daughter of Luman Norton, 41; wife of C. W. Fenton, 50, 60, 103, 111; death, 153.

Norton, Luman, son of Captain John Norton, 13; becomes member of Norton firm, 15, 16; at dissolution of firm, 17; and John, Pottery owned and operated by, from 1823 to 1827, 19; becomes sole proprietor of Pottery, 20; held to be the equal of his father, 36; birth, 36; schooling of, 37, 38; a constant reader, 38–40; enjoyed thunder-storms, 41; marriage of, 41; children of, 41; his family life, 41; fond of playing on flute and fife, 41; a man of quaint charm and ceremonial politeness, 42; his title of 'Judge,' 42; legend concerning, 42, 43; transfers responsibility to Julius, 42, 59; considered shrewd and

capable man of business, 43, 44; a Freemason, 44; a craftsman of the old school, 44, 45; purchases 'Chatfield property,' 57; builds house on Pleasant Street, 59; legend concerning business connection of C. W. Fenton with, 60; approximate date of his withdrawal from business, 64.

Norton, Luman Preston, son of Julius Norton, 68; taken into firm of J. & E. Norton, 89; ability and character of, 92, 93; retirement of, 95.

Norton, Luman Spooner, 8.

Norton, Mrs. Luman S., 7.

Norton, Norman J., son of Captain John Norton, 16; becomes turner, 52; assists in management of distillery, 52.

Norton, Thomas, settles in Guilford, Connecticut, 4.

Norton, William, 3 n.

Norton (E.), Bennington, Vt., pottery mark, 95.

Norton (E. & L. P.), 92; mark of, 92; fire of 1874 in pottery of, 93, 94; the pottery wagons of, 94, 95.

Norton (Edward) Company, mark, 97.

Norton (Edward) & Company, pottery mark, 95, 96.

Norton (J. & E.), 88; mark of, 88.

Norton (J. & E.) & Co., 89; mark of, 89.

Norton (J. & L.), firm name, 15.

Norton (John) & Sons, firm of, 15, 16; dissolved, 16.

Norton, Julius, pottery mark, 88.

Norton (L.), mark of Norton ware 1828–1833, 20.

Norton (L.) & Co., firm name, 19.

Norton (L.), & Co., earliest mark used by Norton Pottery, 19.

Norton (L.) & Son, Bennington, Vt., mark of Pottery after removal to East Bennington, 59.

Norton & Fenton, firm of, 66, 81; dissolution of partnership, 80–85; marks of, 83, 240; contribution of, to development of pottery industry, 85–88.

Norton family, enterprises and interests of, 16–19.

Norton Pottery, the first in Bennington, 3; establishment of, 5; the earliest piece made at ('Aunt Mindy' Gerry's jug), 5, 6; other pieces of original pottery of, 6–8; Harwood's first entry concerning, 11; red earthenware